Alec Baldwin
Doesn't
Love Me

Alec Baldwin Doesn't Love Me

Other Trials of My Queer Life

MICHAEL THOMAS FORD

alyson books
LOS ANGELES • NEW YORK

Manufactured in the United States of America.

This trade paperback original is published by Alyson Publications Inc.,
P.O. Box 4371, Los Angeles, California 90078-4371.
Distribution in the United Kingdom by Turnaround Publisher Services Ltd.,
Unit 3 Olympia Trading Estate, Coburg Road, Wood Green,
London N22 6TZ, England.

First edition: January 1998

02 01 00 99 98   10 9 8 7 6 5 4 3 2 1

ISBN 1-55583-431-0

Library of Congress Cataloging-in-Publication Data
Ford, Michael Thomas.
  Alec Baldwin doesn't love me & other trials of my queer life / Michael
    Thomas Ford.
  1. Homosexuality—Humor. 2. Gay men—Humor. 3. Gay wit and
    humor. I. Title II. Title: Other trials of my queer life.
  PN6231.H57F67 1998
  814'.54—dc21   97-46050 CIP

"I Wish We'd All Been Ready," words and music by Larry Norman,
© 1969 by Beechwood Music Corp. and J.C. Love Publishing Co. All rights
controlled and administered by Beechwood Music Corp. All rights reserved.
International copyright secured. Used by permission.

Contents

Author's Note . . . . *vii*

My Queer Life

Diary of a Would-be Porn Star *3*
Too Much of a Good Thing *12*
Adult Education *17*
Dyke the Halls *26*
Taking the Credit *35*
The Nonwriting Life *44*

Men and Other Obstacles to Happiness

How Alec Baldwin Ruined My Life *53*
The Sound of Music *61*
Why I Hate Shopping *70*
The Perils of Dating *77*
Picture Imperfect *84*
When I Grow Up *90*

Adventures Among the Straight People

Trial by Fire *101*

Singing a Different Tune *114*

Homo Improvement *119*

A Model Queer *125*

Separation Anxiety *133*

Cyberslut *141*

The Way I See It

No Splashing in the Gene Pool! *151*

Games People Play *159*

A Sporting Chance *167*

Just One of the Girls *176*

I'm Not Saying It's Wrong... . . . . *184*

A Slightly Dented Childhood

If Jesus Loves Me, Why Hasn't He Called? *195*

Confessions of a Don't-Bee *205*

Packing for the Second Coming *214*

The Crown of Heaven *223*

The Theory of Relativity *233*

Saying Good-bye to Grandma *242*

Author's Note

TRUTH IS ALMOST ALWAYS STRANGER THAN FICTION, AND I have often been told that I have a very strange life, although to me it has generally seemed perfectly ordinary. This, of course, is the paradox of having odd experiences — you don't realize how truly odd they are until you tell someone else about them and then see that look of disbelief staring back at you. Only then do you begin to think that maybe something queer is going on after all.

The pieces in this book are all true. Well, mostly. At the heart of each one is a piece of reality. My reality, anyway. I've heard people say that being queer doesn't affect how you view the world. I beg to differ. I don't think you can grow up in this place as a gay person without developing an interesting perspective on things.

Here, then, are some pictures of life as I see it, ranging from the childhood days when I was convinced Jesus was going to come and snatch me up into the clouds to more recent adventures navigating the waters of being a queer person in America today. As anyone who's ever looked around can tell you, it's a weird place.

Many thanks must go to Kathleen Vickery, late of *Our Own* newspaper, and to Margaret Maree, who first suggested I write the My Queer Life column and then encouraged me to syndicate it. The same goes for Robert

Thomson and Jim Armstrong of *Fab* magazine, who let me rant every issue in my The Way I See It column. Thanks also to the other editors at magazines, Web sites, and newspapers across the country who gave me a place to tell my stories. (By the way, I'm still waiting for the checks.)

None of this would have happened without Katherine Gleason, who all along has said I have the most peculiar life of anyone she knows and insisted I put it all down; and Gerry Kroll, who kindly believed me when I said people would be interested in reading about it. And I am, I suppose, especially indebted to my family and friends, who are responsible for many of the events in this book. I told you I'd get even some day.

My Queer Life

Diary of a Would-be Porn Star

For a short time a few years ago, I reviewed porn movies for a now-defunct magazine. Once a month a package would arrive, discreetly wrapped in brown paper, containing five or six new flesh flicks for me to watch and give my opinions of. The pay was almost nonexistent, but I did it anyway, happy to be able to do my part in educating the smut-viewing public about the merits of these fine pieces of cinematic beauty. "Anything for art," I told my friends when they pretended to be appalled.

Watching these entertaining videos provided more than the occasional moment of pleasure, but after a while I had a disturbing thought: None of the things I saw in the movies ever happened to me. Oh, sure, the men in the films did things that I did. They went to the beach. They went grocery shopping. They took their dogs for walks. But that's where the similarities ended. When I took my dog for a walk, no handsome man asked me if I needed help burying my bone. When I returned books to the library, the shy man behind the desk didn't follow me into the periodicals section and show me his Dewey decimal system. It just didn't happen.

Because I firmly believe that life imitates art, I knew that the filmmakers couldn't possibly be lying. Surely all across America, men were having hours of hot, oily fun with pool boys, pizza deliverymen, and neighbors they happened to meet in the hall while wearing nothing but a jockstrap. Behind every bush there had to be two guys engaged in carnal knowledge of each other with barely a hint of polite introduction preceding it. Clearly, I was just going about things the wrong way.

I decided that with a little effort, my life too could be as exciting as a porn movie. Even better, it could actually be a porn movie. All it would take was a little bit of planning and some derring-do. If I just put my mind to it, I would soon be romping from one exciting sexual encounter to another. I anticipated days of endless orgies with beautiful men who fulfilled my every fantasy.

I chose a Friday to begin my new life, since I had deduced from my film watching that on Fridays everyone in North America becomes incredibly horny and ready for fun. I woke up that morning raring to go and leapt from my bed in search of the first orgasm of my porn-star life. Wearing nothing but my bathrobe, which was strategically left hanging open so that any men I happened to encounter would have easy access, I strolled to the front door and opened it.

Now, I'm sure the paperboy (who of course had just celebrated his eighteenth birthday) didn't mean to scream as loudly as he did. Still, at such an early hour, it was a little unsettling. And certainly there was no need for running away in such a hysterical manner and leaving all of those papers on my lawn. As I shut the door, I made a mental note not to leave a tip at Christmas. In porn films the paperboy was always most accommodating. To find that mine wasn't was a bitter disappointment indeed.

I decided I was going to have to take a much more active approach if I was going to be successful at porn stardom. I sat down and made a list of the most popular locations for finding sex, based on the porn films I'd seen. The list went like this (in order of frequency):

1. Apartment complexes in Laguna Beach.
2. Beaches on deserted islands.
3. Gyms.
4. Locker rooms in high schools after football practice.
5. Video stores (X-rated sections).

This, as you might well imagine, was not entirely helpful. California was on the other coast. Deserted islands are hard to come by. And high school administrators are not frequently as open-minded as one might think. In the end the gym and video store were the only real possibilities. I decided to try the gym first, since the video store didn't open until noon and I was ready for action immediately. Throwing on some shorts, I packed up my bag and left.

The gym at 9 o'clock in the morning bore little resemblance to the stud-filled athletic facilities of my porn-viewing experiences. Instead of rooms crammed with well-built men wearing tight shorts, no supportive gear, and lots of oil, I found myself surrounded by fifty-two middle-aged women in floral-print leotards and headbands gyrating to Paula Abdul while attempting to get in shape for their daughters' weddings. It was hardly the stuff of homo fantasy.

Undaunted, I checked out the sauna, which, according to porn movies, was frequently the site of some vigorous groping. Inside, it was just as misty and hot as the porn films had promised. And hidden within its steamy interior, a scantily clad man was reclining on one of the wooden benches. Casually carrying my towel (no one wears them in porn movies), I went in and sat down next to him. To my satisfaction he was quite a looker. Just my type.

I nodded, and he smiled. In porn movies this always means, "I want to suck your cock." So I did what any good porn star would do — I spread my legs and waited for him to pounce.

"Hey," he said, putting a hand on my waiting thigh, "have you ever read the *Book of Mormon?*"

I was out of there in a flash, leaving my towel behind as I hightailed it onto the street. This was not the way things were supposed to go. I checked my watch — only fifteen minutes until the video store opened. I started walking.

Entering the store, I ducked behind the black curtain separating the adult videos from the rest of the store. To my surprise and joy, a cute college jock type was busily looking at the covers of the boxes. I looked at the one in his hand and, seeing that it featured two men and not a silicone-laden, red-lipped woman, congratulated myself on my good luck.

I played it cool, knowing full well that these things had to involve a little bit of play before the kill. I walked a few feet down the row and picked up a tape. Out of the corner of my eye, I could see that Mr. Frat Boy was taking quick glances my way. I moved closer, reaching for a tape near him.

"That one isn't so good," he said.

He'd taken the bait. "Really?" I said. "Is there one you like better."

He turned and smiled. "Why? You interested?"

Finally. Sex was imminent. "Maybe," I said, already ripping his rugby shirt off and sucking on his nipples in my mind.

He looked around to make sure we were alone. "I really like to do it to *The Little Mermaid,*" he said. "Disney makes me hard as a rock. Especially if you can talk like the crab."

Clearly, it wasn't my day. I suddenly remembered somewhere I had to be and excused myself before Jocko could launch into a chorus of "Under the Sea."

As I walked home, I pondered my plight. I couldn't understand why it was so hard to get laid. In porn movies men with brontosaurus-size erections practically fell out of the sky. It was impossible to turn a corner without tripping over a luscious piece of beefcake, rump in the air and ready for fun. But all I seemed able to find were the rejects who never made it past Dropping and Sucking 101.

Back in my own home, I tried to think what Ryan Idol would do in my situation. After a minute it came to me. I picked up the phone and dialed the cable company.

"Something seems to be wrong with my box," I said when the weary operator's voice crackled through. "It isn't working. Can you send a guy over?"

Much to my delight, it worked. The operator said a man would be by in about twenty minutes. I hung up, thanking the porn gods, who obviously had decided to smile upon me after all. I then raced into my bedroom and set the trap. I grabbed a tape from the pile by the VCR, shoved it in, and hit PLAY. My plan was simple: I would pretend the cable was out. When the technician tried to turn on the television, a porn film would be playing. Then I'd make my move. I'd seen it once in a movie, and it worked brilliantly.

I paced around the apartment until I heard a knock on the door. Still wearing my gym shorts, I opened it. Standing outside was a hunky young stud fair near bursting out of his uniform. I ushered him inside. His shirt had BILL stitched on it.

"Right this way," I said in what I hoped was a husky voice dripping with innuendo. "I'm not sure what's wrong."

I led Bill into the bedroom, where he went straight for my cable box. I watched as he turned it on and off, checked the wiring, and did something with a little tool he pulled out of his back pocket. He never once turned the TV on.

"That should do it," he said, turning to go.

"Wait a minute," I yelped. "Shouldn't you check it? I mean, what if it's not fixed?"

"Oh, it's fixed," he said. "Trust me." He headed for the door.

"No!" I yelled, practically pushing him back into the bedroom. "Please, just check it."

Bill gave me an odd look as he turned on the television. I held my breath, waiting for a shot of Zak Spears doing what he does best to appear and get the ball rolling, as it were. Instead what came on was a close-up of Mary Tyler Moore tap-dancing madly in an elevator in *Thoroughly Modern Millie*. Her big toothy grin spread across my TV where Zak's hard-as-iron cock should have been thrusting in and out of some lucky orifice.

"Happy?" Bill asked, glaring at me.

Dejected, I nodded. It just was not meant to be. I watched as Bill left the house, pulling the door shut behind him.

"You bitch!" I screamed at Mary as I turned the tape off. "Why couldn't you at least have been a come shot?"

I was running out of possibilities. It was now midafternoon, and I still hadn't gotten off. I sat down to think, wishing bitterly that I had an outdoor pool to lounge beside naked, a gardener with poor English skills and hours of staying power, or at least a handsome neighbor whose wife just didn't like to do certain things. But all I had was a faulty sprinkler, a pimply kid who raked up the leaves once every October, and old Mrs. Krumbach, who complained ceaselessly about her joints. The stuff of wet dreams, my life was not.

Then I had an idea. I'd once seen a movie in which a young man had engaged in a stimulating encounter with another man in the men's room at the local mall. Surely I could do that too. I hustled out the door to the local galleria. Then it was but a quick turn past the Sunglass Hut to the rest room. I threw open the door and commenced scouting out my lucky partner.

There were a couple of possible candidates lined up at the urinals along one wall. I picked the one who seemed the most pornlike (he had on work boots, which I was convinced was a sign) and squeezed in next to him. As I unzipped I tried to remember what the actor in the movie had done. I casually looked over at my neighbor and smiled slightly.

"Hey," I said.

"Hey," he said, smiling back.

I had no idea what to do next. I couldn't for the life of me remember how it had been done in the movie. I reached inside my fly so I could at least pee and pretend to be doing something. But there was no fly. As I scratched around frantically inside my jeans, I realized that in my haste to leave the gym earlier in the day, I'd put my boxers on backward.

Mortified, I tried to free myself from my underwear. My waiting partner watched as I ran my hand around inside my pants, looking for a way out. I looked at him and tried to manage a lighthearted chuckle. Hoping to distract him, I winked seductively.

My contact tumbled out of my eye and fluttered gently into the urinal, where it swirled around in the water, bobbing over the fluorescent pink disinfectant tablet like an inner tube. I squinted, trying to locate it while simultaneously attempting to rearrange my boxers from the outside. With only one good eye, I found that it was proving difficult.

Finally I managed to pull the waistband of my boxers down. Even tough my contact was way past rescuing, I decided that I could see well enough for my thrilling encounter to continue. I looked at the guy next to me.

Unfortunately, he was gone, and in his place was a burly mall guard. He took one look at my half-closed eye and the rapidly deflating erection in my hand and frowned.

Now, in the movies, security personnel are notoriously horny and ready for all kinds of fun. I was disheartened to discover that in real life, this is seldom the case. Noting the look in the man's eyes and sensing that somehow trying to explain things to him would probably not help matters any, I beat a hasty retreat from the bathroom. Using my good eye, I managed to make it home, where I collapsed onto the couch.

My day had not gone at all well, and I blamed it all on porn movies. They had promised me a fun-filled existence of sexual freedom, but they had lied. Grabbing an empty box, I moved through the house, gathering up all the videos I could find. When the box was full, I taped it shut and hauled it out to the curb. Dusting off my hands, I went back inside and slammed the door shut on the world of randy men and their empty promises. It was time to come back to reality. Picking up a copy of *Pretty Woman*, I slipped it into the VCR and sat down.

Now there, I thought happily, *is something I can believe in.*

Too Much of a Good Thing

My name is Michael F., and I am a Marthaholic. That's right, I am addicted to Martha Stewart, Goddess of the Art of Living Beautifully. It started innocently enough. I would catch a glimpse of Martha's television show as I was flipping channels. She would be briskly dipping French toast into batter speckled with cinnamon or deftly winding sage leaves into a cunning wreath. *I could do that,* I thought, and I did. It was easy. It made my life a little brighter.

Things went on in this way for a couple of months. I was satisfied by the occasional fix of Martha's helpful hints and her winning smile. Like a freshly baked muffin brimming with ripe blueberries, my encounters with her left me feeling content and happy. But then I found that these small Martha doses just didn't do it for me anymore. I looked at my perfectly poached salmon reclining on its bed of blanched endive, at the cheerful stencils dancing merrily along the edges of my walls, and I wanted more.

So I subscribed to *Martha Stewart Living,* the magazine devoted to my guru and her ways. Each month I had delivered to my mailbox a new installment of the Gospel According to Martha. What a joy it was to rip off the protective plastic bag and stroke the glossy pages with trembling hands before delving into the mysteries awaiting me inside that only She could reveal.

With Martha's guidance I whipped up lemon tarts so light and fluffy, they practically floated out the window. I learned how to refinish and install the claw-foot bathtub I'd always wanted. I tossed together a kitchen herb garden in no time and discovered everything there was to know about Fiestaware, which I began to collect with abandon.

Soon editors began to phone, frenzied when promised manuscripts failed to arrive. "It's almost done," I'd lie, cutting out gingerbread men with my free hand. Worried friends left pleading messages that went unanswered as I experimented with making my own lavender-scented soaps or devising plans for constructing a charming Italianate grotto in the backyard. Finally I unplugged the phone.

Free to immerse myself entirely in Martha's spell, I devoted my every waking moment to her. I copied her personal calendar (helpfully provided in each issue of the magazine), making sure that on the day Martha was ridding her gutters of fall leaves, so was I. On Martha's birthday I built a chicken coop in celebration. I pictured Martha pruning her apple trees, the stray hairs of her carefree bob clinging to her slightly damp brow, and wished for an orchard of my own.

Things finally came to a head the night of my annual Christmas party, which I went forward with only because it was an opportunity to celebrate all things Martha. The handmade invitations, addressed in my finest calligraphy, had gone out two weeks earlier. The fudge was finished, all eighteen kinds individually wrapped in glistening cellophane boxes and decorated with found objects. Presents, all of them handmade according to Martha's own specifications, sat under the tree.

And oh the tree! How it sparkled with the ornaments I'd spun from glass and carved from wood into fantastic shapes! The tiny hand-dipped candles twinkled as I sat sipping my mulled wine and waited for guests to arrive.

By midnight, when no one had come, it hit me. After months of scorning my friends for the company of Martha, they had abandoned me. I looked at the dilled shrimp and plum pudding languishing untouched on the gaily laid table and wept. I was alone on Christmas Eve, and even the spirit of Martha couldn't save me from my despair. I needed professional help.

The next day, after a fitful night spent tossing and turning on the crisp linen sheets that graced my antique sleigh bed, I plugged the phone back in and called the mental health clinic. "Help me," I sobbed when someone picked up. "I can't take it anymore."

Much to my surprise the young woman on the other end quickly referred me to a local chapter of MA — Martha Anonymous. It was held at a nearby address, and there was to be a meeting that very afternoon. Knowing that I needed help to break my Martha addiction, I went.

The room was full. Men and women of all ages sat in folding chairs in front of a podium. Some chatted quietly among themselves. Others sat, hands neatly folded, looking at the floor as though they were picturing in their minds exactly how it would look sanded and refinished in knotty Carolina pine.

A cheerful woman approached me. "Hi," she said. "My name is Anne, and I'm a Marthaholic. Is this your first meeting?"

I nodded. She seemed normal enough. I wondered what her addiction had cost her.

"Thanks for coming," she said. "Have a cookie."

My eyes widened in terror. A cookie! Wasn't that exactly what a Marthaholic would want? I pictured slim fingers of chocolate, delicately beaded with candied violets, or perhaps the thinnest of butter wafers dusted with vanilla sugar.

Anne sensed my alarm. "Don't worry," she said reassuringly. "They're Oreos."

I sat down, sipping reluctantly from a styrofoam cup of bland instant coffee, and Anne began to tell me her story. "It started with the Good Things," she said. "I made little labels for my kids' clothes, covered old shoes with shells and painted them gold, wove ribbon into the edges of my pillowcases. Then it got worse. Soon I was making peach-pie kits for people I barely knew. I emptied the kids' college accounts to pay for terra-cotta planters. I wore gloves so no one could see the marks on my fingers from pushing cloves into orange pomanders. It was sad."

"But you're okay now?" I asked hopefully.

"Oh, no," Anne said gently. "Once a Marthaholic, always a Marthaholic. I still can't walk past a yard sale without breaking into a sweat. But don't worry, we can help."

That afternoon I heard story after story of people whose lives had been devastated by Martha. People who, like me, had been brought to ruin by her promise of enchanted living — losing lovers, jobs, and friends in the process. From them I gained the courage to face my problem, and Anne became my sponsor. We started with the First Step. "I am powerless over Martha," I would repeat to myself every morning as I ate plain cornflakes from a plastic bowl, resisting the craving to improve it with fresh berries and honey from the hive I'd installed out back.

It was hard, but I was determined. Out went all the back issues of *Martha Stewart Living*. I emptied my closets of potpourri, the kitchen drawers of arcane Japanese cooking utensils. I ate store-bought baked goods, gagging on their mass-produced taste. *Arugula* became a forbidden word in my home.

Slowly my system rid itself of Martha's insidious poison. I no longer felt the need to marble every bare inch of wall space. I found that I could indeed eat vegetables that were not grilled over mesquite and doused in raspberry vinegar. After several months of daily phone calls with Anne, I was even able to part with the collection of animal-inspired egg cups I'd collected in my heyday.

I am still not completely cured. Anne was right: Marthaholics never are. I still sometimes pine for a perfectly trained grape arbor, and some mornings I think I won't be able to get out of bed unless I have transplanting pearl onions or creating whimsical picture frames from antique ribbon to look forward to. Holidays are the hardest. But I persevere.

Besides, the other night I was watching PBS and discovered Norm Abrams and *The New Yankee Workshop*. Watching Norm turn ordinary pieces of lumber into beautiful pieces of furniture, I couldn't help but think that the grotto would look so nice with a Shaker table in it.

Adult Education

I did something recently that made me realize how far I've fallen. I became an adult education student.

Time was when I looked upon people who partook of adult education classes as a sort of hopeless breed of, well, completely pathetic losers with nothing else to do but make feeble attempts at learning French or spend six weeks sculpting unidentifiable objects from clay. In my mind they were all forty-somethings named Bernice or George, wore ill-fitting clothes, and smelled faintly of onions. Suddenly keenly aware that they were never going to become ballerinas or stock-car drivers, they would do the next best thing — take a twelve-week seminar on writing a screenplay, which would concern either a lonely housewife trying to fulfill her dreams or a high school baseball star who finds himself twenty years later still employed at the gas station he once saw as a job to tide him over while waiting for major-league clubs to come calling. Seven weeks into the course, stuck at a crucial point in the script's plotting, both Bernice and George would fail to return to class.

But then the catalog came from the local adult education center. At first I tossed it aside derisively, annoyed that I had even been included on a list of people who might have the slightest interest in exploring their dream lives through yoga or attending a series of six minilectures on wines of the world. I wasn't yet thirty. I'd written a dozen successful books. I was, I thought, far too busy living my dreams to go about analyzing them.

A few days later, however, I reached an impassable point in the novel I was working on. Taking a break from it, I sat down and began leafing through the catalog. I thought that seeing what I would become if I failed to finish my book would spur me right through my temporary block. Just looking at the number of "So You Want to Get Published" courses would put the fear of adult ed into me and get me back to work.

And at first it did. I shuddered at the pages listing "Italian Conversation for Beginners" and "Fun With German, Sections I, II, and III" with Mathilde Von Rottgutten, native speaker and author of *Germany: Playground of the Blondes*. I whizzed through the seventeen pages of dance classes (Brazilian, Thai, and two-stepping open to singles) and on past "Quilting a Winning Baby Pillow," "Knitting for Left-handers," and "Tai Chi as Stress Relief."

Where I got stuck was in the cooking section. Now, I love to cook, and I'm pretty good at it. But there are a lot of things I'd like to know how to do that I have just never found the time to learn. Perhaps the pressure of writing full time finally got to me, but for some reason, a cooking class suddenly seemed potentially amusing, even useful. I pictured myself whipping up fantastic dinners for all of my witty friends, where we would sit around contentedly eating and saying very funny things that would have everyone rolling on the floor.

The trick was to select the perfect class. There were some real losers — "French Toast for Cereal Eaters,"

"Bran New Day," and "Salad Roundup," for example. But tucked among the "Barbecue Blowouts" and "Melon Manias" were some things that actually appealed to me. I could hardly believe it as I scanned the listings and found several classes that didn't make me wince. I made a list.

I finally decided on "Sushi!" Not only was it exotic but the Zenlike title, complete with festive exclamation point, reassured me that I would have fun while learning how to create something I'd always wanted to be able to do. As I picked up the phone to make my reservation, I imagined myself deftly handling sharp knives and obscure culinary apparatuses as I sliced up a lovely piece of fish into works of art and served them to amazed acquaintances. Besides, it met for only one night.

I did not, of course, tell anyone that I had sunk to the depths of adult education. Most of my friends are still talking about those Ph. D. s they insist are forthcoming or working diligently toward their master's degrees in folklore or ancient Incan burial rituals. Even their children take ballet and regularly attend postmodern poetry seminars. To admit to signing up for a continuing-ed class would be cause for endless torment. So I kept it to myself.

As the day of my class neared, I found myself growing fearful. What if it turned out to be awful? Did going mean I'd joined the ranks of those who, like my parents, spent their evenings searching for the best fish fry? Worse, what if I couldn't do it? I almost didn't go.

But go I did, and my exploration into the world of ongoing learning almost ended at the door. When I walked into the lobby, I was greeted by the sounds of music. Bad music. Very bad music. It was, I saw by the sign on the wall, a performance of the second-level mandolin class. All thirty-eight of them were sitting on cheerful blue cushions, joyously picking their mandolins and singing "Leaving on a Jet Plane" in several different keys. It was my worst nightmare come true. I suppose I should have just been thankful it wasn't the first-level class.

I would have turned around and fled, but an elderly woman grabbed me and hauled me inside. Apparently this was her job, and she was very good at it. Try as I might, I couldn't pry her wizened little fingers away from my collar. "Now what class are you here for, dear?" she asked, grinning at me over her bifocals.

" 'Sushi!' " I whispered, afraid someone might overhear me.

The woman riffled through a box of index cards. She found the one for my class, checked off my name, and handed me a name tag.

"Fill this out with your name and class, and wear it at all times," she said. "We like to be friendly around here."

I did not feel at all friendly, but being rather intimidated by matronly women wearing running shoes and CLINTON/GORE T-shirts, I obliged. I peeled off the back and stuck the MIKE/SUSHI badge to my chest. The woman smiled again.

"Good," she said. "Now go right through that door. Your class is in the third room on the right."

I waded through the sea of warbling mandolin players and pushed open the door. Thankful to be free of the awful singing, I started down the hall. It reminded me of being in third grade, where everything is painted the same peculiar shade of green and trying to find homeroom produces waves of nausea. I found what I thought was the right door and went in. A group of thirteen people stared at me. I glanced at the nearest name tag. ELISE/PAST-LIFE REGRESSION it read. I excused myself. I have enough trouble with this life.

Eventually I found the correct room and went in. Sitting around a table were seven other people sporting badges bearing their names — TREVOR/SUSHI, MITZI/SUSHI, SHANIQUA/SUSHI, and so on. I took a seat next to SASHA/SUSHI because I liked the sound of it. Sasha, like almost everyone else in the room except myself and ELIZABETH/SUSHI, who looked to be about sixteen and appeared to be sporting a hat of her own design, was at least sixty-seven years old. She had an enormous quantity of white hair, which she wore in two long braids.

"Hi," I said, remembering that I was supposed to be friendly. "I like your necklace." Sasha was wearing a peculiar-looking piece around her neck.

"Thanks," she said brightly. "I made it in my last class — 'Body as Art.' It's a replica of my vagina in bronze."

I stared at her, not knowing what one was supposed to say when forced to comment on a new acquaintance's privates. She looked so hopeful, like my dog when he's actually fetched the stick and wants my praise. "Well," I said finally. "It's certainly shiny."

Sasha beamed. "I love adult ed, don't you?"

"This is my first class," I said.

"A virgin!" Sasha yelped, a little more loudly than I would have liked. The other students looked over at me. I waved tentatively, still trying to be friendly, as I thought about strangling Sasha with her vagina.

Thankfully I was saved by the arrival of the instructor. I was a little bit surprised to see that he was about as Japanese as I am — which is not at all — and was sporting a Red Sox T-shirt and Bermuda shorts. "Good evening," he said. "My name is Morty Rosenblum, and I'm your instructor."

I raised my hand. "Are you a sushi chef?" I asked.

Morty gave me a withering look. "No," he said. "But I spent time in Japan as an exchange student."

While I was immediately dubious, this answer seemed to satisfy the other students, all of whom nodded and smiled at Morty and at one another. We then went around the table and introduced ourselves while Morty spent a lot of time shuffling some papers back and forth. As I'd expected, everyone else in the class had taken at least three other continuing-ed courses, sometimes more than once. ELIZABETH/SUSHI had taken "Motorcycle Repair and Maintenance" six times.

After these pleasantries, the class began in earnest. Things seemed to pick up as Morty introduced us to the various pieces of equipment we would need to make flawless sushi. We passed around a *makisu* (bamboo rolling mat), *kijakushi* (rice paddle), *hashi* (chopsticks), and other intriguing items, the names of which Morty read from a piece of paper and which I wrote on the back of an envelope I found in my backpack. The other students diligently wrote everything down in little notebooks.

We were then instructed in the centuries-old art of making sushi rice. Apparently in Japan the making of sushi rice is a sacred event, second only to the making of Godzilla movies in its attention to detail. It involves heating the rice to exact temperatures, adding just the right amount of vinegar, turning it frequently with a specially designed kijakushi handed down from generation to generation, and watching it every single second so that it comes out the desired consistency with every grain going in the same direction. Years are spent teaching would-be itamae (sushi chefs) how to make rice, and poor sushi rice is a shame no itamae can bear.

Luckily for those of us without several decades to spend stirring and paddling, Morty suggested that Uncle Ben's with a splash of rice vinegar would do just fine, thus saving us years of toil and resulting in perfect rice in ten minutes every time.

We then moved on to what most people think of when they think of sushi — raw fish. Morty produced a nice length of fresh tuna and proceeded to show us how to slice it up into tender morsels fit for any tsu (sushi lover). He then presented us each with a small piece of our own and told us to go to it. I watched as SASHA/SUSHI picked up her knife and quickly turned her tuna into five glistening pieces of equal thickness and length. Reaching into the rice pot, she deftly formed five fingers (as the lengths of compressed rice are called, we learned) of perfect size and laid her tuna cross them without a problem.

Spurred on by her success, I tackled my piece of tuna. Ten minutes later I had one ragged-looking rectangle of fish and a pile of scraps. Undaunted, I reached into the rice bowl and pulled out a fistful. This I turned into five blobs reminiscent of my first encounters with Play-Doh in kindergarten. I dumped my fish pieces on top and looked at it. It was sad.

"Maybe it will look better with some pickled ginger on it," SASHA/SUSHI said, her vagina tinkling against her chest.

I had even worse luck with rolled sushi. Try as I might, my pieces of nori (seaweed) refused to cooperate, and my rolls ended up looking like some kind of amputated limb from a leprous sea creature, the cucumber strips and imitation crab spilling out like so much offal onto the plate. SASHA/SUSHI peered over her pyramid of perfectly rolled pieces and gave me a sympathetic smile.

My adventure into adult ed was beginning to wear on me. Everyone else seemed to be having a good time, slicing up yellowtail and rolling bits of eel into fantastical shapes. Their knives flew, their bamboo mats whispered, and out came sushi fit for even the most discriminating gourmand.

My last chance came with hand rolls. Essentially a hand roll is a sushi ice cream cone. You simply roll up a piece of nori, drop some rice and fish into it, and there you are. Foolproof. I was determined to make one. Looking out of the corner of my eye to see what SASHA/SUSHI was doing, I snatched up my seaweed, formed a cone, and filled it slowly with its fish contents. I did everything she did, down to the last folding of the nori to keep it all together. When I was done, I laid it on the plate and gazed upon it with pride.

Approximately three seconds later, it fell apart. The rice spilled out like an avalanche, the fish slipping down it like some fleshy sled gone out of control until it coasted to a stop at the side of the plate next to the lumpy blob of wasabi (horseradish paste) I'd stuck there. I wanted to cry.

Morty walked around the classroom, observing our accomplishments. He gave each student little pieces of advice to think about the next time she or he delighted in the art of sushi. When he came to me, he looked at the pile of rice and fish on my plate and patted me on the back. "I hear two-stepping is fun," he said consolingly.

SASHA/SUSHI offered me a ride home on the back of her moped, but I declined. I went home that night alone and dejected, an adult-education failure. All I had to show for my effort was an old envelope with lists of arcane Japanese sushi terms and a fish stain on it. *What will I ever do with this?* I thought, crumpling it up.

I flipped on my computer and opened the file with my novel in it. I was on page 173 and still hadn't broken through the barrier that had caused my initial foray into the realm of ongoing learning.

I typed for a while but with no success. The story just wouldn't come. Glancing over at the desk, I saw the course catalog lying where I'd left it next to the phone. I picked it up and turned to the writing classes.

Dyke the Halls

I have always had a close group of lesbian friends, so having the girls over for a little Christmas get-together seemed like a fine notion. Perhaps encouraged by faulty memories of my own childhood holidays, one day I decided to invite some of them to come help me select and decorate a tree. We would, I thought, go out and cut one of the many pines that grew wild on the land around my house. Then, warmed by goodwill and vast quantities of hot chocolate, we would trim it while listening to carols and eating homemade cookies, perhaps even with green and red sprinkles on top. It would all be wildly fun and a wonderful way to celebrate with our extended gay family before the annual horror of going home to our real ones. Really, it seemed like a good idea at the time.

The first sign of trouble came with the first telephone call, made to my friend Willow.

"Christmas is an Anglo-patriarchal holiday that bastardizes traditional goddess-worship celebrations," she said after I asked her.

"I always thought it was about presents and singing and elves," I said.

"Furthermore," continued Willow grimly, "the whole Judeo-Christian concept of the season is a reprehensible fallacy that completely minimizes the spiritual belief systems of other cultures. All of those horrible Nativity scenes that pop up all over shopping malls across America — they're just representations of what the church would like us to think Christmas is."

"But the presents..." I countered.

"I just can't condone participating in that kind of perpetuation," said Willow. "I mean, this whole celebration — which really you should call 'Yule' anyway — is supposed to be about the coming of the horned god and the cold winter months, not about some fat white man in a suit abusing endangered animals by making them pull a sleigh, which is really probably far too heavy for them anyway."

"Okay, so it's a Yule celebration," I said.

"But the point I'm trying—"

"We're having cheesecake," I said.

Willow said she'd be there by 6.

Next on my list was Rachel. She had just finished meditating and seemed to be in a good mood. I took this as a positive sign. "I'm having a Christ...er...Yule party," I said warmly. "I was hoping you'd come."

"I'm Jewish," she said. "We don't do Yule. Christmas either."

I sighed. "What do you do?"

"Nothing," Rachel said. "Well, there's Hanukkah, but I find the whole thing ridiculous. People rushing all over buying crap no one wants just because they feel bad that their kids don't get to visit Santa. It just makes me crazy."

She was warming up for a lecture, so I cut her off. "Look," I said, "this isn't about presents. We're just getting together, and it happens to be Yule or Christmas or some damn thing. I haven't seen you in a month. Are you coming or not?"

"Well, if you're going to make me feel guilty about it, I guess I have to."

I took that as a yes and told her what time to be there.

Anne was the last person to call. Prepared by my encounters with Willow and Rachel, I told Anne I was having a holiday party, which I would like her to participate in so that we could nondenominationally celebrate nothing and have a good time communing in one another's company.

"Fine," she said.

"Fine?"

"Yes, fine. What did you expect me to say?"

"Um, I don't know."

"I'll be there," she finished, adding before hanging up, "I'll bring my new girlfriend." So excited was I by her smooth acceptance that I failed to register the last part of her sentence. I would live to regret it.

The day of the festivities dawned cold and gray. By noon a light snow was falling, the perfect backdrop for what I hoped would be a pleasant evening with my friends. As the hour neared, I made the last batches of cookies and set them out to cool. Everything was ready, and all I needed was the guests. I began to think happy thoughts. I put on a Windham Hill *Solstice* sampler album, pleased that it contained no religious connotations whatsoever but still sounded wintry.

They all arrived simultaneously, bustling into the house like a pack of cats caught in the rain and trying desperately to get out. "It's snowing," Rachel said glumly. "It's practically a blizzard."

Willow handed me a package wrapped in brown paper and tied with twine. "Here," she said. "It's a candle to burn for Yule. It brings happiness."

"I thought we weren't giving presents," Rachel said defensively. "I didn't bring anything because you said—"

"It's not a present," I said hurriedly. "It's a...a...a ceremonial object."

"I thought we weren't doing anything religious," Rachel started again but was cut off by Anne, who entered accompanied by a tall, thin woman wearing an Army surplus jacket and John Lennon glasses.

"This is Hannah," she said. "We met at the co-op."

Thankful for the distraction, I picked up a plate of cookies. "Nice to meet you," I said. "Would you care for a gingerbread boy?"

"Person," said Hannah.

I looked at her blankly. "Gingerbread *person*," she repeated. "Not *boy*. Do they have sugar, butter, or eggs in them."

"Yes, yes, and yes," I said. "Why?"

"I don't eat anything with animal products or processed sweeteners. No wheat, either."

I glared at Anne over Hannah's shoulder. "Would you like some mulled wine then?"

"I don't drink alcohol," Hannah said. "But never mind. I brought my own soy milk and some rice cakes." She pulled a bag from her oversize Guatemalan peasant's pouch and proceeded to snack.

Thankfully no one else had any qualms about sugar or fat, and we all dived into the piles of cookies. After a half hour or so of munching and chatting, I announced that it was time to go get the tree.

"Tree?" Rachel said, her mouth overflowing with chocolate chip–macadamia nut crunchies. "You didn't say anything about a tree."

"I forgot," I said. "We're going to get a tree." I looked over at Willow, who seemed to be chanting under her breath. "It's a Yule tree."

"Oy," said Rachel, heaving herself out of her chair. "The things you goys do."

Eventually I got everyone dressed and out into the yard. After a short trek through the now-snowy woods, we came to the tree I'd preselected earlier in the week and tied with a red bow so I could find it again. "Here it is," I said proudly. "The Yule tree."

"You're going to cut down a tree?" said Hannah. "A living tree?"

I smiled at her, gritting my teeth. "Yes," I said evenly. "Why?"

Hannah snorted. "Well, go right ahead. But what with the destruction of the rain forests in South America and all, I'd think maybe you'd want to leave this tree in peace."

I produced the handsaw from the bag I was carrying. "I'm sure this one tree won't cause the ozone layer to instantly evaporate," I said, waving the saw menacingly in Hannah's direction.

"She's right," said Willow. "I mean, you didn't tell me you were going to cut down a real tree or anything."

I looked at her through squinted eyes. "Just where did you think Yule trees came from?" I asked. "Do you think the Yule people or goddess worshipers or whatever they were made them out of old newspapers?"

"At least say a prayer to its spirit," Willow insisted. "Really, if you're going to kill it and all, the least you can do is tell it you're sorry. You owe it something."

We all joined hands around the tree. I stared at it, wishing it would just fall over on its own.

Everyone was waiting for me to say something. I cleared my throat. "Dear tree," I said, feeling like the biggest ass on earth, "thank you for giving your life that we might have a joyous Yule season."

I looked over at Willow. "Happy?"

She nodded. I picked up the saw and knelt beneath the tree. I put the edge of the saw against the trunk, only to hear Willow and Hannah break out in violent weeping.

"Okay," I said, standing up. "Everyone into the Volvo."

We piled into the car and drove to the tree stand set up at the end of town. My Christmas/Yule/holiday celebration was turning into one gigantic nightmare, but I was determined to have a good time. We all got out and started to walk through the aisles of trees, searching for the perfect specimen. Although Willow still sniffled a little as she ran her hands over the branches of the fallen trees, she behaved herself.

After looking at every single tree in the entire place, we were finally able to select one that looked decent. Although Hannah said she was sure it was some kind of endangered fir and threatened to turn the owner of the place over to the Sierra Club, Greenpeace, and Robert Redford, I plunked down $45 and tied the hapless tree to the roof of the car. Everyone got back in, and we went home.

With a minor amount of fuss, we got the tree into its stand and settled into a corner of the living room, where it seemed a little overwhelmed. I hauled out a box of ornaments, and we set to work trimming it. I put Rachel in charge of stringing lights, Anne was responsible for hanging balls, and Willow and Hannah volunteered for tinsel detail because it involved the least amount of physical contact with what they insisted on calling "the wounded soul." Cookies were eaten and drinks were drunk, and soon things were humming right along. At least for five minutes.

The lights were the first problem. I should have been watching Rachel more carefully or at least been suspicious when I heard her cackle every few minutes as she bustled around the tree. "There we are!" she said triumphantly, plugging them in so the room filled with merry color. The lights were on the tree, all right, and for once they all worked. But they were arranged in a strange pattern that defied explanation.

"What did you do?" I asked. "It looks funny."

"I arranged them in the shape of a vulva," she said proudly. "See how the labia wrap around the sides? Isn't it great?"

I sighed. "It's lovely," I said. "Let's just hang the decorations."

"I don't know about these," Anne said, looking doubtfully at my box of ornaments. She held up a frosted glass ball in one hand and a hand-blown icicle in the other. "How come these are all phallic-oriented? Don't you have any pink triangles or labryses or busts of Gertrude Stein?"

"Pretend the balls are breasts," I said. "And the angels are drag queens from the Stonewall Riots."

Anne was skeptical, but she went to work, hanging balls and icicles and angels with abandon until she'd gone through the entire box. "Are there more?" she asked.

"In the guest-room closet," I said, busy trying to arrange holly on the mantel. "Top shelf."

Anne disappeared. I stood looking at the tree, munching on a cookie. "This hasn't been so bad after all," I said to Rachel, who was trying to get a red light to line up with where a clitoris should be.

All of a sudden, Anne ran back into the room crying. She grabbed her coat and headed out the door. "What's wrong?" I asked her.

She turned around. "Willow is in the guest room teaching Hannah the basics of tantric yoga!" she sobbed before getting into her Subaru and pulling out of the driveway.

A moment later Hannah and Willow appeared in the doorway, looking slightly flushed. "Hey, what's going on?" Willow asked.

"Anne saw you two playing 'O Come All Ye Faithful,'" I said. "Now she's gone."

"Oh, shit," said Hannah. "She still has my WOMYN FOR A FREE TIBET T-shirt in her trunk."

Willow snatched up her coat and left, followed closely by Hannah, who ran down the driveway yelling "Wait, I need a ride!" her Birkenstocks making patterns in the snow.

I shut the door and turned to Rachel. "Well, that was fun!" she said. "Now, shall we hang this tinsel or not?"

I grabbed a handful and flung it at the tree, where it landed and hung like some cheap stripper's bedraggled fright wig, reflecting the changing colors of the lights as the vulva twinkled gaily. I sank into a chair and moaned.

On the table cheesecake sat untouched, while the wine mulled on in silence.

"Look on the bright side," Rachel said, unwrapping Willow's Yule candle and lighting it. "There's always New Year's."

Taking the Credit

I read somewhere the other day that the average American owes $3,450 in credit card bills. That information alone is unsettling. Then, using all kinds of charts and formulas, the article went on to prove that if the original debt were paid off using only the minimum payment due each month, it would take more than thirty years and require almost $6,000 in finance charges to completely pay it off. In other words, you would have paid for whatever it was you bought almost two times over. So those towels you got for 15 percent off at the Macy's white sale really ended up costing you $128. 53. Did you really need them that badly?

In the '70s, when credit cards first started to become really popular, I would stand in line with my father and listen to him rant and rave about how long it was taking to check out because someone ahead of us had decided to use Visa. In those days paying with plastic required a prolonged procedure involving eighteen slips of carbon paper, a call to get the card number approved, and sometimes even a little dance to invoke the finance spirits, who would, if provoked, cause the receipt machine to jam. I recall quite vividly the grumbling and foot tapping that ensued whenever anyone dared utter the terrible words, "I'd like to charge that, please." My father said it was just a fad and would never last. He said the same thing about men wearing earrings.

Now, of course, you can't leave the house without plastic. In my wallet are two credit cards (American Express and Visa), an electronic library card, a card to use at the supermarket to get surprise bargains, a card for making telephone calls, a card for renting movies at the video store, a card that gets me a discount at the vitamin store, and a bank card that allows me to do amazing things at ATM machines and that also somehow functions as a MasterCard. I haven't touched actual cash in months. The money just flows in and out of my account electronically, like a tide of cybernetic krill being swallowed up and regurgitated by a gigantic computerized whale.

And I'm fairly streamlined. I have friends who have dozens of credit cards, store cards, frequent-flier cards, gas cards, and bank cards. Their accumulated debt is in the tens of thousands, yet they never seem to worry. They just keep transferring balances from one card to another, gaining an extra sixty days before payments are due again. On day fifty-nine, they simply switch again, generally to a card with lower interest. When one card turns its weary back and says, "Not tonight," there's always another one waiting with open arms.

Not me. I've learned my lesson the hard way. For years I had only one credit card — American Express ("Member Since 1989"). The plain old green card. I got it when I got my first job. I trusted it because, since the balance has to be paid every month, I knew I wouldn't go overboard. And this worked very well for a long time.

I bought what I needed; I paid it off. Signing the receipts at restaurants or in stores, I felt very grown up and responsible.

But after a few months of happy bliss, the onslaught began. As soon as I got my American Express card, others began wooing me. All of a sudden a plain old credit card wasn't good enough. The really cool cards didn't just pay for things; they gave you stuff too. Seemingly every day another offer came in: free flight miles for every dollar spent, a percentage donated to worthy causes, "bonus credits" that could be traded in for gifts, even cash back at the end of the year. The more I bought, the more I earned. (That logic escapes me now, but at the time I fell for it.) In the face of such temptations, my little green AmEx card seemed pale and weak.

I called American Express. "Why can't my card earn me free car rentals?" I demanded. "Why does it just sit there while the other cards do magical tricks and cough up goodies left and right?"

The operator was cheerful. "What you need," she said, "is the Gold Card."

Until then I had no idea such a thing existed. A Gold Card. It sounded so regal. So chic. So much better than a boring old green card. Why, it was even capitalized, while the green card, like some obscure East Village poet, had to be content with going about lowercased. I signed up on the spot.

My Gold Card came a few days later, sealed in a smart-looking pouch and stamped with an official-looking gold seal. I even had to go sign for it at the post office, which made it all the more thrilling. Once home, I tore open the pouch and gazed at my new treasure. When I moved it around in the light, it sparkled promisingly.

According to the booklet that was enclosed with the card, my upgrade came with all kinds of features I would soon find indispensable. I could, for example, purchase $100,000 worth of travel insurance just by asking for it. Or I could take advantage of the many holiday travel packages put together on a regular basis by the thoughtful folks at American Express, who had reserved a cabin in Montana just for me. I was assured that holders of the ordinary old green card had no such perks and were a decidedly inferior lot. They, of course, weren't paying $75 a year either, but I didn't dwell on that for more than a moment. It seemed a small price to pay for a cabin in Montana.

I couldn't wait to use my Gold Card, so I took my friend Katherine out to dinner. When it came time to pay, I whipped out my shiny new card and placed it gently on the table. "Where'd you get that?" Katherine asked.

"They gave it to me," I said. "All I had to do was ask. Isn't it pretty?"

"But you make no money," she said, shocked. "I thought the Gold Card was for all of those business majors we hated in college, the ones with jobs on Wall Street now."

"They said my credit rating was superb," I answered proudly.

Now, Katherine wasn't as off the mark as you might think. It used to be that things like Gold Cards and $15,000 credit limits were reserved for people who actually made enough money to buy things worth $15,000. Not anymore. These days a mere child can get a $20,000 limit simply by asking for it. In fact, the deeper into debt you go, the higher they raise your limit. When my friend Jesse surpassed his $12,500 Visa limit, they sent him a cheese log and a $5,000 upgrade.

I was to find out just how this worked about a year later. I had been happily using my Gold Card for everything. I had even — once — taken advantage of what the company cryptically referred to as my "membership privileges," a term that implied all manner of clandestine activity, like secret handshakes and meeting strange men on dark corners to exchange packages. I had used my card to purchase tickets to an Indigo Girls concert, where I was assured that I would have the absolute best seats at Radio City Music Hall, reserved especially for people who, like me, were good enough to have been given the Gold Card.

The night of the show, I arrived and found my seats. They were very good indeed. Very near the stage. But they weren't the best. In front of me a herd of teenage girls sat chatting, waiting for the show to begin. Certain that they couldn't possibly have Gold Cards of their own, I casually tapped one on the shoulder and asked where she had gotten her tickets.

"Oh," she said, "my father has an American Express Platinum Card."

I felt as though I'd been slapped. A Platinum Card? Until then I'd assumed that a Gold Card was the pinnacle of success. I thought I'd arrived. Now, if the girl was to be believed, I discovered that I still had a ways to go. Distressed, I was completely unable to enjoy the show, even when Amy and Emily encouraged the audience to sing along on the chorus of "Least Complicated." I tried, but my heart just wasn't in it.

For weeks I was disconsolate. Then out of the blue, an envelope arrived in the mail. At first I thought it was a wedding invitation because it was very thick and hand-addressed in fine calligraphy. Then I noticed the American Express address on the back. Opening it, I pulled out an engraved card. "You are cordially invited," it said on the outside. Inside it went on to inform me that "in the next few days you will be receiving a special invitation." It didn't say to what.

The next few days were tense ones as I waited expectantly to see what was coming. Finally, a large vellum envelope arrived. Inside was another engraved invitation. "Because you are in the top 1% of the financial elite," it read, "we are extending to you our greatest honor."

It was, remarkably, an invitation to accept the Platinum Card. Along with the invitation was a book — an actual book — outlining all the pleasures the Platinum Card could bring me if I "choose to accept this wonderful distinction." The whole package was more extensive than any of the college prospectuses I'd received in high school.

"You, a Platinum Card?" my roommate said, looking over my shoulder as I read. "What did you make last year, $20,000 or something?"

"It doesn't matter," I said, caressing the soft leather cover of *The Guidebook to the Platinum Card*. "I'm one of the financial elite."

I spent all night reading the book. I discovered, among other things, that owning the card would give me guaranteed reservations to the world's trendiest restaurants. Never mind that an evening out for me usually involved mediocre Indian food and a frozen yogurt —

now I had my very own table at the Four Seasons. Not only that, but Platinum Card owners could get, with no fuss whatsoever, tickets to any show in any city, just by calling one easy-to-remember phone number. It was all too good to be true, especially for a little boy from Barneveld, New York.

The thing that finally hooked me, however, wasn't the guaranteed seating or the marvelous tickets. It was the "Personal Assistant" service. According to the book, if I were to become a Platinum Card owner, the entire American Express company was at my disposal should I ever need help. Say, for example, I was on a business trip and feeling a little tense. All I had to do was call American Express and within minutes a masseur would be at my door, ready to knead the worry away. Or suppose I required a unique and thoughtful gift for a client or loved one. One call to AmEx and a personal shopper would scour the world's best shops for a one-of-a-kind item, wrap it, and send it by overnight mail, along with a personally written card bearing my name.

How could I pass up such a wonderful thing? I pictured myself in a strange city — Singapore, perhaps — and discovering that I'd just left my briefcase with my new novel in it in the backseat of the cab that was speeding away. Not to worry. Stepping into the lobby of my hotel (four-star, of course), I would pick up the phone and dial 1-800-PLAT-CARD. A courteous employee would pick up on the first ring. After hearing my story, she would immediately dispatch a young man to comb the city for my missing briefcase while I repaired to the finest restaurant in town and enjoyed a lovely dinner. Upon my return to the hotel, my briefcase would be waiting for me at the desk. Not only would my manuscript be safely in my hands once more but my thoughtful personal assistant would have taken the time to copy-edit it for me and rewrite the ending, which had been troubling me on the flight over.

Ignoring the small print about the $300-a-year membership fee, I returned my RSVP card and waited. The card arrived a week later, ensconced in a blue velvet box embossed with a platinum AmEx logo. After washing my hands, I carefully pried off the lid and beheld my new card in all its glory. Surely Mary herself had not beheld the baby Jesus with quite the same awe. It was lovely, bearing a gentle silver finish with my own name stamped in sharp relief. I cradled it in my hands and sighed.

If I'd been excited about using my Gold Card, I was orgasmic over the Platinum Card. Once again I took Katherine to dinner. This time we went to a restaurant with a two-month wait for tables.

"How'd you get reservations?" she asked, examining the real silver place settings. "Have you been sleeping with a waiter again?"

"No," I said casually, sliding the Platinum Card out of my wallet. "I just used this."

Katherine's eyes went wide. "Good lord!" she whispered. "Is it real?"

"Yup," I said. "Want to touch it?"

Over the next month, I used my Platinum Card often and well. Every time I looked at it, I got a warm feeling inside. Whenever I handed it to a sales clerk or waiter, I beamed with pride. Then the bill came. All $2,326.78 of it. I opened the envelope (which disappointingly was not vellum but the same plain old paper they sent the green card bills in) and nearly fainted. I couldn't believe things had gotten so out of control. And I'd never even used the masseur or the personal assistant!

In the end, I never did use them. That one bill was enough to knock some sense into me. After taking out a cash advance from another card (at 19. 8 percent interest) to pay off AmEx, I called and canceled my Platinum account.

"Just give me back the green card," I said sadly.

"The green card?" the operator replied incredulously. "You're giving up the Platinum Card for the green card? But we're offering Platinum members box seats for the Rangers' games for only $4,000."

For a moment I was tempted. Then I remembered my 19.8 percent interest. "No, thanks," I said, trying not to cry.

It took me two years to finally pay off the cash advance. With interest, my little Platinum Card party ended up costing me $3,342.18. Now I'm back to the green card, which is fine with me. I'm still so shaken I can barely take it out of my wallet without weeping. But I still have that Platinum Card, resting in its little blue velvet box. And sometimes, when I'm feeling down, I take it out and remember a time when I was one of the financial elite.

The Nonwriting Life

Writers who claim they've wanted to write since the age of six and would die if they couldn't write are pathological liars.

I hate writing. In fact, I will do almost anything to avoid doing it, and actually getting me to produce something is no less a miracle than it must have been to construct the hanging gardens at Babylon. If it wasn't for the simple fact that I am totally unemployable in any other capacity, I probably wouldn't write at all. And if someone were to offer me a vast sum of cash to stop, I would. Why Joe Eszterhas, the screenwriter of such classics as *Showgirls* and *Basic Instinct,* and the highest-paid writer in Hollywood, refuses to make the same concession, I cannot understand. He's probably written since he was six.

Discovering this about me amazes people who know that I have made a living as a writer for several years now. This is because people have interesting ideas about writers. Most think we spring from our beds each morning and leap to the keyboard to get down all the fresh ideas that have been birthed in the subconscious while we sleep. They envision us spending joyous days at the computer creating marvelous new worlds and turning out witty phrases left and right until, breathless from the act of creation and weak from forgetting to eat, we repair to the kitchen for a light snack of leftover sushi before settling down to watch something stimulating on PBS.

I do know writers like that, but they are not to be trusted, and I do not speak to them. My own life, and that of most full-time writers I know, is far less glamorous. How books are written remains a mystery I do not fully understand, even though I have produced close to two dozen of them. I know only that, in my case, they generally are pieced together in fits of activity that come between extended periods of not doing anything at all.

Take, for instance, this past Tuesday, which is fairly representative of most of my days. At 5:30 I got up and, after stumbling about in the dark trying to find my clothes, took Roger, my black lab, to the park for a swim and a run with his friends. Now lest you think my getting up at this early hour is an admirable display of affection for my loyal pet, I should explain that we do this because predawn is the only time the park is not overrun by joggers and fishermen, two groups of people whom neither Roger nor I need added to our morning experience. It also means I don't have to make elaborate excuses for going to bed at 8:30 in the evening and refusing to have dinner with people I don't like.

When we returned several hours later, Roger enjoyed a leisurely breakfast on the porch while I ate potato chips and Lotsa Lemon yogurt and wondered why all the geraniums were yellowing. I then spent from 8:30 until 9 examining the plants and trying to cheer them up, unsuccessfully, by spritzing them with a mixture of fish meal and bottled water. What I was really doing was not working on the book that I'd promised my editor would be on her desk by Friday but that in truth I had not even begun to write.

At 9 o'clock I turned on *Oprah,* which I watch because my agent says that authors who appear on her show make million of dollars, and I figure tuning in each day will give me some tips on how to write books Oprah likes. On this particular morning, the guest happened to be Toni Morrison. I had sort of been hoping for Zack, a seventy-pound two-year-old who had been making the talk-show rounds of late, but I settled for what I could get. Besides, it was literary and was therefore not a waste of time. Everything went well until Oprah asked what Toni liked best about being a writer. "Oh, I don't think I can call myself a writer," Morrison said. "I don't think anyone can make a living by writing these days. It's just too hard."

I turned off the TV. Toni Morrison has several bestselling novels and a Nobel Prize to her credit, and she still won't call herself a writer. I don't even have a savings account. And I've written more books than she has. Surely it was a sign that I should just stop. I started to scan the help-wanted ads but decided it was too much effort because they weren't listed alphabetically.

From 10 to 11, I checked my E-mail, none of which was important but all of which was deeply fascinating in comparison to trying to write something. I then answered it all, writing thoughtful and incisive responses in the event that a century from now someone will want to know what I had to say about things. Having sent it, I opened WordPerfect and began to look through all of my files, deciding that it was a wonderful opportunity to clear things out and, thus newly organized, begin my writing work with a fresh outlook.

At 1:30, while I was deeply engrossed in reading a self-help book on visualizing success (deleting the files had become boring when I realized there was nothing new since the last time I'd cleaned them out), the phone rang. Visualizing someone calling with an offer of cash, I picked it up. Still, ever wary that it might be a disgruntled editor, I disguised my voice.

"Hello?" I said gruffly, adopting a slightly irritated tone, as though interrupted in the middle of composing something utterly brilliant.

"Relax, it's me," said my friend Katherine. She is a writer too and is almost as good at avoiding actually writing as I am.

"What are you doing?" I asked, pleased to have something to rescue me from almost working. Since Katherine had called me, I had the passive-aggressive advantage of having her to blame later for my unproductive day.

"Nothing," she said flatly. "I got up at noon and watched a *Murphy Brown* rerun. I was thinking about going to the library, but I'm too tired."

Being tired is a central quality of all full-time writers. I cannot recall the last day on which I did not have a nap.

"Maybe you should write something," I suggested lightly. I was hoping Katherine might actually believe for a moment that I was really working.

"Right," said Katherine instantly. "When's the last time you wrote something?"

I thought about that. "I handed a manuscript in at the beginning of February," I said. "A novel. Rent was due."

Katherine was impressed. "I haven't handed anything in for months," she said. "In fact, I forget what it is I'm supposed to be working on."

"The article about lesbians in China," I reminded her. While we seldom do any of our own work, writers can always remember the details of what our friends are not working on. That way we always know who would be ahead if anything were actually written.

"Oh, yeah," she said sleepily. "That's been due for weeks."

I sighed. "You know, I wish I had something interesting to work on," I said. "That would make it so much easier to be motivated."

"You have three books under contract," Katherine said.

"But none of them are interesting," I complained. "I didn't think they'd actually buy them when I sent in the proposals. I just needed to feel like I was doing something."

"Just write them," Katherine said. "What about your column?"

I needed to change the subject. Being reminded of everything I wasn't writing was making me tense. "Do you think Joyce Carol Oates and Stephen King have conversations like this?" I asked.

"Probably," said Katherine. "I bet she eats Oreos all morning and then calls him to see what he's doing."

"And he's sitting there playing solitaire on his Mac," I added. It made me feel better to imagine writers more famous than myself sitting around not writing too.

Katherine and I talked for a long time about not writing and about what Joyce and Stephen were doing. By the time we were done, we had them engaged in trying to create a stained-glass effect on their office windows while avoiding finishing first drafts of their new books, something Katherine and I had actually done a few years back. Then I looked at the clock. It was 3 o'clock, time for Roger's walk. I said good-bye to Katherine and hung up.

After Roger's walk, I gathered the mail and scanned it hopefully for (1) letters from publishers with checks, (2) letters from readers with kind words and/or checks, and (3) magazines that would give me something to do for the rest of the afternoon. Sadly, there were no checks or kind letters, but there was a new issue of *Entertainment Weekly*. Grabbing the cookies from the kitchen, I sat on the porch and started to read while Roger dozed in the sun. It would, I thought, help me relax for all the writing I would not do later in the afternoon.

About halfway through the magazine, I came across an article about a young writer, who was not Joe Eszterhas, who had just been paid $2 million for a script that apparently featured neither plot nor characters. I snatched up the phone and speed-dialed Katherine's number. She picked up immediately, using the same mock-annoyed tone I had adopted earlier.

"It's me," I said. "Listen to this." I read her the article. When I was done, I sighed. "It's not fair," I said plaintively. "I could have written that."

Men and Other
Obstacles to Happiness

How Alec Baldwin Ruined My Life

I'm saving myself for marriage. My mother would be so proud. Unfortunately, there's one small problem: The man of my dreams is taken, and I'm not getting any younger waiting around for him. Yes, the world is a sorry place indeed. Crime is rampant. Children can't read. People are homeless. It's enough to make any sympathetic person weep for days. But while these things are indeed terrible, they are not the worst things about the world, not by a long shot. No, the worst thing is that Alec Baldwin is married, and not to me.

Don't laugh. This is a serious issue. You see, Alec was my first and only real love. Ever since I was seventeen and saw him on television in the homo-oriented TV mini-series *Dress Gray*, I've known I would marry him. From the moment he slipped off his attractive officer's uniform and I saw the dark line of hair peeking out over the edge of his crisp white T-shirt, I was hooked. Then there were the eyes, so blue and inviting. The secretive smile. And the voice. So sensual. So masculine. I could just imagine how it would sound whispering my name as he slipped into bed and put his arm around me. After the scene in which he lowers himself into a hot bath, I was a believer in love at first sight.

Once I'd found my man, I set about getting ready for him. Having grown up with two older sisters whose primary objective in life was getting married as quickly as humanly possible, I knew how it was done. I prepared a hope chest, filled with everything my man could desire. I embroidered little linen guest towels with my new initials. I collected flatware in an appealing design and chose a china pattern that was both homey and elegant. I loaded up on sheets I knew Alec would look the most handsome reclining on in his white boxer shorts on our honeymoon night.

Then I waited. I knew that if I was patient, Alec would come. No matter that we moved in two different worlds. I had fate and little linen guest towels on my side. In the meantime, I saw all of his movies — *The Alamo: Thirteen Days to Glory, Beetlejuice, Married to the Mob, She's Having a Baby, Working Girl, Talk Radio,* and even *Forever, Lulu.* No matter how brief Alec's appearances in a film, in my eyes he was the star. *Great Balls of Fire. The Hunt for Red October. Miami Blues.* With each movie, my love for Alec deepened. I sat in the audience, eating popcorn and wishing I could reach out to pat his thigh and tell him how magnificent he was on screen, even in the smallest roles.

Then came *The Marrying Man.* Oh, sure, I admit that I'd heard all the stories about his off-the-set romance with costar Kim Basinger. I'd secretly read the tabloids while waiting in line at the supermarket and seen the pictures of them kissing. But I knew it was just hype, a carefully orchestrated publicity stunt to boost the buzz around what was, with the obvious exception of Alec, a terrible film. I didn't sense any real danger. After all, surely Alec would never sully himself by touching lips that had touched Mickey Rourke's.

What a blow, then, when I turned on the television one awful evening to hear Mary Hart chirpily announcing that not only was Alec really dating that horrible bitch but he was going to marry her. My man — my Alec — was actually going to give himself to the woman who not only couldn't act to save her life but who had gone out and bought a whole town. Even on my worst shopping days, I had never returned home with more than a pair of shoes. And I sincerely doubted that Kim even knew what a little linen guest towel was.

I didn't understand it. How could Alec — my Alec — the man who spoke so eloquently about politics, acting, and human rights — the man who won accolades for his serious stage work, be marrying the human equivalent of cotton candy? It was yet another senseless act in a world gone awry. I went into a tailspin.

Lest you think that my love for Alec is based solely on his on-screen image, I should tell you that I have met Alec in person twice in my life. Okay, I've seen Alec in person twice in my life. The first time was when he played Stanley in the revival of Tennessee Williams's *A Streetcar Named Desire* on Broadway. I was first in line the day the box office opened. When the woman behind the ticket window asked me what kind of seats I wanted, I answered breathlessly, "As close to Alec as I can get" and flung my Gold Card at her.

Now, normally I wouldn't bother to plunk down $75 to watch some guy in a play. But the real genius of Tennessee Williams is that he was, when it came down to it, a frustrated queen, and consequently most of his leading men spend a great deal of time running about in undershirts and boxers. Because the parts are so gripping, the male stars seldom realize that the entire point of a Williams play is to see hunky men seminude. This makes it all a great deal of fun for the rest of us, who are in on the joke and wish that more actors would venture into live theater.

I do not actually remember much about the play. I'm sure Jessica Lange, who was also in it, was brilliant. After all, she won raves for it, even though I suspect the critics applauded her simply because she was able to touch Alec's chest while still retaining the ability to speak complete sentences. And I'm told that the writing is very good for that sort of thing. All I can vividly recall is that Alec took his shirt off six times during the two and a half hours he was onstage. In fact, the entire production seemed to have been conveniently choreographed around opportunities for Alec to undress. Whoever staged the thing should have won a Tony for it.

Alec himself was nominated for a Tony, and I have no doubt that this had less to do with the forcefulness with which he screamed out "Hey, Stella!" than it did with his nightly striptease. I am not exaggerating in the least when I tell you that every time Alec reached for the buttons on his shirt, the entire house fell completely silent. When he casually shucked off the shirt and peeled his sweat-soaked T-shirt over his head to reveal his beautiful hairy chest, there was an audible gasp from every sensible person in the audience, the vast majority of whom were male. It was a moment I will never forget. Had my American Express card allowed it, I would have bought box seats for the entire run.

This brings us back to the night I discovered Alec was getting married. Tragically, the second time I saw Alec was on the day before his wedding to She Who Is Unworthy to Run Her Tongue Over His Chest. After hearing the news of the impending nuptials, I had called in sick for a week, unable to get out of bed except to change the Alec tape in my VCR. Finally, after wearing out my copy of *The Hunt for Red October,* I'd pulled myself together and returned to work. It was my first day back, I had somehow muddled through despite my pain, and I was coming home from my office in Midtown. I'd managed to get a cab at Second Avenue and 52nd Street. It was raining, as well as a Friday afternoon, and this was no small accomplishment. For a brief moment, I thought maybe things were looking up.

As the cab rushed past the corner of 48th Street, I noticed a man waving for a taxi. In the true manner of a New Yorker possessed of a cab while others wait in the rain, I laughed wickedly to myself. Until we got closer, and I realized that it was Alec — my Alec — standing there, rain running down his manly face and onto his coat as he vainly tried to flag a ride. Suddenly, everything seemed to move in slow motion. It was just like a scene from a 1940s love story. I pressed my face against the glass and wailed his name as we raced by. Try as I might, the Pakistani driver would not stop the cab, even when I grabbed him by the hair and screamed, "You don't understand — I must get my hands on that chest!" We sped down Second Avenue as I cursed the fact that real life seldom turns out like a Billy Wilder film.

Little did I know that Alec was, in fact, at that very moment on his way to his wedding in Long Island. When I saw it on the news later that evening, with a triumphant Kim smiling as she dragged an obviously confused Alec down the aisle, I wept bitterly. Fate had thrown me

another chance, and I'd blown it. When I'd left him on
that corner, I'd ruined forever any chance we might have
had. I knew it was all over for me and Alec. I did the only
thing a jilted lover can do. I bought sixteen bags of
Reese's Peanut Butter Cups, put my worn-out copy of
Beetlejuice in the VCR, and ate myself into a stupor.

In the days after, I tried to cope as best I could. At
first, I hoped the marriage would fall apart in the tradition of so many other ill-suited Hollywood couplings.
Surely Alec would quickly see what a mistake he'd made
and divest himself of the walking Barbie he'd given
himself to. Then I would rush in to comfort the man
who obviously had been destined for me all along,
laughing cruelly at Kim as I put Alec's bags in my trunk
and drove away to a secluded cabin in Vermont. Smiling
sweetly, I would roll down my window and reduce her
to tears with the two cruelest words I could think of:
"*Boxing Helena.*"

But he didn't leave her. In fact, over the next year or
so, Alec and Kim seemed to become one of those rarities
in Hollywood — a bizarre couple who manage to
remain together despite the fact that they have absolutely nothing in common. Just like Bruce and Demi, they
inexplicably weathered everything from financial ruin to
critical potshots at their films without a scratch. Not only
did they thrive in the face of adversity but they did it
shamelessly.

Kim Basinger, of course, became my enemy. I rented
her movies, searching them for some sign of the elusive
quality possessed by the shameless hussy who had stolen
my husband right out from under me. Like Venus
Williams watching tapes of Martina Hingis to prepare a
game plan, I studied her every move. She had to have

something I didn't have, something that drove Alec crazy, and I was determined to find it and duplicate it. I watched *9½ Weeks, Batman,* and *Cool World* until I was sure my eyes would begin to bleed. I analyzed the way Kim flipped her hair, dissected her amazing ability to speak without ever moving her lips, and strived to copy her capacity to render a full range of emotions meaningless with the same vacant stare.

My friends begged me to stop my madness. "Please," my friend Katherine said. "Switch to Billy. At least he isn't married." This, of course, was pre–Chynna Phillips. But I wouldn't hear of it. "His face is too bony," I said, kissing my picture of Alec with a full day's growth of beard. "Try Danny," said another well-meaning soul, and I was briefly tempted, until I heard him talk. "Too stupid," I said decidedly, replaying my tape of Alec fervently discussing environmental issues on *Crossfire* with John Sununu and imagining myself walking a picket line with him, his manly hand gripped in mine. I suspected Kim's idea of saving the environment was using biodegradable bleach.

In the end, of course, my battle proved fruitless. Despite numerous voodoo dolls, rituals, prayers, and candle burnings, as of this writing Alec remains with Kim. They've even managed to produce a child, dashing my long-held hope that perhaps the relationship was never consummated and that Alec was holding out for me, wondering why I was so late in coming. When he decked the photographer trying to snap a photo of him on the way home from the hospital, I knew in my heart that it was out of frustration at not having found me.

Unable to have him for my own, I have devoted my life to celibacy. If I can't have Alec, I want no one. No other mouth will kiss mine. No other hands will caress my flesh. I have resigned myself to an existence devoid of love. Oh, sure, I've tried dating, but inevitably it ends up the same way every time. No matter how witty, charming, and handsome the man, at the end of the evening when he asks for another date, I sigh, look into his eyes, and say sadly, "I'm sorry, but you're just no Alec." Like an unlucky princess in one of the sadder Grimm's tales, I am cursed to wander the world alone while another enjoys my beloved's bed.

Still, there may be signs of hope for me yet. A few weeks ago, I read in a gossip column that Alec had started going to a salon to have his back hair removed, after Kim said it repulsed her and refused to do it for him anymore. All I have to say is, Kim, you better watch out, you bitch. Because I, for one, will be waiting outside the door with hot wax in hand.

The Sound of Music

During the decade in which I lived in New York, I saw three Broadway shows. One was *Lettice and Lovage,* a play that starred Maggie Smith and Margaret Tyzack and was very, very funny. The second was *A Streetcar Named Desire,* which starred Alec Baldwin's chest and was very, very refreshing. The third was *Gypsy,* which starred Tyne Daley and was neither of the above.

You see, I dare to stand in defiance of one of the most cherished of gay male traditions: I do not like musical shows. In fact, I will stretch my neck out even further and announce once and for right-here-in-public all that I dislike Barbra Streisand as well. There, I've said it. Start throwing stones.

Now, everyone knows that the only reason homosexuals live in New York is so they can attend Broadway shows. Therefore, being someone who doesn't even know who Patti LuPone is proved to be a decided disadvantage in my life there. While my friends rushed off for evenings of *Sunset Boulevard* and *Phantom,* I mumbled excuses and bolted for home and safety. When out-of-town acquaintances would phone, asking advice on what to see when they came to The City for the weekend, I feverishly pawed through the Sunday *Times,* hoping the ads would provide some clues and I wouldn't be revealed as the theater dunce that I am.

This aversion to musical theater began early in my life, when my mother decided it would be fun for the family to trek out to a production of *The Music Man* starring the odder half of *The Odd Couple,* Tony Randall. I sat, horrified, as grown men and women twirled and bounced across the stage in costumes straight out of *Mary Poppins.* Even worse, they all sang, including Tony. They sang while walking. They sang while dancing. They just kept singing. I knew this didn't happen in real life, and it confused me. Why, I wondered, didn't our mailman belt out a jaunty chorus as he popped letters into the box? How come my father, spurred to heights of joy by the appearance of a parade, never produced a cane and hat and did a little dance? A decidedly cynical child, I immediately suspected that someone was having a joke at my expense, and I didn't appreciate it.

A few months later, my mother announced that we were going on a trip to Vermont. Completely unsuspecting, I eagerly hopped in the car and went. When we arrived at a quaint mountain inn, I was indeed surprised. Then we went inside.

"Do you remember that movie we saw about the children in Austria?" my mother asked as she registered at the desk. "You remember, *The Sound of Music?*"

I nodded, confused. I did remember the movie. I had even enjoyed it to some degree, mainly because the children in it were horrid and had gotten, albeit accidentally, to swim in a river, something I was forbidden to do at any costs. I had no idea what it had to do with the inn or Vermont or me.

"Well," my mother said, "have I got a surprise for you. When that family escaped from Austria, they came here and started this inn. We're going to meet them."

For a moment I was completely thrilled. Although I had little use for musicals, I was easily overwhelmed by the thought of celebrities. Once my father had wrangled us seats in the presidential box at the Kennedy Center, and I had taken great delight in peeing in the same toilet Jimmy Carter used. The thought of meeting actual movie stars made my head swim.

I was beside myself until dinner, when the Von Trapps were to make their appearance in the sitting room. At the appointed hour, the guests gathered in the room and waited. A door opened, and in walked several elderly people dressed in costumes. None of them was wearing shorts made out of draperies.

"Who are they?" I asked my mother, pointing at the aged women and men seating themselves in chairs.

"Those are the children," she said.

"Where are their costumes?"

"That was just a movie," she said. "These are the real people. Now look, here comes Maria."

I turned and looked, expecting a young woman to frisk into the room with a guitar. Instead, what came in was the oldest woman I'd ever seen, led by two slightly younger but equally wrinkled women. They took her to a chair, where she sat down heavily and smiled wanly, as though being trotted out as an exhibit was hardly the most exhilarating thing she had to do that day. "Welcome," she said in a whisper, as though speaking any more loudly would cause her to crumble into dust.

One by one, the guests went up and shook hands with the eldest Von Trapp. Some of them wept openly.

All of them hugged her. When it was our turn, my mother took my hand and dragged me up to the chair. Eyeing Maria dubiously, I stood and scuffed the floor with my shoe.

"This is Michael," my mother said. "He loved the movie about you."

"Did you?" she asked.

I stared at her for a long moment. "Why aren't you dead yet?" I asked finally, unable to think of anything else.

The trip home was a grim one. Years later, my first editor would tell me that in elementary school she had as her teacher one of the youngest Von Trapp daughters, who had become a nun like her stepmother. Seeing the cheerful *Sound of Music* children on television and then facing the ruler-carrying real-life Von Trapp specimen in class had so unnerved this woman that she couldn't hear even a single song from the movie without going into hysterics. I know how she feels.

Things got worse as I grew older and realized that I was surrounded by people who not only liked musicals but who thought it was fun to participate in them. My sisters listened endlessly to *Jesus Christ Superstar*. Annual viewings of *West Side Story* were encouraged. In high school, which unfortunately for me coincided with the popularity of films like *Fame* and *Flashdance,* one enterprising teacher informed us that we would be putting on a show he'd written based on the wretched Styx album *Paradise Theater.* I was told I would have to sing, solo, some absurd song, which after hearing the words of I was convinced had to do with a man taking his mother to Africa and not enjoying it very much. Perhaps I was wrong, but we'll never know. I conveniently broke my arm and got out of it. I still insist I fell out of the tree by accident.

College was better, as I attended a highly religious school where, among numerous other things, we were forbidden to attend Broadway musicals because the content was considered less than seemly. Since the school was only half an hour from New York by train, this was a very real concern to the God-fearing folks who supervised our education, and the moratorium on musical theater was one of the only edicts set down by the school's governing body that I accepted as plain good sense, even if I didn't wholly agree with the reason.

Imagine my horror, then, when after graduation I went to live in Greenwich Village and discovered that not only was the singing of show tunes considered acceptable by reasonable people but it was practically mandatory. Just as in *The Music Man,* I could barely walk down my block without someone breaking into song and tossing flowers into the air. On my first visit ever to a gay bar, I entered warily, only to be surrounded by a chorus of manly voices belting out the words to "Over the Rainbow." I stood, staring at the crowd around the piano, and wept.

I tried to fit in. I really did. I spent evenings at bars like Eighty-Eights and Don't Tell Mama. I bought the original cast albums (which I very quickly learned never to call sound tracks) to popular shows and played them. But it was no use. I just didn't like it. While others laughed lightly and called out their favorite songs to the piano player, I sipped my beer and wished I was home watching TV. I didn't get the sly references to *Guys and Dolls* and *Showboat.* I felt like Herbie, that elf in *Rudolph the Red-nosed Reindeer,* the one who wants to be a dentist instead of making toys. Eventually, of course, I had to move out of the city in shame.

I don't like musicals for the same reason I don't like opera: I do not believe that sane people should express their feelings in loud tones of voice. If you are sad, I do not want to hear about it in sweeping movements accompanied by a thirty-piece orchestra. If you have just fallen in love with the most wonderful boy or girl in the world, chances are you're the only one who thinks it's really swell, and leaping onto a bench and crowing about it will not make you any friends. Do you have a problem so intense you feel you must share it with the world? Trust me, singing about it won't help. Shut up.

Now, I'm not totally against musicals. I do recall with some fondness purchasing the sound tracks to *Grease* and *Saturday Night Fever* and singing along in the rec room. And somewhere in my record collection is a copy of *Xanadu*. But that's the extent of it. And I was ten. I also thought Farrah Fawcett was really cool, and I wore a green satin baseball jacket because Shaun Cassidy did. I have since moved on. Unfortunately, some of my contemporaries seem not to have and are now bombarding the world with things like *Rent* and revivals of *Hair*. They should be ashamed of themselves.

Part of the problem is that this is not the '70s, when things like musical theater seemed perfectly natural and, in comparison to Vicki Sue Robinson and *Welcome Back, Kotter*, positively brilliant. Everyone was singing then, so why not put it on stage, dress it up in fun costumes, and sell tickets? But we know better now. Sure, we think going to the Kiss reunion tour is fun, and it is. But do we really need to drag *Grease* back out of the trunk, put Brooke Shields in it, and pretend it was the greatest moment of our lives? At least Gene Simmons knows he looks silly in his platform dragon boots, and we love him all the more for spitting blood at us while we rock and roll all night just one more time.

I think perhaps I would like musical theater if it didn't take itself so seriously. For example, what if instead of Maureen McCormick and John Stamos as Sandy and Danny in the *Grease* revival we had, say, the Dalai Lama and Camille Paglia? "You're the one that I want," the Dalai would croon as he boogied in the Shake Shack. "Tell me about it, stud," Camille would say, pitching her cigarette to the ground and throwing her shoulders back. The audience, shocked out of its stupor, would go wild. Or what if instead of Julie Andrews romping around on stage hamming it up in *Victor/Victoria* we had, oh, Al Gore accompanied by some gaily dressed members of the Senate as a chorus. Now that would be fun. And I bet he'd show up at the Tony's ready to perform.

But no, what we have instead is *Cats*. Okay, I admit the idea of a bunch of singing cats was entertaining when I was six. But at twenty-nine, I find it merely irritating. And I have seen *Cats,* although I have spent many years in therapy trying to forget the event. All I recall now is that the entire row ahead of me was filled with a group of high school students from Ohio. They all wore the same outfits they'd worn to their prom, and they thought they were very sophisticated. The theater crackled as satin-covered behinds settled into the seats, and the air was heavy with the smell of Aqua Net and Obsession for Men. The enthusiastic theatergoers clapped after every "meow" and swish of a tail. When the time came for Betty Buckley to sing "Memory," one of the boys fainted.

See, that's the problem with musicals. They pretend to be real art enhanced by some catchy songs, but all they really are underneath the costumes and sets are the Enchanted Tiki Room and Country Bear Jamboree from Walt Disney World shoved into a building with a grand name, peevish ushers, and no legroom. But because the ticket costs $85, people who should know better think it's something to get excited about.

In fact, if you look closely, you will see that underneath the pretty costumes and lavish sets, all musicals are really Disney movies. Think about it — every successful animated Disney film has relied heavily on catchy tunes to sweep the action along. Where would *Snow White* be without "Some Day My Prince Will Come" or *Lady and the Tramp* without "The Siamese Cat Song"? Sure, musicals were around long before Disney, but isn't it suspicious that more and more, Broadway shows look like cartoons come to life? Is it so difficult to imagine Andrew Lloyd Weber's phantom singing "Whistle While You Work" or *Les Mis*'s Cosette warbling "When You Wish Upon a Star"?

This is Broadway's secret shame. Writers and producers will do anything to convince us that their shows aren't just expensive versions of movies we could rent for $3 and enjoy in the comfort of our own homes, but mostly they're just variations on *Pinocchio* and *Bambi*. The truth of this is evidenced by the fact that when Disney announced plans to open a theater in New York and put on a production of *Beauty and the Beast,* the Broadway elite proclaimed the show nothing more than candy for the masses of unwashed tourists (much as the filmmaking community cried foul when the movie version was nominated for an Oscar and did better box office than the other four nominees combined). Undaunted, Disney went ahead. The show went on to be the season's biggest and only hit, undoubtedly due to millions of people from Ohio wearing prom dresses and plastic shoes. But fans of musical theater refused to accept this young upstart into their arms, insisting that their own shows were, well, just better.

I'm curious to know where the Broadway glitterati draw the line. Is Tony darling Nathan Lane darting about in a toga that reveals far more than anyone wants to see really any more dignified or deserving of praise than a giant singing candlestick dancing with a talking clock? Given a choice of the two, I'd be hard-pressed to choose, although I give the edge to the candlestick and the clock simply because I haven't quite forgiven Lane for singing "Hakuna Matata" in *The Lion King*.

And hey, now that I think of it, wasn't that a Disney movie too? Perhaps that line between Hollywood and Broadway is blurring a little bit more. Or maybe the folks on the Great White Way are finally accepting the inevitable — if they want to keep working, they have to get their noses out of the air and take a look at what America really likes to watch. It seems that in the battle between high art and popular culture, the little mouse with the funny pants and the squeaky voice is still kicking everyone's ass.

Why I Hate Shopping

I do not like to shop. At all. For anything.

I used to think this was because as a child I spent a great deal of my life being dragged around by my mother while she searched for the perfect pair of navy blue pumps. Any shopping trip inevitably turned into a quest for The Pumps, with my mother scanning store after store for the elusive footwear while I wailed pleas for mercy. "Aren't those the right color?" I'd sob as she picked up the three thousandth pair of perfectly adequate-looking blue shoes we'd seen that afternoon and examined them closely. I'd hold my breath and wait, collapsing into hysterics when she shook her head and said brightly, "Just this one more store."

Many years and much therapy later, my mother still does not have her navy blue pumps and I understand this is not the reason I hate shopping. I hate it because being in the proximity of so many things to buy makes me hyperventilate not because I want them but because the idea of so many lives spent making all the things and then even more lives spent convincing people they need the things and then even more lives spent selling the things and working to be able to buy the things makes me twitch with rage. Every time I see something truly awful — for example, a T-shirt emblazoned with kittens drawn in glitter — I am struck by the realization that not only did someone have to sit down and consciously decide to create that T-shirt, but then someone else had to spend at least part of her or his life manufacturing it, someone else designed a marketing strategy for it, someone else ordered it, and now someone else was actively selling it to someone who would actually buy and wear it. The fact that the sum total of probably one whole life was spent making that stupid glittery kitten T-shirt makes me want to cry. That's why I do not go shopping.

On the rare occasions when I *do* go shopping, inevitably I am overcome by the horror of being surrounded by so many useless things. And the frightening part is — I am fairly easily convinced that I need to purchase them. Obviously I have to own another pair of sandals; the current ones are running down a bit. A new linen shirt from J. Crew? But of course — you never know when you'll be invited to that clambake on the Vineyard. Before I know it, I've become a maelstrom of buying, flinging my Visa card at unsuspecting sales clerks as I dash from store to store until, breathless, I stagger out loaded down with parcels and bags, boxes and receipts. Then I look down at my perfectly good sandals and weep.

It's happened again. The last time I tried to go to shopping, I needed only to pick up Q-Tips. (The dog had an ear infection.) Three days later, I returned with seventeen pairs of socks, a baseball glove, three candles shaped like winged horses, a white-noise machine, four kinds of freshly baked cookies, a goose-down duvet, and all of Olivia Newton-John's albums on CD. The only thing I didn't have was the Q-Tips.

For many years I lived in New York, where shopping is not a problem, primarily because everything is far too expensive to actually buy. And since stores in New York invariably specialize in just one thing, shopping is easy. Limited as you are to purchasing the single item you need, there is no temptation to "just pick up" additional things or to browse through aisle after aisle of other things you hadn't thought to buy but are suddenly overcome with a need to purchase. If you need new shoes, you go to the shoe store. A nice ham, the ham store. Intriguing new sex toys, the sex-toy store. In New York, consumerism, like everything else, is very regimented. There are, of course, enormous department stores like Macy's and Lord & Taylor's, but they are to be avoided at all costs because they are crawling with thin young people dressed entirely in black who spritz you with various perfumes while chanting, "Obsession for Men," which is not, as it might at first seem, a question. The experience, I imagine, is probably not unlike attending a Hitler Youth meeting where everyone smelled nice and worked on commission.

But I no longer live in New York. And in the rest of America, shopping is a far deadlier undertaking. You can imagine my horror, then, when one day I went to change the sheets and realized that there was simply not a pair left with the elastic intact and without various unidentifiable stains mottling them like some kind of weird body fluid-food-pet stain batik. It just wouldn't do. I had to buy new ones, and that meant going shopping.

I decided to go to Filene's, primarily because it was the only store I could actually remember ever seeing in Boston, and it was close by on the subway. I could get off, get my sheets, and be home within an hour. While it wouldn't be enjoyable, it would at least be painless.

Or so I thought.

Getting there was fine. I got on the T when it came and got off again eight stops later at Downtown Crossing. I exited the turnstile and proceeded immediately to the entrance to Filene's. This was when I realized my first crucial mistake. Upon exiting the T station, I found the street swarming with people. It was lunch hour, which meant that approximately 8 billion people were scurrying about downtown Boston trying to complete their errands before grabbing something to eat and returning to work.

Taking a deep breath, I darted across Winter Street, weaving between men in dark suits and women with smart dresses. Arriving on the other side relatively unharmed, I congratulated myself and headed for the door to Filene's.

That was when I stumbled upon my second crucial mistake. You see, I'd forgotten that, like Macy's, Filene's is really just an entire mall crammed into one store. This means that everything detestable about a mall is amplified about 10,000 times by the mere fact of being contained in a smaller space. Once I got through the door, I was met not with the sounds of Prozac-like music of the 1980s but by the feverish screams of a frenzied mob of Hispanic housewives. They were all running about excitedly waving their arms in the air, as though someone had just caught a glimpse of the Virgin Mary in a Wonderbra and everyone was dying to see it before it degenerated into just another 32A cup.

I flattened myself against the wall as a large woman charged past, her arms filled with half slips and her eyes rolled back in her head. "What the hell is going on?" I said.

"It's a sale!" someone screamed as she sailed past me on her way to a table overflowing with black knee socks. Before I could thank her for the information, she went down like a wounded deer, felled by a woman holding up the last pair of socks in triumph.

Apparently I had wandered smack into the middle of some kind of radio promotion being put on by a Latin music station. A deejay had taken over the center of the floor and was chattering ceaselessly as the shopping women swarmed around him. "Who'd like another ten percent off?" he crowed in his faux-masculine deejay voice.

"We do!" screamed the women as one, the spittle flying from their lips as they ran panting from rack to rack.

I spied the escalator across the room. There was no way I was going to reach it what with all the women creating crosscurrents everywhere I turned. Like sharks worked up into a feeding frenzy, they were out of control, grabbing and pushing in the quest for bargains. I needed to create a diversion.

"Hey!" I shouted. "Isn't that a size sixteen Lanz nightgown over there?" I called out recklessly.

The flow turned instantly, with every woman in the store charging for the sleepwear. As the aisle near me cleared, I took advantage of it and sped across the floor. As I ascended into the upper reaches of Filene's, the din of voices became a dull roar.

Upstairs, things were calmer. I leisurely made my way to linens and started to search for sheets. I wanted plain white cotton sheets. Nothing fancy. What I saw were rows and rows of gaily colored sheets in vibrant colors. There were displays of cheerful sheets created by designers such as Ralph Lauren and Laura Ashley. Their bright flowers and sporty plaids called out, and I felt the familiar spell falling over me. Maybe I did need some nice green-checked Polo sheets.

I picked up a package. $129.95 for a sheet. Just one. And I needed at least two, plus pillowcases. The spell lifted. But they were very attractive, as was the man in the photo on the package. Maybe if I had sheets like this, I could have a man like this as well. Maybe he came as part of the set. I quickly moved away. Somehow, the spell became weaker the farther away I got. I wondered briefly if there was some chemical included in Ralph Lauren sheets that made them irresistible to gay men. Pheromones, maybe. That could explain Calvin Klein underwear as well.

I searched the entire section, to no avail. I found purple sheets, sheets with birds, abstract sheets, even black sheets. But no actual white sheets. I did find a lot of sheets that looked white to me, but they all had names like china, bone, and, still inexplicable to me, Marilyn. The closest thing they had to plain old white was a set of creamy linen sheets with satin ribbon edging. They were called angelwhite, and they cost $85. Maybe for Martha Stewart's country home, but not for me.

Finally, a clerk appeared from the recesses of the store like a prophet sent to deliver the wisdom of Jehovah to the ignorant. His hair was neatly greased back, and he looked like he knew a lot about bedding. His name was Geoff.

"Can I help you?" he asked politely.

"I need sheets," I said confidently. "White sheets."

"White?" Geoff said, as though he'd never heard of the color before.

"Yes," I said. "White."

"How about eggshell?" he suggested, starting for the Laura Ashley section.

"No," I said quickly. "Just white. Plain white."

"What about this lovely buttermilk Vera Wang bed ensemble?" he tried, waving a $625 set at me.

I could see where this was heading. "No buttermilk," I said. "And no ensemble. I just want sheets. White sheets. No eggshell. No winter. No ennui. Definitely no Marilyn. No whatever they call it. Just white."

Geoff's demeanor changed. "Fine," he said shortly. He led me to a dark corner of the store. "Normally we don't put these out," he said, "but we had some left."

He pointed at a stack of sheets carelessly tossed in a jumble on the floor. They looked a lot like the Laura Ashley, Ralph Lauren, and Vera Wang eggshell-buttermilk-Marilyn-winter sheets. But they said WHITE on them in little letters, like it was a guilty sin to be so ordinary.

"Most of our customers prefer the more unique shades," Geoff said, as though I'd just asked for Cheese Whiz and Wonder bread.

"Most of your customers are downstairs wrestling over a bra," I informed him. I picked up a set of sheets (only $39.95), paid, and left. As I exited the store, I rejoiced in what was, for me, a successful shopping trip, made even happier by the fact that I wouldn't have to repeat the endeavor for another five years or so. I hopped onto the T and breathed a sigh of relief.

Back at home, I pulled my hard-won sheets from the bag and looked gleefully at the package.

They were the wrong size.

The Perils of Dating

I am not good at dating.

Mind you, this isn't just some sudden gloomy thought brought on by an annoying dry spell between thrilling romantic encounters. This is based on the indisputable fact that over the last seven years I have had approximately three dates, none of which I can actually recall and none of which was repeated.

I suppose it's my fault, really. I never know how it's all supposed to work. My parents, from all accounts virgins on their wedding night, had exactly one date, which consisted of attending a church picnic surrounded by beaming elders. One of my sisters married at nineteen after dating only two men, and the other ran off with an unsavory character just to prove some point that, much to her enduring annoyance, none of us every fully got. Even my forebears are no help — one grandmother became pregnant, and I swear I am not making this up, while living in a convent; the other had four husbands, leaving me forever in doubt as to my mother's maiden name when asked for it by surly bank managers. With such meager experience to draw on, it's a wonder I haven't ended up padding around a trailer in a muumuu while my ex-con boyfriend bellows for another Hostess Snowball and a can of Genesee Creme

Ale so he can thoroughly enjoy the breathtaking thrill of *Cops*.

Let us also not forget that I am of the generation reared on the magic of Disney. Countless viewings of *Cinderella* and *Sleeping Beauty* as a child left me with the firm impression that all I'd have to do to attain romantic fulfillment was lounge around pining and eventually some handsome man with perfect teeth would happen by and be struck by my lonely beauty. We would then repair to some fabulous castle, accompanied by the chirps and trills of cartoon birds, and spend the rest of our lives being deliriously happy in a generally cheerful, if not sexually explicit, kind of way.

Imagine my horror, then, when I found out the whole affair actually involved the wanton exchanging of phone numbers and trying to fall asleep with my hero's slumbering head making my arm numb. I have a difficult time accepting that Snow White was forced to endure Prince Charming's suggestions that water sports might be interesting, and picturing her going through his drawers while he was out hunting to see what other princesses he'd been slipping it to ruins the whole dream utterly. If you ask me, being a cartoon heroine isn't all it's cracked up to be when the curtain comes down and the prince goes back to hunting Bambi's mother with the guys.

Walt's lies aside, I am willing to accept some of the blame for this problem of not yet being partnered. My friend Grace says it's because I'm not serious enough. Maybe she's right. With the exception of supermodels and Playboy bunnies, who inevitably list humor as the most desirable quality in the man of their dreams, most people seem to rank it far beneath being steadily employed and having perfect abs. The thought that

Naomi Campbell would find me utterly enthralling has its appeal, but on the whole I'd rather have George Clooney banging on my bedroom door.

Nor does it help that I'm completely oblivious when someone is interested. I do not know when I am being cruised. I think men who smile at me knowingly are looking at something amusing behind me. I once had a man I was intensely fascinated with kiss me for a full three minutes on a crowded New York street in front of a whole phalanx of firefighters battling a restaurant grease-fire inferno. Afterward, I politely said good night, went home alone, and wondered for days if he liked me. It never occurred to me that sticking his tongue down my throat before an audience of toasting diners might be a clue. I thought he was just being nice. By the time I figured it out, months later, he'd moved on to someone with more highly developed dating skills.

Curious to see if I was the only one with this deficiency, I called my friend Sybil, also single. "Are you dating anyone?" I asked innocently, hoping she'd say she wasn't and we could then bitch about it for an hour or so.

"No one special," she answered. "A couple of different people."

A couple of different people! She said it so casually. The thought astounded me. How can anyone date a couple of different people. Maybe it's just me, but the minute I start dating someone, or even get introduced in passing, I instantly become a neurotic mess. Okay, I was probably neurotic long before the dating even started, but the first date inevitably sets off a predictable pattern. No matter that we've shared only one night of Thai food — I must know where it's all leading. If he doesn't call, he must hate me, or he's sleeping with someone else. If he does call, I wonder why he doesn't have anyone else to hang out with. You can see the dilemma. I would hardly have the time to stalk more than one person at a time.

The casual dating thing may be what the carefree queers of the '90s are into, but it just doesn't do it for me. I don't like being around strangers enough to date someone if I don't think that joint checking and rooms filled with IKEA furnishings aren't a definite possibility. I don't need to sit through boring movies or endless hockey games just so we can get to know each other and feel that we have fulfilling interpersonal relationships. I am quite secure in my dysfunction and do not need to pretend that my life has meaning outside of watching Bruce Willis movies. I have an entire owner's manual already typed up. I simply hand it over on the first date and tell him to call with any questions.

This whole notion of casual sex also leaves me cold. In the time it would take me to find someone, discuss who would do what to whom, and do it, I could have eaten an entire Entenmann's pound cake and spent several amusing hours replaying the scene in *The Color of Night* where Bruce Willis pulls off his boxers and gives an all-too-brief shot of his ass and willy. As for the sex part, I could accomplish the same thing by myself, and without having to take a shower, leave the house, or wonder why there were two toothbrushes in his bathroom and a second pair of glasses on the bedside table.

No, I am looking for more. In pursuit of this dream, I trotted dolefully to the local gay bookstore and picked up a copy of a self-help book whose blurbs promised that reading it would ensure romantic success. I will not embarrass the author by revealing his name, because he is a frightful liar. To be sure, the book was filled with all manner of sage advice about seeking out the mate of one's dreams. I learned that I must first love myself if anyone was to love me and that I have no one to blame but myself for consistently passing over well-adjusted, happy men for those with criminal records and enormous endowments. But this I already knew.

Where the book really failed was in its suggestions for actually finding a man once I'd cleared away all of the emotional debris I'd built up over the years. I should, the author suggested helpfully, think of men as squirrels. And squirrels, naturally, are searching for nuts. In particular, squirrels want large, attractive, meaty nuts. *Don't we all,* I thought as I turned the page, curious to see where this whole squirrel thing was going. It was there that I learned that I am, in fact, the nut, which was not as disconcerting as it probably should have been. Furthermore, if I wanted to attract a squirrel with a particularly bushy tail and a cheerful outlook on life, the book said, I must be an especially wonderful nut. Because the best squirrels always have the best nuts. *Maybe I should just date squirrels,* I thought joylessly as I tossed the book aside.

The problem, ultimately, is that dating involves men, and men are hard to find these days. Oh, sure, there are scads of annoying fellows doused in Obsession for Men just lying about for the taking. But the really good ones, the ones who like big dogs and don't care what Madonna is up to today, are fair near extinct. When I do find one that might be interesting, his wife always comes along to spoil it.

It also does not help that I am the least social human being on this planet, making the normal avenues of meeting people closed to me. I do not go to parties. I do not attend readings and literary functions, usually wonderful places for writer types to meet men, at least men who can read. Unfortunately, these types of men have never appealed to me, as they are frequently disposed to having ideas about things, which they want to discuss at length. This is intolerable. Bars are also not an option, if only because I do not see well in dim light and become easily confused by the noise and smoke common to such places, which within minutes renders me into something of a cross between a hysterical beaver trying to remove itself from a leg trap and a political prisoner being forced to stare at a naked bulb while unpleasant people with loud voices ask questions to which I do not know the answers.

I've tried the volunteer route as well, spending several months working at a community center hoping that, while doing some good, I might also encounter some nice ex-jock with a house in the country and the courtesy to think that everything I do is amazing. Sadly, while I did learn lots of clever cheers to toss around at rallies of all kinds, in the end I found it difficult to relate to men whose primary concern was for which nipple to get pierced. And forget meeting men through friends. My friends do not know anyone I would ever want to go out with. In fact, I don't even want to go anywhere with them, so why would I trust their judgment.

When I do, by chance, meet someone who might even possibly be date material, I have developed a remarkable system for going through an entire relationship with the person in my mind in thirty seconds flat. I whiz through dating and the first sexual encounter to moving in together and buying a dog in no time. By the time I've even walked across the room, I already have us fighting over the VCR as he packs his things to leave, making introductions irrelevant because we are no longer speaking. It saves a lot of time.

It's not that I'm particularly fussy. In fact, I don't ask for much. But what I do ask for is hard to find these days — a man who is independent, believes in himself, and questions the state of the world. Unfortunately, these men are almost always either married to Kim Basinger or they're career criminals. As my friend Dan cruelly pointed out recently: "Your problem is that your ideal man is the Unabomber." Sad, but true.

Still, ever the romantic, I refuse to stop believing that somewhere out there is a man I can, if not love madly, at least tolerate. So here's the plan: I am having an essay contest, and the grand prize is me. Anyone interested is free to submit. All you have to do is tell me in 750 words or less how you are going to make me wildly excited forever. Essays will be judged on originality, penmanship, and ability to amuse me. Presents are also a nice touch, especially cash. The winner will be notified by my arrival on his doorstep.

Okay, so it isn't Ed McMahon handing you a big check with lots of zeros. But at least you don't have to lick seventy-three different stamps and put them in the right places to win.

Picture Imperfect

I do not like to have my picture taken.

This is not a mere paranoia; it is an out-and-out mania. I do not pose for group shots during outings with friends. I do not think spontaneous camera clicking is cheery and whimsical. I firmly believe that people who were the photo editors of their high school yearbooks all grew up to work for the Department of Motor Vehicles and wear unpleasant fabric blends.

The analytically inclined among my friends say this aversion to being photographed is because I have issues with how I look. That's not true. I'm perfectly happy with the way I look. I simply have issues with being locked in a frame and stared at by people I only marginally like.

When I was a child, this wasn't the problem it might at first appear to be. For one thing, I was a third child, with ten years coming between me and my two older sisters, whom my mother had enthusiastically conceived less than a year apart. Despite my being of a different gender, and thus a novelty, my parents apparently decided that all babies do, in fact, look like Winston Churchill, and chose not to add any further pictures to albums already crammed with close-ups of infants with interchangeable expressions.

Thankfully, neither of my parents was particularly interested in capturing our lives on film anyway. While there were reams of photos taken of the first few birthdays and holidays of my sisters' lives, this ended abruptly somewhere around the time of my eldest sister's sixth birthday, as though having finally figured out how to keep the camera in focus, my father had decided that the game was no longer amusing. After that, all there is to mark our growth are a few shots taken at random moments, generally by people other than our parents. The sole picture of me from those dreamy years of childhood shows me shaking hands with Ranger Rick, the raccoon mascot of the nature magazine of the same name. It was taken by an overenthusiastic friend of my mother's, whose child was also along for the historic event. Despite my joy at meeting this hero of my youth, my face sports a decidedly bitter look.

Besides, even if they had been inclined toward picture-taking, neither my father nor my mother could ever accurately recall what was depicted in any given photo anyway. Never ones for writing the dates or occasions on the backs of snapshots, a typical look through a stack of pictures went something like this.

"Oh, look, that's our house in Hawaii," my mother would say, peering at the blurry shot of something resembling palm trees and water.

"No, it's not," my father would counter. "It's from our trip to Kenya."

"But that's your mother there, standing by the palm tree."

"I think that's a native totem, actually."

Inevitably, after half an hour of trying to distinguish old houses from long-deceased pets and children from national monuments, they would give up in disgust, tossing all of the photos back into the box and storing it once more on the top shelf of the linen closet, where it would languish until the next time someone worked up the courage to do it all again.

It was a simple matter, then, to prevent any photos of myself from being taken. If for some reason inspiration struck and someone produced a camera during a family event, I quietly hid behind my uncle John, who was easily wide enough to conceal a small boy. And when that annual horror known as school pictures rolled around, I just never brought the forms home. On the one occasion when my mother mentioned that she'd like an image of me, I took one of my cousin Jay, who was my look-alike, and gave it to her. Unsuspecting, she kept it on the refrigerator for years, much to the puzzlement of my aunt Pat.

Thus I rode out my adolescence and teen years safe from the glare of flashbulbs. And I escaped my college years unscathed as well, save for one unfortunate shot showing my friend James in drag, looking eerily like Bea Arthur, while I leer at a phallic-shaped balloon gripped in his hand. The negatives of this print, taken shortly before we attended a Halloween party at the local Episcopal church, are still running around somewhere and are certain to come back to haunt me at my Nobel Prize ceremony.

With that one startling exception, photos were not an issue again until I got my first and only job in the professional world. Upon my arrival at the office, I was told I needed to have a picture ID taken if I wanted, as I was assured I did, to enter and exit the building without having to be searched each time by the hulking guards who flanked either side of the one door in and out. Deciding that it would be unwise to throw a fit on my first day of gainful employment, I sat sulkily before the camera and got it over with. Thankfully, the picture was the size of a postage stamp, and it remained safely in my wallet for the entire five years I worked at that company. I shredded it the day I left for good.

I was quite pleased at myself for having made it through almost three decades without being photographed more than absolutely necessary. Of course, not having a driver's license or passport had posed the occasional problem, but then the joys of travel are overrated anyway, and staying in one place for a lifetime seemed a small price to pay for my convictions. Then, one awful afternoon, the phone rang. Never one to sense danger early on, I picked it up innocently, only to be greeted by the editor of a book I'd recently finished.

"Hi," she said airily. "We're doing the jacket for your book this week, and we need you to send over a photo."

I gave the little harmless chuckle I'd always used for such requests in the past. "I'm afraid I don't have one," I said. "Just use copy."

She was adamant. "We have to have a picture," she said, an edge in her voice. "We always have pictures of the authors."

I will not bore you with the details of the next half hour of conversation. Suffice it to say that this horrible woman, who should have never been given a job where she can viciously abuse innocent writers by threatening to withhold advance checks, would not back down. She even had the rudeness to point out that my contract specifically required my cheerful cooperation with this matter, a point I was sure to take up with my agent when I fired him later in the day. By the time I hung up, I'd agreed to hand over a suitable photo of myself by the next week, my suggestion for using the Ranger Rick photo having been soundly rejected.

Not only did I not want to have my picture taken but this was a most unfortunate time to need one. Smack in the middle of a sweltering summer, I had shaved all of my hair off a few weeks earlier. It was growing back, but it was at a stage where I looked suspiciously like a worried hedgehog. Now, thanks to the demands of being a world-famous author, the entire known universe would be able to enjoy my bad hair day.

Distraught, I called my friend Becket, who takes very moody black and white pictures of people who do not like to be photographed. Almost all of his clients are writers, and he has developed a wonderful touch with those of us who would rather rewrite an entire novel for the third time than sit in front of a camera. We scheduled a photo session for the next day. "It will be fine," he said.

It was not fine. I was crabby. I complained. I whined. But Becket was patient. He settled me on the stool and arranged my collar. He even gave me a shirt to wear after deciding that the HOTHEAD PAISAN T-shirt I walked in with was totally inappropriate. The shirt was a black polo shirt. I hate both black and polo shirts, but Becket said it was arty, and I believed him because he said it so sincerely. Besides, he promised me an Oreo if I behaved.

The session took two hours. It consisted essentially of Becket imploring me to smile and my refusing to do so.

"Just try," he said. "You'll look great."

"I will not," I said grimly. "I look ridiculous when I smile."

"Just try," he pleaded. "Please. Pretend Alec Baldwin is reading your book and finds you absolutely fascinating."

I tried. Anything for Alec.

"Okay," he said instantly. "Smiling isn't the only look. Let's try something else."

Becket took four rolls of film. By the time I left, he was whimpering softly, and I had a headache. I did not get my Oreo.

When Becket developed the contact sheets, I went back and looked at them.

"They're all the same," I said, looking at row after row of my unsmiling face.

"I know," he said. "It's amazing. How do you do it?"

I took two of the least agonized-looking photos and put them in an envelope. I sent them to my editor with a short note: "I told you so."

When I Grow Up

I was walking down the street shortly after my twenty-eighth birthday when suddenly it dawned on me: I will never be an astronaut. This is simply a fact. At my age I am too old to begin the NASA training program. Normally this wouldn't be any big deal, no real cause for alarm. But for some reason, this discovery set off a disturbing chain of thought as I realized to my horror that at some point I had quietly crossed the line where there are now many, many things I am too old to do or too far along to start learning.

When I got home, I made a list of careers that, in all probability, were no longer options for me:

> Child prodigy
> Someone in the 18–25 range on surveys
> Teen model
> Serious novelist under 30
> Ingenue

Okay, so perhaps I never wanted to be any of those things in the first place. And being a certain age does have its advantages. I cannot, for example, be drafted in the event of war. I no longer have to pay outrageous insurance premiums on my car. I am almost old enough to run for Congress. But when it comes to having a career, my options are dwindling rapidly.

Remember those glorious days of youth, when everything seemed possible and nothing stood in your way? Why, I changed my future occupation on an hourly basis. One morning I wanted to be a fireman, that afternoon a doctor, and later that evening an explorer. I went through a whole week of looking forward to life as a cowboy, only to pitch it in an instant to be a Barnum & Bailey circus clown. It was a thrilling time, filled with endless possibilities and limitless horizons. When anyone asked me what I wanted to be when I grew up, I had an answer, and usually several. "But," I always pointed out afterward, "I haven't exactly decided yet." I didn't want to fence myself in when there were so many exciting options.

But all of that quickly ended sometime around my twelfth birthday. (Interesting how discovering the joys of masturbation is followed so quickly by an avalanche of unpleasant awakenings, isn't it?) While wanting to be a pro baseball player is fine when you're five, when you hit your teens people generally start expecting more from you.

I still vividly remember taking a career test in high school in which we were instructed to answer questions designed to gauge our interests. Using some odd sort of number system taken directly from a *Cosmopolitan* test on relationships, we then added up our results and plotted two points on a graph. Scattered about the graph's field were various types of careers — exciting things like architecture, biological sciences, nursing, and, most appealing of all, government. Wherever our points met on the graph, that's the field we were destined for. I feverishly found my two plot points and moved my fingers together to find which of the many thrilling futures would be mine.

Imagine my dismay when, instead of coming together on economics, veterinary medicine, or even the arts, my fingers met over…empty space. There was one small corner of the graph that remained empty, and I was smack in the middle of it. All around, marvelous careers circled like glorious, shining prizes, but they were just out of my reach. I checked my points again; they were correct. Somehow, the answers I'd given to the questions resulted in absolutely no career prospects at all. When I presented my empty, futureless graph to my guidance counselor, he chuckled wryly. "Don't you worry," he said. "It just means you have a lot of interests. You can be anything you want to." I didn't tell him that I had no idea what I wanted and had been hoping the chart would give me some hints.

Things picked up a little a few months later, however, when a military recruiter came to the school to administer the ominously titled Armed Services Vocational Aptitude Battery test, called ASVAB for short. Taking the ASVAB test was entirely voluntary, but the time it was offered coincided with gym class, which that week involved square dancing. While most of us had little interest in the military as a way of life, when time came for the test, the library was packed.

Given the amazingly grim nature of the armed forces, the ASVAB was remarkably fun. Unlike the SATs or the other standardized tests we took on a regular basis and loathed, the ASVAB involved lots of problems taken directly from everyday life. At least everyday life in the Marines or the Army. For example, one section involved looking at lists of items that might be found in a military storeroom, things like uniforms, tents, flashlights, rifles, jeep parts, and gallon jugs of mayonnaise. Next to each item — and there were about a hundred of them — was a number. Our job was to run through a list of random numbers on our test papers, find the items to which they corresponded, and write them down. We had three minutes to see how many we could match up.

Apparently, I did very well on matching up blankets (number 00789), gas masks (13986) and boots (87602), because several weeks after taking the ASVAB, I received a letter informing me that I had been recommended for Navy nuclear engineering training. I was assured that my ability to match up numbers with their corresponding items was unsurpassed in my school, and probably in the entire world, and that the Navy would give me just about anything to enlist. I was ecstatic. Finally I had proof that all of those hours playing Concentration as a child had paid off.

In the end, at the insistence of my father, I never did get to enter the breathtaking world of nuclear technology. Instead I went off to college where, set upon by the same evil people who insisted I couldn't be a clown, I was forced to pick a major. For many reasons, not the least of which was that it seemed the easiest and you didn't have to do fractions, I chose English. Even then I had no idea what I would do with my degree when I was done. I figured I had four years to figure it out.

Four years later, with nothing to show for myself but a working knowledge of Milton and a much-praised critical variorum on a Keats ode, I still had no idea. I went so far as to fill out an application for the seminary, in the vain hope that it would give me another four years to make up my mind. Throughout it all the Navy had continued to call my home during my college years to tell me there was always a bunk waiting for me aboard one of their spiffy submarines. While it was nice to have this safety net, by that time I knew there were other reasons I didn't want to head out to sea with a lot of men in close quarters besides the fact that I dislike water.

Then, one night I was driving a visiting lecturer on writing back to her home in New York City. She asked me what my plans were after graduation. When I mumbled something about not having decided yet, she gave me her publisher's phone number and insisted I call the next day. I did and subsequently got my one and only actual job in the business world. Finally, I had a direction, even if it was completely by accident. When people asked me what I did, I promptly said, "I'm an editor." The pressure was off. It stayed off for five years, at which time the company was purchased by another publisher and we were all given the option of either moving to New Jersey or being fired. Being a sensible person with no tolerance for big hair and toxic waste, I chose downsizing and was thus dumped into the world once more with no idea where I was headed.

That was several years ago, and in that time I seem to have become, by default, a writer. This is fine with me. But it seems to upset a lot of other people, to whom writing is clearly not so much a profession as it is something to do when you aren't really working. No matter that I've published upwards of twenty books and won a handful of awards or that I manage to support myself entirely on the words that come out of my head. I'm still suspect. I'm still cheating somehow. Writing is nice as a hobby, but as a career? It's as though I'm still hanging around in that empty space on the career graph, and no one is very happy about it.

This is most evident when I am introduced to people for the first time. "What do you do?" they ask politely.

"I'm a writer," I say flatly, knowing what will come next.

I get one of two responses. The first, "Have you written anything I might have read?" is the least unpleasant of the two, as it at least displays some sort of acceptance on the part of my new acquaintance of the fact that I really do this for a living. Things inevitably go downhill, however, when it is revealed that I have not written anything that has either reached the number one spot on *The New York Times* best-seller list or been turned into a television movie featuring Tori Spelling.

The second response, "Oh, a writer. I hope you publish something someday," is more typical, implying as it does that I could not possibly have written anything yet because the speaker has never heard of anyone foolish enough to admit that he actually writes for a living. It is almost always accompanied by an indulgent little smile of the sort reserved for children who have just announced that they fully intend to become Supreme Court justices or rock stars.

Even my family doesn't quite get it. "How's it going?" my father says cheerfully when he calls. "Are you still doing that thing you do?"

"You mean write?" I say.

"Yes, right, that's it. Is it working out yet?"

"Well, I just published another novel."

"Really? Did they pay you for it?"

"Not enough, Dad."

"Well, that's okay. It's always a place to start, right? You have to begin somewhere. One of these days you'll figure out what it is you want to do."

I'm curious to know what the cutoff limit is for when certain ambitions and careers become unacceptable. For example, it seems absolutely thrilling for a six-year-old to say she wants to be an Oscar-winning actress. "That's right," we say, "you keep practicing that acceptance speech." But when those same words are mouthed by a 34-year-old waitress whose biggest part to date was as a silent extra in a community theater production of *Our Town,* we tend to disbelieve them. An eight-year-old boy whose greatest ambition is to be the star of the Rangers is encouraged to bash his way around the rink. His seventeen-year-old counterpart is told to start thinking of trade school as a viable option.

At the same time, please note that we lavishly reward those who refuse to give in. Actors. Sports stars. Supermodels. All highly paid. All fawned over. All because they refused to advance beyond the age of four while the rest of us put away the basketballs and dog-eared scripts and learned how to do accounting and fix cars instead. We don't love these people because they're great; we love them because they didn't listen. You can bet their parents still call them up and want to know when they're getting real jobs.

I used to attempt to explain my work to people, spouting lists of my books and pointing out my various magazine and newspaper columns as proof of my claim of being a real, full-time writer. But that was simply too much effort. Besides, if you have to work that hard to get people to take you seriously, you're too defensive. Now I don't bother. Whenever anyone asks me what I do, I remember my five-year-old self and respond happily, "I'm thinking of being a clown, but I haven't decided yet."

Adventures Among
the Straight People

Trial by Fire

As a queer man, I've made a concerted effort to stay away from that harpy of gay life — the Fag Hag. I'm referring, of course, to that peculiar breed of heterosexual woman who finds it some kind of thrill to hang around men she'll never get into bed with and who remarks frequently that spending time with her beautiful but untouchable boyfriends is just like having a pajama party with all her girlfriends, minus the thrilling conversations about tampons and armpit shaving that we men missed out on in our teens and that it can be argued some segments of our population have been making up for ever since by clumping around in glitter wedgies and dresses that would scare Gloria Swanson back up her staircase.

While some men find the company of these women amusing, I am not one of them. I grew up in a house with two older sisters, and consequently the feminine mystique was demystified for me very early on. The esoteric rituals of depilatory creams, sanitary napkins, and the appeal of a smart vinegar and water spray hold absolutely no fascination for me, and the world of straight women is one I haven't wanted to spend time in since I first discovered the joys of man-to-man sex in a men's room at the local Sears.

As a result, over the years I've carefully honed my Hag Radar to the point where I can spot clingy heterosexual women immediately and avoid them like an ex walking on the street with a new, more handsome lover. I refuse to spend a minute with any woman who begins a sentence with "If only you weren't gay," forces me to go shopping to help her pick out something for her nephew's bar mitzvah that is both tasteful and will make Stacey Schermer green with jealousy, or asks me to share oral sex techniques that will make her boyfriend babble uncontrollably and promise her emerald earrings. If I wanted to hang around a lot of straight women, I'd have a Tupperware party.

Because of this aversion, the fact that Grace and I are such good friends surprises most people. Thoroughly heterosexual (except for one drunken confession about a fantasy involving Cindy Crawford and a bottle of lemon-scented oil that I promised never to tell another living soul), Grace is one of the few straight women I know who doesn't expect me to be able to offer decorating advice. She never asks me to go to weddings with her as her "special friend," never teases me for not knowing anything about opera, and not once has she asked me if her favorite actors are gay. We met on line waiting to buy tickets to a k.d. lang concert. Each of us thought the other was a dyke.

What enables Grace and me to remain friends is that we respect each other's views. She knows not to try to make me appreciate modern painting, and I in turn have stopped trying to explain to her why hockey is the only perfect art form. Her idea of indulging in Italian food involves sun-dried tomatoes and basil-infused olive oil; mine is eating SpaghettiOs straight from the can. I cannot understand her fascination with nerdy academic men who take her to lectures on the underlying Christ figure metaphors in Renaissance sonnets. She finds my obsession with big jocks who like to go to Steven Seagal movies appalling.

Despite these differences, we have managed to stay close, and for five years this partnership has run smoothly. But a few months ago something happened that tested the strength of our friendship, and it was the last thing either of us expected.

It started when I dragged Grace to Sam Goody to look for the latest John Michael Montgomery album. She had just forced me to sit through an agonizing French movie involving subtitles that had no pronouns and featured lots of pale men and women throwing leaves at one another while weeping, all set to a score composed mostly of bassoons and what sounded like small children being crushed to death by stones. I had fallen asleep halfway through and was still aching from a persistent cramp in my left leg that made me limp around like a wounded bear. As my revenge, I had brought Grace record shopping because I knew she would hate it. As expected, she was being a pain in the ass.

"You just didn't understand it," she said as I pulled her though the doors. "It was all about how men and women relate to one another."

"Nothing blew up," I said. "There were no cute men and far too many breasts for my liking. And what was that business with the nun and the bowl of tomatoes?"

Grace snorted. "Just because Harrison Ford didn't run through wearing a fedora and fending off a bunch of natives with only his manhood and a short piece of stick doesn't mean it was stupid. Not everything is about sweating and saving the world. You know nothing about art."

I ignored her, rounding a large Garth Brooks cutout whose considerable cardboard bulge poked invitingly over a display of his latest album. "I don't know why you have to listen to this stuff anyway," Grace was droning as I pulled her down the aisle of the country section. "It's so...twangy."

"Shut up," I told her venomously as I tugged on her upper arm. "It's better than that Eurofag–Pet Shop Boys–mindless computer dance crap you listen to. And I think you need to do some more water aerobics; you're getting a little thick up here, and you'll look doughy in that off-the-shoulder thing you bought to pick up boys at the opera."

She responded by kicking me viciously right where my cramp was, so that I stumbled and lost my hold on her arm. Sensing an opportunity for escape, she made a worthy attempt at dashing back toward the jazz section while I tried to regain my balance. Fortunately, I was able to cling to a surprisingly sturdy Mary Chapin Carpenter stand-up and regained my balance quickly enough to give Grace a head start of only a few feet. Before long I was right behind her.

I had just managed to get a good grip on her hair and she was in the process of trying to step on my foot when the fireman came into view. He rounded the corner near the vocals section and made his way toward us, striding by the Anne Murray section briskly. Without a word, we paused midbattle, an unspoken truce brought on by the appearance of the only thing on earth that could get us to stop — a Fire God.

I should explain that Grace and I both have a thing for firemen. More precisely, we have an obsession with anything remotely to do with firemen. We walk the long way to the subway so we can go past the firehouse and linger while we watch the guys wash the trucks or straighten the hoses or even put the recycling bags at the curb. We always stop to pet the dalmatians at our respective houses — Highrise at mine, Domino at hers — and chat up their owners, Fireman Steve and Fireman Robert. When the fire department had a big subway ad campaign last year, we had a contest to see who could steal the most posters. STAY BACK 200 FEET means nothing to us when the sound of sirens calls.

This man fully lived up to my vision of what a fireman should be. His very broad shoulders were packed into the telltale blue fire department T-shirt, the rest of him into jeans and boots. His short dark hair begged to have someone's hands — preferably mine — run through it. He had the shadow of a beard. He was the most beautiful thing I'd ever seen. I glanced over and saw that Grace's eyes had practically rolled back in her head, and she was beginning to drool like one of those pictures of a medieval saint in ecstasy over being pierced by God.

We stared in awe as our firefighter walked through the aisles, both of us carefully searching for signs that he might be available. Whenever he passed behind a pillar or display, we held our breath waiting for him to reappear. We bobbed and ducked and scurried after him, following silently. After a minute of watching him, I surmised that there was no one near him who might be a potential significant other, and a quick scan showed that the ring finger of each hand was bare.

"It's not real," Grace murmured.

"I can practically smell the smoke," I said.

We looked at each other suspiciously. There was only one fireman and two of us. The answer to the problem was simple, and we both knew it. One of us would have to die.

"I'll invite you to the wedding," I said and started after my soon-to-be husband.

I got about five feet before a violent force knocked me flat against a display of Amy Grant Christmas CDs. In my daze, I could only vaguely wonder where Grace had learned to bodycheck like that. I felt like the casualty of a Ranger-Canuck run-in as I peeled myself away from Amy's oversize smiling face.

"Get out of my way," Grace hissed as she streaked by. "This one's mine."

Pausing momentarily to check her lipstick in a metallic theft-prevention sticker on the back of Juice Newton's *Greatest Hits*, Grace made her way across the store, softly humming "On Top of Old Smoky." She was wearing her short skirt, and I knew I was in trouble if I didn't think of something fast. My mind raced as I ran through a list of possible diversions, watching in horror as Grace moved closer and closer to my intended. Finally, when she was halfway down the aisle, I stopped her dead in her tracks by shouting, "Forget it. He's heading for the show-tunes section."

The fireman, who was in fact intently perusing that area of the store, turned around, the original cast album from *Carousel* in his manly hand. I quickly ducked behind a stack of Judds boxed sets, leaving Grace to fend for herself and congratulating myself on my cunning.

Forced to think quickly, Grace relied on her years of experience in dealing with men. "You know," she said cleverly, "I just loved *Backdraft.*" She followed this with a little laugh and a swing of her hair. The fireman smiled. *That bitch,* I thought bitterly.

Peering out from behind the Judds, I could clearly see every move Grace made. She was standing as closely as possible to the fireman, laughing at everything he said and swinging her hair thirteen times a minute. Her hand rested lightly on his masculine forearm, her nails purposefully stroking the soft dark hair as she babbled on and on, holding him captive. At that moment, I hated her more than I'd ever hated anyone in my life. She wasn't my friend; she was a husband stealer.

I had to think of something to get her away from the man I was sure I would spend the rest of my life with. Grace was working herself up into her "if you take me home I'll do things to you that you only thought were possible in European soft-focus films" mode. I'd seen it before and was all too familiar with her success rate. Unfortunately, I was too busy thinking about the fireman's hairy forearms to concentrate fully on my next move.

"Can I help you find something?" a voice asked from behind me, startling me back to the real world.

I turned around to find a store clerk watching me. I stared at his wide, innocent face and blinking eyes. He reminded me of a big, stupid dog waiting for a bone. What I did next was the act of a desperate man.

"Actually, Walter," I said, glancing at his name tag and whispering conspiratorially to gain his trust, "I'm just watching that girl over there."

Walter looked over the stack of grinning Naomis and Wynonnas with their big red hair and squinted at Grace, then looked back at me. "She sure is pretty," he said.

I put my hand on his shoulder. "No, Walter," I said seriously, "you don't understand. I think I saw her stick some blank tapes in her backpack."

Walter blinked again while his brain processed this new information. "Are you sure?" he asked, his demeanor growing bolder as the enormity of the situation sunk in.

I nodded, hoping I looked innocent and believable. Walter, eyes gleaming, pulled his pants farther up his belly and squared his shoulders. Then he walked over to where Grace was playing out her seduction scene. "Excuse me," he said politely, interrupting a gale of girlish laughter as he tapped her sharply on the shoulder, "but would you please come with me."

Grace looked as if he had slapped her. "Why?" she said defensively, her eyes narrowing. Walter, his adrenaline churning out of control from this unexpected power opportunity, turned stone-faced. "Just come with me, please, ma'am. We'll talk about it downstairs. In the security office."

I knew Grace wanted to put up a fight, especially over being called "ma'am," but she also didn't want to make a fool of herself in front of her prey. The fireman was looking from Walter to Grace, and she knew she was in trouble if she said anything unladylike. She went quietly, remarking over her shoulder to the fireman as she left, "There must be some mistake. I'm sure it will be cleared up in a minute. Don't go away."

As Grace marched past me, I avoided looking at her, pretending to rifle through some Patsy Cline CDs. She tried to stop and say something, but Walter pushed her ahead of him. "It's always the innocent-looking ones," I said, shaking my head sadly as they went by.

Once Walter and Grace were out of sight, I made my move. I knew she would be back once Walter opened her backpack and found nothing but breath mints and notes for her doctoral thesis in early English pastoral poetry. I had only a few minutes to get the job done and get Mr. Fireman of My Dreams out the door before Grace would be on the loose again. I strolled over to my beloved, my heart beating wildly as I planned my strategy.

"I wonder what that was all about," I said casually as I sidled up next to him, checking out the way his butt looked in his jeans and resisting an urge to run my tongue down his neck.

He looked over at me quickly, then looked again. A good sign. "I don't know," he said. "She seemed like a nice enough girl. I can't imagine she did anything wrong."

"I'm not sure," I said, determined to crush once and for all any positive thoughts he might have about the evil vixen who almost took my man. I was pretty sure he was playing on my team, but these days it's hard to tell, and I always end up going for the straight ones anyway. If I was going to end up disappointed, I was going to make damn sure Grace was right there with me. "I think I smelled liquor on her breath."

He looked at me again and grinned, his perfect lips parting to reveal white teeth that appeared to have benefited from years of orthodontia as a child. I thought I'd pass out when I saw the way his chin dimpled. Then, just as I was getting a good look at his beautiful brown eyes, he went back to his work. He appeared to be looking for a particular album, pawing through the stacks of CDs intently.

I know absolutely nothing about musical theater apart from the fact that at some point someone sings something, but I decided to improvise. If my man liked musicals, I could learn to like them too. Besides, I'd seen that movie where Mary Poppins dresses a bunch of kids up in curtains and takes them on a bicycle tour through the Alps while they're all pursued by nuns and eat strudel while playing the guitar, and that had to count for something. I hummed something I thought sounded vaguely show tune–like and snatched up the nearest CD without looking at it, pretending to read the back intently.

"Isn't this the show Liza was in?" I asked, throwing out the only name I could come up with that I knew might have anything even remotely to do with musicals. I saw her sing in a Diet Coke commercial once and figured she must have been in something along the way to deserve that kind of exposure.

He glanced over. "I doubt it," he said, looking at me strangely. "That's the sound track from *Terminator 2*. You must be thinking of *Cabaret*."

"That must be it," I said lightly. "I'm always getting them confused." I put it down again and wondered what he'd do if I just tackled him and threw him to the floor. Things were not going well. Then, to make matters worse, before I could come up with another conversation starter, Grace reappeared at the top of the escalator. I could see by the way her lips were set as she stormed up the aisle that whatever was left of Walter would regret the day she walked into his store. I quickly moved to the other side of the fireman so that he was between us. I knew she wouldn't risk damaging him just to get at me.

"It seems," she said pointedly as she came to a stop and rearranged her face into a mask of sweetness, "that someone made a mistake."

I tried my best to appear sympathetic. "That's terrible," I said, leaning in to smell my fireman's manly scent and noticing the hair that peeked over the collar of his T-shirt. "Some people will just do anything to get noticed."

"Some people," said Grace, shredding a CD wrapper with her nails, "are going to be sorry forever when I get my hands on them."

The fireman had made his way to the R's and seemed to have found just about everything he wanted. Grace and I glared at each other balefully over his back as he bent to retrieve one last item. We both knew that time was running out, and both of us were desperate to get the man's clothes off. Now it wasn't even about him; it was about which one of us was a better flirt. Grace decided to go for broke. She brushed the hair out of her eyes and pretended to see the fireman's shirt for the first time.

"Oh, wow," she gushed, "a fire department T-shirt. What company are you with?" We both know the location of the Manhattan fire departments by heart. I held my breath, hoping he was closer to my apartment than hers.

"Oh, it isn't mine," he said. "It belongs to my brother. I would never go near a burning building. I'm in the Shearson-Lehman accountant training program."

Grace and I looked at each other, our eyes welling up and our bottom lips trembling. Our mighty fireman was a fraud. It was all a cruel joke. This was worse than finding out there was no Easter Bunny or even that Newt Gingrich was running for president. Far worse. This was as bad as finding out that the hole in the ozone layer was caused by excessive chocolate consumption.

After that, it didn't matter whether the guy had a boyfriend, a girlfriend, or a golden retriever named Jack.

He had the shirt, he had the boots, and he had the look. But he wasn't the real thing. He would never come home from work sweaty from a practice run. He would never let us wear his T-shirts around the house. We would never be able to make love on top of the hook and ladder with him wearing nothing but his heavy black boots. We both knew that, despite his looks, there was nothing exciting about tax-exempt status or itemized deductions or plant amortization and that sex on a pile of account ledgers would never be as exciting as the feeling of yellow rain gear on bare skin.

Once again, we united in our desperation.

"Look at the time," I said miserably. "*60 Minutes* is going to start soon."

"I'd better get going then," Grace played along. "I don't want to miss Steve Kroft's piece on the decline of family values."

The faux fireman waved farewell, oblivious to the fact that he had broken our hearts, and we headed off. Dejectedly, we walked out the door of Sam Goody and into the black night. Outside, we looked up at the empty sky and cursed our bad luck.

"Just think," I said after a minute in which we both contemplated our mutual loss, "we almost killed each other over an imposter."

Grace put her arm around me. "Why don't we go get a beer and laugh about it. I'll even let you drink out of the bottle instead of forcing you to put it in a glass."

Arm in arm, we headed down the street to our favorite bar. We might not have firemen, but we were content to have each other as friends. Before we'd gotten half a block, we had already started to laugh about it and were finding fault with the man we had so recently thought a god. "His nose was a little crooked," I pointed out.

"And that single-eyebrow look isn't for everyone," Grace added thoughtfully.

Then we spotted the hunky policeman standing next to the subway entrance, handcuffs gleaming seductively against his thigh. I could feel Grace stiffen next to me as she thrust her chest out to maximum advantage, and her arm slipped from mine. This time I wasn't giving her any chances.

"Well," I said cheerfully, breaking away from her. "I think it's time to ask directions to somewhere."

As I dashed toward my God in Blue, I heard Grace's heels clicking on the pavement right behind me.

Singing a Different Tune

When my nephew, Jack, was about to turn ten, I called my sister well in advance of the actual date and asked her what he would like for his birthday. The tenth year is a big one for any child, marking a transition between the dreamlike world of kick-the-can and paper dolls and the horrors of adolescent life like spontaneous erections and big bullies named Kurt, and it should be commemorated accordingly. I still recall vividly the gold eagle pendant my cousin Jay, my childhood hero, presented me with on my tenth birthday. I wore it religiously, until one sad day the clasp snapped and it was lost forever, improving dramatically my choice of accessories but leaving me cheerless. I wanted Jack to have such a moment to remember.

Karen knew instantly what Jack would cherish above all else on this earth. "CDs," she said promptly. "He's really into music now."

This was good news. Children as a rule have no taste whatsoever, so when buying music for them, it's just a matter of going to the record store and picking up whatever is hovering at number one for that given week. Even if they have no idea what it is, kids will play it loudly and thrash about in some semblance of dancing, feeling very grown-up and pleased with themselves. The week of my tenth, it was the sound track to *Grease* burning up the charts, and I received it with delight and some surprise, considering that my mother had forbidden me to actually see the movie after learning that the word "shit" was uttered freely. I played it endlessly (taking Olivia Newton-John's solos, naturally), and to this day I wonder how my life would have turned out if, instead, AC/DC or Bruce Springsteen had ruled the airwaves in the fall of 1978.

"So what should I get him?" I asked. "Hootie and the Blowfish? Coolio? Maybe Garth Brooks?"

Karen laughed. "Oh, no," she said cheerfully. "Nothing like that. He likes sound tracks."

"Great," I said, visions of *Grease* filling my mind. "So maybe the music from *The Lion King* would be good." I had this vague notion that every ten-year-old thrilled to all things Disney.

"Actually," Karen said, "he wants the albums from *Cats* and *Les Mis.*"

I was speechless. I wondered if my sister had any notion of the implications of what she had just said. Maybe, I thought, I'd just heard her incorrectly. "You mean the Broadway shows?" I asked doubtfully.

"Yep," she confirmed. "He loves those. We went and saw a touring show of *Cats*, and he's been humming the songs ever since."

I didn't know what to say. This was my sister talking, the one whose only response to my coming out was "Well, you know I'm okay with it, but God says it's wrong, so you're probably going to hell." Now she was telling me, in effect, that her very own son was exhibiting early signs of becoming a raging queen. And not only did she not seem to mind; she was enthusiastically supporting his bid for queerdom.

Okay, I know the stereotype of the gay man singing show tunes is one many people find offensive. I know I don't happen to like them very much. And we all go out of our way to reassure kids that just because some boys like ballet and some girls like softball they aren't necessarily going to end up with rainbow flag stickers on their Volvos and mineral water in the fridge. But really, when's the last time you saw a little boy who could belt out "I'm Just a Girl Who Can't Say 'No' " grow into a fascination with Pamela Anderson Lee's breasts? Can you blame me for being suspicious?

Still, I knew I had to be careful. I certainly didn't want to out the kid to his mother, especially so near to his birthday. If he really was tripping gaily on the heels of Dorothy's ruby slippers, I didn't want her to freak out, which I knew she would. She was already worried about the effect it might have on him being raised by a single mother, and she'd probably go out and buy him a rifle to compensate. She still harbors a suspicion that I'm gay because our father never built a tree fort with me.

"Um, Karen," I said, trying to determine exactly how serious the situation was. "Does Jack just kind of hum the music, or does he know all the words?"

"It's amazing," she said ingenuously. "He knows every word to every song. He hears them once and has them down. He can even do the motions Grizabella makes when she sings 'Memory'. You should see it; it almost makes me cry. Why?"

"No reason," I said casually. "I'll see what I can do."

I hung up and ran to the record store. Now I'm not saying it's right to actively hope that a young child is gay, and far be it from me to suggest that we push those showing the slightest indication of a queer aesthetic along in any way. All I will say is that I skipped with a glad heart to the show-tunes section and snatched up Jack's requested discs. For good measure, I added *Phantom of the Opera* and briefly paused at *Gypsy* before deciding that would be too much even for me. He had to be broken in slowly.

Once home, I wrapped the CDs and shipped the whole mess off to my sister with a prayer to the Patron Saint of All Young Queens — Charles Nelson Reilly. On Jack's birthday, I called to see how things were going.

"Hello?" Karen shouted when she picked up the phone. In the background I could hear the swelling tones of "Music of the Night" filling the apartment.

"Hi," I said briskly. "How's the birthday boy?"

"Just great," Karen said. "He's absolutely thrilled with the CDs. You didn't have to send so many, you know."

"That's okay," I said. "You only turn ten once. What's that shrieking?" In the background I could hear what sounded like a recent castrato bemoaning his fate.

"He's singing," Karen said proudly. "All morning it was 'On My Own' from *Les Mis*. Now he's learning *Phantom*."

I tried not to crow in triumph. "That's really great," I said. "He'll be a singer in no time." I imagined what my sister would think when Jack started renting Joan Crawford movies. She'd probably blame it on me, but I didn't care. Score one for our side.

"Oh, he already is," Karen said. "You should hear him try to do 'Evergreen.' "

This was more than I could stand. "He sings Streisand?" I said incredulously.

"Oh, yeah," Karen answered. "He's been getting into my Barbra records since he was six. In fact, my present to him was his own copy of *The Broadway Album*. We sing it together."

I had to hang up.

So maybe ten is a little young to know for sure. Still, I think the fact that I asked for an Easy-Bake Oven when I was seven was probably some kind of early indicator, sexist or not, of what would come. My friend Anne agrees. She gave her Barbie a crew cut and rechristened her Alix when she was four. Now Anne drives a UPS truck and plays rugby for her wimmin's collective team. You can't ignore the facts. Jack's birthday is coming up again, and this year he wants to visit the Smithsonian to see the exhibit of first ladies' gowns. Karen say she's glad he's showing such a healthy interest in American history.

Homo Improvement

I love working around the house. Blame it on some rogue butch gene roaming my system, probably the same one that periodically commands me to watch baseball or have an overwhelming desire to buy a pick-up truck. Whatever it is, I find that I am constantly doing things like rewiring the outlets, replacing the grout in the bathroom tiles, or installing faucets with spray attachments to the kitchen sink. I freely admit that I don't always do these things well, but I do approach them enthusiastically, flinging open my how-to books with abandon and going at the old wallboard with my trusty hammer and a merry heart. At the moment, every window in the house is covered in shrink-wrap plastic to increase energy efficiency, and I have a half-formed plan to put built-in bookcases in the office.

Naturally, my favorite place to indulge my obsession with all things handy is hardware stores. I love them and find myself wandering helplessly inside whenever I pass a particularly fine one. There's just something about a well-ordered collection of hand tools, gardening implements, and fasteners of various types that can fascinate me for hours, even when there's nothing in the store I actually need. If the place also carries lumber, I'm lost in rapture as I inhale the scent of freshly sawed pine and envision a Sunday afternoon constructing a deck.

My favorite hardware store of all is Home Depot. Not just any old hardware store, Home Depot is the Valhalla of home improvement centers. It floats majestically in a concrete parking lot sea, calling to the thousands of do-it-yourselfers who flock there from morning till night, drawn by the siren song of circular saws and the magical lure of easily assembled kitchen cabinets. Like enchanted heroes in a Norse legend, weekend carpenters and professionals alike follow the beacon of the twenty-foot-high orange letters that make up the Home Depot sign. "Come to me," they beckon seductively. "I am the promised land."

And indeed it is. My first visit to Home Depot was nothing short of a religious experience. A cavernous space, it is crammed from floor to ceiling with every conceivable hardware, gardening, and plumbing product. I had gone there for a simple screwdriver, but by the time I wheeled my cart to the checkout line several hours later, I had also picked up such indispensable items as a butane fireplace starter, new wallpaper for the bathroom, assorted lengths of nylon hose, iris bulbs in various colors, and a tool of which I had not even the vaguest notion of its use but that leapt unbidden into my arms as I passed by. Such is the magic of this wondrous place.

Nor is the appeal of Home Depot limited to the items that can be purchased there. Not the least of its charms is the large number of attractive young men who work there. Invariably clean-cut and hunky, they are all clearly designated by their festive orange aprons and by the fact that, at least here in Boston, they are all named Tom. The Toms swarm all over Home Depot like ants over a fallen peach, appearing at regular and often-startling intervals to say hello and ask if they can be of service. Surprisingly, they actually do seem to know where things are and how much they cost. Once I decided to test a Tom who had asked me four times if he could help me. Picking up a wicked-looking piece of PVC, I asked Tom to explain it to me. For the next fifteen minutes, he entertained me with a demonstration of how one could, by using the remarkable PVC device, change one's ordinary kitchen sink into a cunning garbage disposal. Impressed, I bought two.

Despite their allure, the Toms are not what fascinate me most about Home Depot. What I find even more interesting is the enormous number of queer men who, like me, seem to spend hours roaming the aisles. Home Depot is cruisier than any bar I've ever been in, and this despite the unflattering fluorescent lighting that falls from some nether region far overhead. At any given time, the place is crawling with fellow homos looking for everything from geraniums for the summer house to real Italian marble for the bathroom floor. Yet neither the host of actual repairmen, plumbers, and carpenters who do business there nor the Toms seem at all fazed by sharing their Palace of Masculinity with a bunch of queens. I've often wondered if they don't recognize the gay men in their midst or if they simply don't care.

A few months after my first visit, I had occasion to find out once and for all just how clued-in the Toms were. One Thursday evening I made a happy trip to Home Depot to fetch some padding to lay beneath the host of tasteful yet affordable Oriental rugs I had recently purchased there. In a hurry to get there and back, I had written the measurements of all the rugs on the back of the nearest piece of paper. In this case, it happened to be an envelope that had contained a letter from my friend Hank.

Paper in hand, I entered Home Depot's whooshing doors and made my way through the electrical wiring, past the paint shakers, and down the flooring aisle. There I discovered roll after roll of handy backing just waiting to be cut into perfect sizes for my rugs. All I needed was a Tom to help me. Luckily, one popped up not two seconds later, asking if he could be of use. When I said he could, he seemed genuinely glad, unlike young men whose job it is to ask such questions at, say, Macy's, where an answer in the affirmative is likely to result in an hour of petulant and reluctant service.

Tom and I selected a hefty roll of serious-looking padding and rolled out a length of it in the aisle. It was a beautiful thing, thick and cushiony, and it made me happy just to see it. We then stood there, hands on our waists, looking down at it as we shared a moment of common manliness. We were about to embark on a home-improvement journey together, one that would require both strength and cunning, and when it was all over we would have accomplished something useful. In that moment I understood the appeal of the football huddle.

"Beautiful padding," Tom said, nodding his head approvingly.

"Sure is," I answered. "Looks sturdy too."

Thus invoking the Hardware Gods, we got to work. Tom produced a handy utility knife from his back pocket, and we set to work hacking up the padding. I took out the paper with the measurements written on it and handed it to Tom. He studied it carefully, as though basking in the glory of my penciled eight-by-fours and ten-by-fives, the numeric language of the lumberman.

Then he turned it over, and my heart sank. Hank is a very clever man. Among other things, he makes his own stationery, paper included, and decorates it with a wide variety of amusing pictures and stamps. On the back of this particular envelope, where it had been sealed, was a giant pink lip print stamped in fluorescent ink. I tried to remember if Hank's name had been on the return address but couldn't recall. I wondered if Tom would even notice.

Tom looked at the lips, then grinned. "A love letter, eh?" he said teasingly. "Is she a real Betty?"

I thought seriously about this. Certainly Hank has many appealing qualities, and I'm sure his boyfriend of many years thinks he's just swell. Yet I doubted that he was what Tom would consider a real Betty. As I saw it, I had two choices: I could go along with him and say that no, it wasn't a love letter and she was just a friend, or I could come out and announce that yes, he was a real sweetheart and wasn't it wonderful that so many different kinds of people shopped at Home Depot. Either one would require an explanation I wasn't sure Tom would understand.

Beyond that, I wasn't sure I wanted to shatter the illusion of male bonding we had created there on the floor of Home Depot. I know, I know...it's important for us all to expand the horizons of our straight friends whenever possible. So sue me. Gay men don't get a lot of opportunities to be just "regular guys" in the world of lumber and nails, and it was sort of fun running around such an *über*-butch place blending in. Like Cinderella, I wanted the ball to go on a little while longer before Tom turned into a pumpkin and my fairy godmother took away my tool belt.

I looked down at the envelope and said a silent apology to Hank for the betrayal I was about to commit. "Not so much a Betty," I said to Tom. "More of a Mary."

"A Catholic girl," Tom said, nodding sympathetically as he began to cut pad. "I know how that is."

A Model Queer

The phone rang at 9:30 on a Friday night. It was Stephen.

"Hi," he said cheerfully. "What are you doing tomorrow afternoon?"

I hate questions like that. Having been given no actual information on which to base a decision, I have no idea how to answer. And the risk is high. Should I say I'm busy, it inevitably turns out to be something I really wanted to do, like go to a Bruins game, and I then have to pretend to have looked at the wrong date on my calendar. If I say I'm free, I have unfailingly agreed to participate in something dreadful, like being dragged to a foreign film festival, and I am forced to invent, on the spot, some believable commitment I'd momentarily forgotten about.

Because I am not particularly good at lying under pressure, this often puts me in a difficult position. Once, after having innocently said I was free for Tuesday night and then being told that, in that case, I was accompanying my friend Alice to an eight-hour performance of Japanese opera, I tried to get out of it by saying that I'd just realized I was having my wisdom teeth out that afternoon.

"That's funny," she said evenly. "Didn't you have them out the night we were supposed to go to the

Peruvian puppet festival too? I guess in that case you wouldn't be interested in the extra tickets I have to the Garbage concert on Friday. Bye."

With that unfortunate incident in mind, I decided to go for the middle ground with Stephen. "I'm not sure," I said vaguely. "I have a manuscript due Monday, and it depends on how much work I get done on it. Why?"

"I'm doing this shoot," he said. "It's supposed to be about lust, and I want you to model for me at a strip joint."

"I am not stripping for a national magazine," I told him firmly. "My father might see it. My publisher might see it. Anyone might see it."

"Don't worry," he assured me. "You'll just be sitting at a bar watching strippers. All you have to do is look horny and stick money in their G-strings every so often. No one will even know it's you unless they look hard."

That certainly sounded easy enough. Too easy. "Why me?" I asked suspiciously.

"I need an all-American type," he said. "The magazine wants a mix, and you're the most clean-cut guy I know personally."

"You mean I have the shortest hair."

"Yeah. So, can you make it?"

My first reaction was to say no. Having my picture taken is far from my favorite pastime, and avoiding that very situation is something of a mania of mine. I was about to say I just didn't think it was a good idea and hang up.

But before I could open my mouth to decline Stephen's request, I was suddenly overcome by a vision of my face on magazine covers across the country. Me surrounded by hunky men wearing nothing but lots of oil and the smallest of briefs over their bulging crotches. While I am usually not one to have delusions of grandeur, I found myself swept up in the indulgence. After all, it isn't every day that writers get a shot at fame.

"All right," I said. "Where is it, and what time?"

Stephen told me to show up at 2 and gave me directions to the club. The next afternoon, I dutifully dressed myself in my one and only suit, as Stephen had said he wanted the models to look like Wall Street brokers. There was a brief moment of ugliness when I couldn't button the pants, which I hadn't worn in almost six years, since my one and only job interview. But I held my breath and got them closed, all the while thinking bitterly about lost youth. I hoped I wouldn't have to pick anything up.

I managed to find the club with no problem. It was a splashy-looking place in the heart of the financial district, the windows tinted black and a length of red carpeting stretched from the entrance like a lascivious tongue. There was no sign, and I felt slightly deviant as I walked toward it. Warily eyeing the burly bouncer outside, I went in and made my way to the back. Sure enough, three models were having their pictures taken by a photographer. Three female models. With nothing on but bikini bottoms.

"Can I help you?" one of them asked me, her hands on her hips. "Uh…no," I stammered, trying not to look at her breasts. "I'm waiting for someone. But I'll just wait out front." I beat a quick retreat before she took anything else off.

I don't know why, but the thought that it would be female strippers I was posing with had simply not occurred to me. I knew Stephen was straight, likewise the

magazine he was shooting for. But the image of me surrounded by naked women is not one I am generally
accustomed to envisioning. If I am going to be lusting,
the object of my affections is not likely to be wearing
spike heels and pasties. I'd just assumed that the strippers
would, well, not have breasts.

Once safely back outside, I stood with the bouncer
and watched the hookers working the block, trying to
decide if I should just go home before I got into any
more trouble. Across the street a woman walked up to a
Jeep waiting at the stoplight. She pulled her top down
and laid her breasts on the hood, as though presenting a
cut of meat for inspection. Just then, a police car came
around the corner, lights flashing. The woman took off
down the street, her breasts flying wildly, her purse
under her arm as she set the land distance speed for the
fifty-yard dash.

As the woman turned a corner and disappeared, a
cab pulled up to the club's door. I was so busy watching
the fleeing hooker that I almost didn't notice Stephen as
he got out with another man, camera bag in tow. "What
was that?" Stephen asked. "The Olympic trials?"

He introduced the man with him as Ed, another
friend he had roped into the day's festivities. Ed had hair
much longer than mine, and he hadn't shaved in a few
days. He was, Stephen explained, supposed to represent
the underside of corporate lust. I didn't ask what I was
supposed to represent.

Before we went in, I cornered Stephen. "You didn't
tell me this was a straight club," I said accusingly. "Do you
know how many naked breasts there are in there?"

He just grinned. "I must have forgotten. Look, how
hard can it be to look excited? These girls are beautiful."

"Oh, right," I snarled. "When was the last time you got hot and bothered watching a Mel Gibson movie?" He ignored me and went over to say hello to the strippers.

Stephen set up his equipment at one end of the room. Because it was still early, there were only about fifteen men in the club. They all looked like someone's father, only slightly more rumpled. They quietly sipped drinks and watched the women, who danced on an island in the middle of the circular bar. The men's eyes were fixed on the gently swaying breasts floating above them, as though hypnotized by their movement. I tried to see what they saw, but the thrill escaped me entirely.

For the first shots, Stephen wanted Ed and me to sit at the bar, as though we were relaxing after a hard day on the trading floor. He asked one of the women to dance directly in front of us. Ed and I were directed to look up at her rapturously as she ground her hips and puckered her red lips seductively. I obligingly gazed upward, wondering how she managed to balance in high heels while avoiding knocking over the drink glasses and ashtrays that lined the bar for effect. I hoped the puzzled look on my face would pass for burning passion.

"All right," Stephen said after a few minutes of shutter snapping, during which I'd counted the number of moles on the dancing woman's legs. "It's time for the money." He handed us each a wad of one-dollar bills. "Now, when Sarah bends down, run your hand up her leg and slip a dollar in her garter."

Ed grinned. "This should be fun," he said. I gulped my fake drink, wishing desperately that it were real.

Sarah started dancing again, and Ed and I commenced lusting. The sound system was blasting Blondie's

"Heart of Glass," and every time Deborah Harry surged into the chorus, Sarah would crouch down and either Ed or I would run a hand up her leg and put a dollar under the black garter belt around her thigh, until she had a whole fan of bills covering her leg. When we ran out of bills, she gave them back and we started over again.

We repeated this routine with a number of different women, sliding our hands up various thighs and fumbling with one garter after the next. "Ooh, ooh, ooh-aah," Debbie crooned, and we maneuvered another dollar up another leg. Ed seemed to be enjoying himself, and the women were very pleasant, if somewhat bored. I did my best to appear inflamed by them, but I was really thinking how oddly hairless their bodies were under my fingers.

Stephen then asked two of the dancers to do some one-on-one shots with us. I was paired with Karen, a beautiful woman with long wavy hair and big brown eyes. Stephen gave me a cellular phone, and we pretended I was showing Karen how to use it while she hung on my every word. We pressed buttons and made the lights go on and off, telling each other terrible jokes while trying to appear seriously horny. In the meantime, Ed was being mauled by the woman he was posing with. She was sitting on his lap and running her long-nailed hands through his hair.

During a pause in the shoot, Ed's partner noticed his wedding band. "What would your wife think about this?" she asked teasingly.

"She knows it's for art," Ed deadpanned. "Otherwise she'd kill me."

Karen looked at me. "And what would your wife think?"

"I don't know," I said. "But my ex-boyfriend would probably be very surprised."

I waited for her to rush away and start shrieking a Homo Alert. Instead, she laughed. "You mean all the guys over there watching us are getting hard-ons wishing they were you, and you couldn't care less?"

"Ironic, isn't it?" I said helplessly.

She smiled evilly. "Well, in that case, why don't we give them something to really get off on."

The next thing I knew, she grabbed me by the tie and pulled me up off my barstool. While I did my best to breathe, her hand went around my neck, and she pulled me toward her. Suddenly, her tongue was in my mouth.

Now, there are women that I find attractive. And from time to time I've looked at various women and wondered what it would be like to make love with them. But it's always in a very general, nonexplicit kind of way, sort of like you'd look at a BMW driving alongside you and wonder in passing what it would be like to ride in, even though you probably never will. I had certainly never had the urge to grab a woman and make out with her. Now, purely by accident, I had my chance to find out what it was like.

Karen was beautiful. She was funny. She was a good kisser. She had a lot of the qualities I would find attractive in a man. Except that she was a woman. I tried to feel insanely hot for her, but all I could think about was that her lips tasted like peppermint.

The moment was shattered by Stephen saying very loudly, "I am telling every single person you know about this. And I have the film to prove it."

Karen let go of my tie. "Anything happen?"

"Sorry," I said. "Maybe if you had a beard."

Stephen wanted to take some shots of the dancers in their dressing room, so he left Ed and me to wait for him at the bar. As we sat there, one of the men who had been watching the shoot came over to talk to me.

"You sure got it good," he said sadly. "I'd pay fifty bucks to have one of them do that to me."

I looked at him. "Well," I said consolingly, "some guys have all the luck."

Separation Anxiety

Shortly after my twenty-second birthday and a few months before my parents' thirty-fifth anniversary, my phone rang at 11 at night. It was my mother. My mother hasn't been awake after 8:30 for at least twenty years, so this came as something of a shock.

"Who died?" I asked, since I could think of no other reason for her to be up and talking to me at that hour.

"No one," she said. "What do you think of your father?"

"What?"

"What do you think of your father? I mean, as a husband?"

"What are you asking me for? I'm not married to him."

She sighed. "I'm not in love with him anymore."

To be honest, her announcement was not the surprise it might seem to an outsider. Children generally know when their parents are unhappy together, and my sisters and I had been aware of it for many years. We just assumed that neither could be bothered to find anyone else he or she liked any better. Still, she was my mother, and even though I was aware of the issue, I hardly wanted to discuss it with her. After all, this was the woman whose idea of talking about sex was to leave *The Marriage*

Guide for the Christian Woman in my sisters' rooms shortly before their weddings. Since there was apparently no companion guide for men, I got all of my ideas about sex and marriage from this helpful book, and for years all I could remember was the haunting paragraph suggesting that during the first attempt at intercourse with his wife a man should stop for a minute after penetration and try to calm down so that he wouldn't ejaculate from overexcitement. When, upon my own first sexual experience (which admittedly involved slightly different genders, orifices, and positions), I discovered that this little trick failed to work, I was sorely disappointed.

Given this shaky background, I was not enthusiastic about the possibility that my mother might now decide to discuss with me, in depth, my father's shortcomings in the marriage area.

"Oh," I said helplessly. I was about to suggest that she call someone who could be of more help, like her sister.

"I want to leave him," she said before I could proffer that recommendation. "And I want to marry Rod."

This is where things began to get interesting. First of all, Rod was the pastor of my mother's church. Not only was he about twenty-five years her junior, but he was also married, with two small children.

"You can't do that," I pointed out, ever practical. "Rod is already married." As far as I was concerned, the matter was settled and we could all go back to bed.

"He's leaving his wife," she answered. "He's telling her now, and we're leaving tomorrow for Vermont."

Then it all came out. She wasn't thinking of leaving my father; she had already done it. In fact, she and Rod had been having a passionate affair for months. Apparently, Rod's secretary had found out and threatened to expose them to the church congregation, thus bringing things to a head. Despite myself, I was sort of impressed. I knew she'd been the head of women's ministries at her church, but I had no idea she had thrown herself so fully and completely into her duties.

Still talking in a steady rush, as though afraid I would interrupt her and spoil the whole thing, she said she knew Rod was the man for her because, unlike my father, he went to church and he prayed.

"Well, he sort of has to," I said. "I mean, he is the minister and all."

She ignored this bit of wisdom and informed me once again that in the morning she and Rod were leaving for Vermont, where apparently they were going to set up house immediately. "What do you think of that?" she asked finally.

What do you say when your mother, whose most spontaneous action to date has been changing her haircut of thirty years, informs you that she is leaving your father for a man of God? "Good for you," I said, trying to remember what all the self-help books said to say when confronted with sudden and unexpected news. "As long as you're happy." Then I recalled what she said when I came out to her and couldn't help adding. "But I just want you to know that I still think the Bible says it's wrong."

When she hung up, I immediately called my sister Karen, who at the time lived in the same town as my mother. "What the hell is going on?" I asked. "Is she insane?"

"Don't ask," she said. "She's driving me nuts. Now I know how she felt when we were all in high school and she hated the boys we dated."

"What has Dad said?"

"He doesn't know yet," Karen said.

Until that point, I'd forgotten that my father was away in Burma on assignment for the government. He'd been there almost four months and wasn't due back for another six weeks.

"Didn't she call him?" I asked incredulously.

Karen sighed. "She says she sent him a letter."

As it turned out, my mother never did send that letter. In the end, it fell to Karen to tell my father what had happened when he called a few days later for his twice-weekly check-in. By then, my mother and Rod were happily ensconced in a house in the Green Mountain State that they had bought with the money my mother cleaned out of the bank accounts. When informed of all of this, my father's response was similar to mine. "Oh," he said, then asked how the dog was doing.

When he returned home a few weeks later, my father was oddly cheerful. Assuming he would need some company, and secretly dying to know what he thought about it all, I went to visit him. He looked happier than he had in all the time I'd known him. In fact, he didn't even have time to say hello when I arrived. "I have a date," he said, rushing out the door with a wave.

I later found out that after my father learned of my mother's leaving with Rod, he did two things. First, he had his wedding band cut off, since over the years his fingers had grown and it no longer slipped off easily. Then he made a list of the women he wanted to date when he returned home. He was now busily engaged in working his way through that list. Since neither of my parents had dated much before they married, they were both apparently doing as much as they could to make up for lost time.

Several days after my arrival, my father received in the mail a letter from my mother informing him that she was coming back at the end of the week to pick up some of her things. The letter contained two lists. One of the lists was composed of the items my mother intended to take from the house. It was a long list, taking upward of five or six pages. In it, my mother displayed an uncanny ability to recall accurately the contents of every closet, cupboard, cellar, box, drawer, and chest in the entire house. She even listed, individually, all the items of the junk drawer in the laundry room.

In condensed form, it went something like this:

Furniture
Artwork
Carpets
Kitchen utensils
Cookware
Books
Garden tools
Photo albums, minus pictures of Dad and his relatives
Silver
Christmas tree ornaments
Croquet set
Piano
1 cat to be determined

The second list contained the items my mother had decided my father could keep. It was a far shorter list and looked something like this:

Grill and charcoal
Wood in woodpile
Hay in barn
Snowblower
Dog
1 cat to be determined

A few minutes after reading the lists, my father left the house and went into the barn. We had no idea what he was doing, but we thought it better not to ask. When he returned a few hours later, he was in a decidedly better mood but refused to tell us what he'd been engaged in all afternoon.

On the appointed day, my mother arrived precisely at 10 with an enormous U-Haul van and her sister to help her load it. Rod himself was nowhere to be seen. For the next few hours, they busily emptied the house of most of its contents. As they carried out lamps and boxes and rugs, my father stood looking on, a delighted smile on his face. He didn't say a word as my mother hauled away the accumulated debris of thirty-five years.

When my mother finally finished, she closed the back of the U-Haul, hopped in, and trundled off without so much as a good-bye to my father. Catching her reflection in the side mirror, I could see that she had a very self-satisfied look on her face as the truck turned onto the road. When I looked over at my father, he was grinning madly.

"What's so funny?" I asked.

He started laughing. "Did you see those big cardboard boxes? The ones marked 'dishes' and 'garden stuff'?"

"Yeah, why?" There had been about ten very large, very heavy boxes that my mother had gone to great lengths to get onto the truck. In fact, she had left out the piano she'd planned on taking just so she could fit them on.

"Well, I put those there," my father said. "They were all filled with bags of horse shit from the barn."

This is the fun part of divorces that happen when everyone is older: You see sides of your parents that you never knew existed. And because you're no longer a child and have long ago stopped believing that your parents are madly in love, you can, for the most part, enjoy it because it has absolutely nothing to do with you. The months following the separation were filled with all sorts of incidents, accusations, and general anxiety as things were hammered out, but they were always good for a laugh or two. My mother, for example, lost her first two lawyers to heart attacks, one right after the other, dramatically proving what I had suspected all along about her effects on those who worked for her. I also discovered that my father was much funnier than I had ever expected. He immediately took to calling my mother The Wicked Witch of the North and announced that now that she was gone, he no longer had to endure a house that smelled of potpourri.

Much to my surprise, my mother and Rod lasted. Although unable to work any longer as a Baptist minister, Rod found a challenging position as the manager of a pizza parlor. As for my father, in the end he never made it past the first name on his list of women. After dating number one for several months, he informed us that they were getting married. My mother, too, announced her impending nuptials shortly after the various divorces involved were final. My sisters and I were ecstatic on both counts, mainly because since both of the new spouses were considerably younger than Mom and Dad, we wouldn't have to worry about looking after them when they became aged and infirm.

Things didn't work out so cleanly for everyone, however. My nephew, Jack, was forced into a peculiar position. Rod's two little boys were Jack's age and also happened to be his best friends. Now, because of my mother's marriage to Rod, they suddenly rocketed from the status of friends to that of uncles, which confused Jack enormously. "Look at it this way," I said at the wedding as he tried to puzzle out their new relationship, "Now you have two more people to borrow money from when you get older."

Cyberslut

fter years of trying and failing miserably, I have finally become what I aspired to be in high school — a slut. It's true. No one I went to school with would ever recognize me now. Overnight, quiet, innocent little me has turned from a good boy who cleaned his room into a raging nymphomaniac who ties men to beds, takes on three at a time, and has absolutely no limits whatsoever.

All right, so maybe I had to compromise a little to make my dream come true. I admit that the action isn't always exactly as realistic as I'd like. And there is the little matter of my having to become a woman.

It all started the day I innocently decided to check out some of the chat rooms on my on-line service. Signing on and breezily clicking the talking-heads icon that beckoned coyly on the menu bar, I was whisked away into a room where a group of friendly people were talking about their pets.

"What do you feed your bulldog?" asked someone called TashaBarks, and almost immediately several helpful souls responded with their suggestions for kibble amounts and vitamin additives guaranteed to produce a shiny coat. *This is fun!* I thought and began scrolling through the other rooms available. Plant lovers. Football enthusiasts. People who cooked artichokes. It seemed that everyone, in what was no doubt a direct influence of the redoubtable Virginia Woolf, indeed had a room of their own.

That's when I saw it. Tucked away in the corner of my screen was a little, brightly colored button. "Private Rooms," it said ominously, like some discrete sign in a hotel catering to mobsters. "Private Rooms"? I had no idea such a thing existed in cyberspace. I wondered what they could be. Never being one who could resist even the smallest of temptations, I moved my mouse furtively across the screen. I hovered over the button for a moment, pausing expectantly while I made my decision. It was a little like the feeling I used to get whenever I'd find where my parents had hidden the year's Christmas presents and I'd sit looking at them for several minutes, agonizing over my choice. Inevitably, I'd reach for the first one and start shaking.

Of course I gave in and clicked the button. Then I waited while the screen whirled and re-formed until once again I was greeted by a list of rooms. But unlike the harmless pet people and chipper marigold growers of the first chat area, these rooms were populated by a slightly less savory crowd with decidedly prurient tastes. In fact, there were dozens of dens of iniquity to choose from, with names like hairychestedm4m, bicuriousmarried-men, and str8collegemen4gays. It was just like shopping for my own personal fantasy.

I immediately felt slightly guilty, a holdover from the days when I firmly believed that both Santa and Jesus saw my every move. Then, intrigued, I selected a room that sounded promising — hardjocks4u — and entered. To my delight, I found myself in the company of twenty-three other users. The room was filled to overflowing with ready, apparently horny jocks. I sat back, threw off my cybertowel, and waited for the locker room to heat up.

But during the entire time I remained in hardjocks4u, nothing happened. The dialogue screen featured a lot of people typing things like "Who's hard here?" and "Anyone in Toronto?" but no one ever answered. And despite the appealing personal profile I'd created for myself ("Likes Baseball! Ready Now!") not one person asked me if I wanted to hit a few balls with him.

Bored, and feeling slightly rejected, I signed off. I couldn't believe that with all of the horny computer users out there, I couldn't find one who found me worth even a "Want to play coach?" come-on. Then I had a thought. As me, I hadn't had any luck. But maybe on-line sex was like real sex. Maybe I just needed to be someone more interesting.

Thus was born Nikki. Nikki is 23. At 5 feet 3 inches tall and 103 pounds, she cuts quite a figure, especially with her long red hair and green eyes. A design student in New York, Nikki's favorite things are rough men, alternative rock, and sushi.

I suppose I could have made up a male character, but somehow doing that felt like cheating. Improving upon myself just to get laid seemed, well, creepy, like having pectoral implants and getting my teeth bonded. This way I got to be a whole new person, one with no background. It was like playing a character in a television show. I just pretended I was guest starring on *Melrose Place*.

Nikki made her debut in badboyz4naughtygrlz on a Friday night. Within seconds, she was bombarded with

six instant messages from men who found her absolutely thrilling. Every few seconds a bell would ding and
another little dialogue box would appear on my screen
with a message from some admiring suitor. "Hey
Nikki!" said one, "Want to get oral?" "Do U like big 1s?"
asked another.

After a few moments of giddy confusion, I figured
out how to work the little boxes and went searching for
Mr. Right. It wasn't easy. Nikki was turning out to be
more popular than I'd imagined, and every time a new
message box opened, the one I was writing in would
get shoved off to the side and I wouldn't be able to find
it again.

Besides, for each person who contacted me, I had
to take a minute and look up his personal profile to see
what I was getting. I weeded out people who had no
profile at all (probably FBI agents), put down slogans
from the '70s for their quotes ("Keep On Truckin' " was
surprisingly popular), and anyone who said he looked
"like an older Mel Gibson/Kevin Costner/Richard
Gere." (All three are attractive, but really, how well will
they hold up?)

I finally settled on a man whose handle was
JackNOff. His profile informed that he was 34, an
"account executive," and "into ladies who know how to
party." His instant message had said, "Want to sit on it?"
All right, so maybe he was the cyber version of the used-
car salesman at the bar with his shirt collar open to his
waist and the distinct odor of Old Spice hovering around
his head. But he sounded ready. I had no idea Nikki was
so easy. But she insisted on talking to Jack before I could
stop her. What can I say; it's just the kind of girl I am.
Apparently.

"Hi, Jack!" Nikki typed back briskly. "I'd LOVE to sit on it."

"Kool!" Jack fired back. "It's 8 inches with big balls!"

It soon became clear to me that everything that appeared on the instant message screen was required to be followed by an exclamation point, as though the sender was constantly in a state of near orgasm and could barely find the time to misspell common words. It was all so thrilling I had to close my eyes and take a few deep breaths before going on.

"Wow!" Nikki responded, amazed by her luck. "I bet it would feel REALLY good in my pussy!"

"Sure would!" Jack informed me. "What's your pussy like?"

This took me aback. I hadn't really thought about my pussy before. I wondered, if I indeed had one, what it would look like. I tried to recall the pictures I'd seen in *Penthouse* when I was eleven, but my recall wasn't very clear. "Shaved," I said finally, unable to think of anything else.

That's when Jack popped The Question. "Are you a real girl?" he asked.

I thought about this for a moment. Maybe my pussy answer had been unsatisfactory. Did women shave their pussies? I wasn't sure. Besides, I thought, was it right to fool Jack into thinking some hot gal was on the other end of his dialogue box, pussy at the ready? Maybe I should just end it right there. Then I pictured hundreds of men across the country, their wives sleeping unsuspectingly in the other room while they typed dirty messages to girls they'd never get in real life. In solidarity with those sleeping wives, I typed my response.

"Hey — I have a hot, shaved pussy, don't I?"

To my amazement, this seemed to satisfy Jack. "Great!" he answered. "Let's do it!"

Nikki and Jack did it. So did Nikki and BigDkinNY, Nikki and SailorMan, and Nikki and BadDad. Nikki did it with everyone who wanted her and in every way imaginable. And as she did, a pattern began to emerge. First of all, it appears that every single man on the Internet stands six feet tall, weighs 180 pounds, and has an eight-inch cock. It also seems that, to a man, they are willing to do anything suggested to them by a 23-year-old with a filthy mouth.

"I want you to stick your fingers up your ass!" Nikki told BadDad (43, balding, into home brewing), and he did.

"I want you to sit there in your chair and watch me get fucked by my boyfriend!" she informed CopStud (36, Italian, drives a pickup), who was happy to oblige.

"Then I want you to suck my pussy juice off his dick!" she tossed out, despite Cop's earlier pronouncement that he "didn't like fags." To her delight, he was more than willing, and I felt I'd scored one for our side, even if it was only on a computer screen. "His cock tastes SO GOOD," he cooed, and Nikki wondered about the wife and three children mentioned in his personal profile.

After eight straight hours of fornicating in cyberspace, Nikki was exhausted. She'd sucked, fucked, spanked, whipped, bitten, and shaved her way through a dozen men, each of whom had told her she was the hottest sex they'd ever had and asked if they could meet her in person. Laughing lightly, she declined, saying she had to wash her hair (so many men had asked to come in it, it would take hours). Sated, and feeling very naughty indeed, I turned the computer off and went to bed.

I lay there for a while, chuckling at the joke I'd pulled on a bunch of straight guys who were none the wiser. I wondered what they would think if they knew the person getting them off had a dick. I pictured SailorMan (40, divorced, likes schoolgirl uniforms), who had asked Nikki to tie him up and spank him. Thinking of how he'd enthusiastically typed "I'm cuuuuuummmmmmmmmiiii-innnnnnggggg!" in response to Nikki's head-giving capabilities, I wondered what he'd do if, at the crucial moment, she'd written back, "Surprise! My dick is bigger than yours! Have a nice day!"

Then, just before I fell asleep, I had another thought. An unsettling thought. If I was having such fun being someone else, perhaps I wasn't alone. Maybe there were others who, like me, just weren't who they said they were. I thought of RuffPup (28, tattooed, rides a Harley) and how he'd tied Nikki to his bed and made her beg for it before savaging her repeatedly. Suddenly an image came into my mind. Two dykes in Toledo. Bored with the *Murder, She Wrote* rerun. Sitting at their keyboard.

"Hey," says one, sipping her Diet Coke and rearranging her flannel nightgown, "this one sounds hot. Nikki. She likes sushi!"

"Perfect," says the second. "Watch this." She sends Nikki a note reading, "Bend over, I want to shove my big dick up your sweet ass!"

Nikki's reply comes back: "Sure, Ruff! I love it in my butt!" The dykes collapse in gales of laughter and start typing.

The Way I See It

No Splashing
in the Gene Pool!

There's been a lot of talk recently about the possible existence of a gay gene, some little bit of nelly DNA traipsing down our bodily pathways like some out-of-control subcellular fairy godmother who taps her glittery magic wand and turns some of us into queers. Apparently, just as we can inherit from our parents poor eyesight, male pattern balding, or an inability to clot successfully, we can now have passed along to us a fondness for Ethel Merman, an inexplicable affinity for Volvos, and a penchant for going antiquing in Vermont on fall afternoons. Now, while I'm all for expanding our knowledge of this fascinating little world we call the human body, I'm not at all sure I approve of this latest scientific foray into my inner workings.

Before going further I would just like to say in the interest of full disclosure that I am hardly impartial on this topic. I freely admit that I think it's entirely irrelevant. I really don't care why anyone, myself included, is gay. If you want to believe you were born to love other boys, hurrah for you. If you insist that you're challenging socially restrictive gender roles by actively choosing to munch muff, I say munch on, sister. If you're one who has concocted complex theories about nature working in conjunction with nurturing, I say your time would be better spent watching *Xena: Warrior Princess*. It matters not to me. If you really demand an answer, I propose that the same aliens who created Easter Island and crop circles are responsible. After all, who else but queers would think of decorating a barren shoreline miles from nowhere with gigantic festive tikis?

But I do seem to be among the minority on this one. There are a lot of people — both gay and straight — who demand more empirical evidence for the existence of same-sex desire. Much like the seekers of knowledge banging their way through the South American jungles looking for the Nine Insights revealed in James Redfield's *The Celestine Prophecies,* these questing souls want desperately to know where this fabulous state of queerness originates from. For these folks the source of sexual attraction is a puzzle of intense fascination, and they look for answers in hard science. To them the possibility of pinning a queer gene under a microscope is the modern-day equivalent of at last finding the elusive Holy Grail.

And what an eclectic group these earnest wonderers are. First and foremost, we have the throngs of queer women and men for whom being given any definitive reason for their sexuality would be welcome relief. Long bullied by others, or perhaps simply beset with good, old-fashioned religious guilt, these people are simply unable to just get over it already. Haunted by memories of being called "drama club fags" and "softball dykes" in middle school, they ache to know once and for all that it isn't their fault. "See!" they want to cry out in triumph to disapproving families as they wave the latest issue of *Scientific American*. "I can't help it. It says so right here in black and white. With charts."

And let us not forget the anxious parents them-selves. What a boon such a discovery would be to them. A gene to hang it all on would certainly eliminate all those hours of wondering if not enough time was spent playing catch, or perhaps too much emphasis was put on neatness and table manners. Having something concrete to point the finger at would make it seem more like being part of a club, like parents whose children have MS or cancer and who gather together for support. "Oh, yours has it too?" they could say reassuringly to other mothers and fathers whose children were similarly afflicted, free at last from the burden of having caused it themselves. Of course, there would still remain the small question of how that little bit of biological data got inside us in the first place. But never mind; it's a start, and at least we could still blame it all on Mom and Dad when the going gets too tough.

Ironically, perhaps those for whom the discovery of a gay gene would be most agreeable are those who already hate us on general principle. At last, something to explain it all away. Why, we aren't so scary after all. We're just defective. And because that rascally gene is tucked away safely inside us, there's no chance of its spreading to uninfected people through casual contact. What a relief!

Surely once this gene were isolated, a vaccine of some sort wouldn't be far behind, or at the very least a test that would indicate early in pregnancy if a fetus car-ried the awful gene. (And hey, maybe all that talk about outlawing abortions was just a bit premature, don't you think?) One little blood test, and problem solved. Saving future generations of children from the curse would be only a matter of minor surgery, freeing up a lot more time for fretting over racial minorities, unwed mothers, and Hollywood.

Maybe we could even have telethons, like the annual bash Jerry Lewis throws for his kids. Some second-rate celebrity could become our spokesperson — Phyllis Diller might be good, or Sally Struthers now that her correspondence-school gig has ended. One weekend a year, she could take over our local PBS stations and hold a variety show to raise funds for getting rid of this terrible pestilence. I can just imagine her wheeling out children cursed with the horrible gay gene. Holding them up to the camera, she would speak in pleading tones of the awful life awaiting them unless a cure could be found. Dollars would pour in as willing Americans pledged their dimes and nickels to eradicate once and for all what would become the newest birth defect. Instead of perverts, we would be a cause. Undoubtedly, some enterprising soul would come up with yet another colored ribbon (aubergine, perhaps?) for celebrities to wear to show their concern for our plight while accepting awards.

Then again, maybe there are more practical uses for a gay gene. We could, for instance, manufacture it in mass quantity and use it as a biological weapon. Specially equipped Fag Fighters would spray Agent Pink over war zones. Within a matter of hours, the unsuspecting soldiers would all find themselves overcome by the need to redecorate. Throwing down their guns, they would stampede to the nearest Bed, Bath & Beyond, where they would put aside their petty differences and unite in their mission to create a beautifully accessorized Laura Ashley bedroom. Peace would reign planetwide.

But that's all in the future. What about now? What about those who have already been affected? If the fact that I adore Bette Davis can be blamed on a piece of proto-plasmic fruit salad in my basic makeup, what does it mean for the gay youth of tomorrow, the ones born in the last few years and already too old to be fixed easily? I'll tell you what it means: BOCES. Let me explain.

Where I went to school, in the oh-so-progressive wilds of upstate New York, we had a thing called the Board of Cooperative Educational Services, BOCES for short. In theory, BOCES was a nice idea — students who might not be what you would call college-bound would spend a part of each day at the BOCES center, where they would learn practical skills with which they might support themselves following graduation or, more likely, after dropping out when becoming pregnant or impreg-nating someone else.

Each day after homeroom, the BOCES kids would file onto special little buses and be taken away to be apprenticed in their chosen trades. Unfortunately, the BOCES offerings were limited primarily to cosmetology and automotive repair, girls choosing the former and boys the latter. The classes, which focused on such intriguing subjects as the best way to feather hair and the swift rebuilding of carburetors, were far from challenging, and those of us who were more academically inclined, but generally smaller and more timid, delighted in taunting our vocationally oriented classmates by screaming "Bye, botards" out the windows as the buses pulled away. It may not have been kind, but it was our only revenge. And they were, after all, different. "You're so BOCES," implying as it did a phenomenal level of stupidity, was the worst insult in our little social world.

Now, imagine if you will a bus idling outside your average junior high school. Waiting to board is a small group of students, say about 10 percent of the total school population. The boys stand, books clutched to their chests, discussing their recently purchased cardigans. The girls, more casually attired in jeans, T-shirts, and motorcycle boots, are combing their hair and smoking. While in many respects they look just like everyone else, there is something about them that sets them apart from their classmates. They aren't drooling or limping, but something just isn't quite, well, *normal*. When the doors to the bus open, these students plod on glumly and find their seats. The bus pulls away, and as it leaves the school parking lot, a group of students calls out, "Bye, queertards." The kids on the bus cringe in shame.

These are the kids with the gay gene. Not retarded, nor even the more politically correct "differently abled," they are instead labeled "orientationally challenged." While their handicap is not severe enough to prevent them from being mainstreamed with normal children, they do require special classes that meet their unique needs. So for a part of each day, they are shipped off to a nearby school, where the process of helping them overcome their uniqueness takes place.

Fortunately, since the discovery of the gay gene there has been a swift movement to teach educators how to handle the needs of these children. Now that their problem has been recognized as just another physical handicap, lesson plans have been made and ways of teaching them to deal with their differences have been honed. Flashcards are implemented. Phonics are explored. After years of such education, many queertards are able to lead perfectly happy lives among their normal neighbors, where their presence allows the community to feel that they are highly advanced in their ability to forgive the unfortunates their disabilities.

But that comes later. For now, the boys are taken to one part of the building, the girls to another. For the boys, the afternoon consists of learning how to sit with legs spread wide and the best ways to take up more space than necessary, followed by instruction in speaking loudly, thinking of themselves as the most important people in the universe, and enjoying interminably long viewings of team sports. The girls, after being shown numerous episodes of *Beverly Hills, 90210* featuring a shirtless Jason Priestley, are drilled in the finer points of wearing skirts, appreciating the joys of makeup, and being happy with less. The classes are hard, but the promise of acceptance helps the students to persevere. After all, they are told repeatedly, they are simply helpless victims of their degenerate nucleic heritage.

With luck, the queertards will soon learn to see their disability as simply another obstacle on the road to becoming productive members of society. If not entirely normal, they can at least be assimilated. Sure, the other kids back at school might not always be kind, but special ed has prepared them to deal with being social outcasts, and they always have each other.

The highlight of the school year is, of course, the prom. For this lovely event, all of the gay gene boys are required to invite a gay gene girl. Frilly dresses in unnatural colors are the rule for girls, short hair and pressed shirts for the boys. Music is provided by a Carpenters tribute band. Kool-Aid and Nilla Wafers add a festive touch to the converted gym, which has been decorated in a manner befitting the theme: Change Is Good.

Eventually, of course, there would be a cure for the gay gene. Slowly and surely, the last remaining holders of the queer strain would die off, making gays and lesbians nothing more than a footnote in medical textbooks of the future. Like smallpox and the bubonic plague, queerness would be eradicated, rendering special ed for queertards unnecessary and making everyone happy except those who would lament the absence of really stylish designer dresses, women's golf, and popular culture. Until then, it looks like we'll all be riding the little bus to school.

Games People Play

The last time I visited my nephew, Jack, we spent the entire time on the couch, battling each other in a heated bout of Mortal Kombat. This clever video game, which was the subject of no small controversy when it first appeared, involves two combatants going at each other in a variety of martial arts. In addition to normal abilities such as throwing, kicking, and blocking, the different players one can choose come equipped with a multitude of interesting skills, including the ability to jolt an opponent with electricity, spit deadly venom, wield a razor-sharp fan, and (my personal favorite) deliver a crushing fist into the genitals of male characters. (I tried using it on one of the two female fighters; it didn't work.)

The object of Mortal Kombat is, naturally, to kill your opponent, the more viciously the better. With each blow delivered, blood splatters across the screen, until eventually someone loses. When one player lies dead, the other can reach down and rip out his or her heart, holding it aloft in all its dripping glory while uttering a victory scream. It is all very thrilling, and the game is enormously popular, particularly with the under-twelve set. Apparently they do nothing else but practice it for hours. Jack, who is eleven, wielded his joystick with amazing dexterity, slashing and hacking away at me, his beloved uncle, while I tried futilely to figure out how to duck. Within seconds Jack was waving my heart over his head, grinning madly.

My angelic, loving nephew then turned to me and delivered his own fatal blow. "You suck," he said.

See, this is the problem: Games today are mean. And as a result, children are growing up mean. Instead of living life as fun-loving sprites sledding down hills and skipping rope, they are fast becoming bitter little creatures who measure their success by how many hearts they can rip out. They mature into gloomy teenagers, and eventually they become mean-spirited adults and are loosed upon the world. This is not just a random thought caused by my loss of life and self-esteem at the hands of someone whose voice has yet to change. It is scientifically accurate. Bear with me; I have proof.

Once upon a time, there were kind, gentle games like jacks, hopscotch, checkers, and hoop rolling. Like the times during which they were played, these games fostered the notions of joy and carelessness once associated with not being old enough to drive or shave. Free from the anxiety caused by having to excel, children who played them grew up happily and became things like schoolteachers, inventors, and Marie Curie. They might have wanted to be the schoolyard marbles champion or the best double-Dutch jumper on the playground, but in the end it was all in fun. Rarely were noses bloodied over whose kite swooped the most elegantly or whose toboggan ran the hill the fastest.

But the years wore on, not always smoothly, and as the world changed, so did the games. Things became a little more difficult with the introduction of more complicated playthings like Twister, Barbies, and Slinky. Suddenly, the stakes were raised. Social status was determined by who could get the most Barbies and assorted accessories. Who could stand the longest with left foot on blue and right hand on green became a mark of prowess discussed at great length during recess. Whose Slinky was slinkiest was a matter of public record. Faced with the need to improve or be left behind, children became more focused, more competitive, and thus we have things like accountants, dental hygienists, and Newt Gingrich, who I understand once balanced with both right hand and foot on yellow for three hours at a friend's fifth birthday party.

Still, things weren't that bad. The board game reigned supreme, and innocent pastimes such as Candyland, Uncle Wiggly, and Chutes & Ladders filled rec rooms across the country. These were fun games, where nothing really bad ever happened to anyone. Even if you got stuck in Marshmallow Swamp, there was always a helpful friend to pull you out and send you on your way with a smile and a pat on the back. While it was always a thrill to win, playing was what was most exciting — moving the pieces around the board, throwing the dice, choosing a card. In fact, when climbing the ladders and sliding madly down the chutes ended, it was sort of sad.

But then came the '60s, when despite the peace and love flowing freely throughout the land, Americans realized that unless they shaped up, they wouldn't be the smartest or strongest kid in class anymore. The Russians had already sent a dog into space, and all we had to show for ourselves was San Francisco, paisley, and Andy Warhol. If something wasn't done — and soon — the entire country was going to be held back a grade.

Children's games answered the challenge to save America's youth, and soon the shelves of Toys R Us were overflowing with action-oriented creations like Operation and Mousetrap. Unlike their predecessors, these games were hardly soothing. To the contrary, they required a level of proficiency and cunning that sent even the most ferociously competitive six-year-old into hysterics.

For those of us born into this madness, life was harsh indeed. Who can forget holding those oh-so-realistic tweezers that came with Operation and trying to remove the patient's funny bone? Up it would come, the gleaming metal sides of the opening seemingly closing before our very eyes. Yet the patient's life was at stake, and his fate was in our hands. We'd seen hours of *Emergency* and *Adam 12,* and we knew what we had to do. Calming ourselves, we focused on the delicate task at hand. Then, just when we thought we were free and clear, a sudden twitch of a muscle ended it all. The plastic nose glowed alarmingly red. The buzzer screeched hatefully. Completely unnerved, we screamed and had to go sit quietly with a washcloth over our forehead while we recovered from the strain and admitted failure.

Mousetrap was no better, despite the ingenious Rube Goldberg apparatus that made it so popular. After spending sixteen hours setting up the game, we had to sit and watch while our gaily colored mice trudged on to their inevitable doom. Even worse, we had to execute them ourselves, turning the handle of the starting mechanism and watching helplessly as each stage of the trap was set painfully in operation. The boot kicked the bucket. The ball rolled out and down the steps. The little man dove into the pool. Finally the trap rattled down, imprisoning our squeaky game pieces and leaving them to who-knew-what horrible fate. No wonder so many of us grew up to need Prozac.

Think about it. Our favorite games in the '70s all involved imminent demise. Kick the Bucket. Don't Break the Ice! Rock-Em Sock-Em Robots. These games weren't about having fun. They were all about blame, all about survival of the fittest. Instead of having to come up with new solutions or creative answers, we had to be content to simply avoid screwing up. Winning at Don't Spill the Beans had nothing to do with skill or cunning. You simply had to stay out of the way, feeling the tension build up until some other unfortunate soul tipped the scales and finally you had someone to point the finger at. Watching any group of children playing these games, we should have seen the whole S&L scandal brewing.

Then there was the worst of all — Perfection. Even the name was ominously Big Brotherish. Oh, how well I recall that devilish little box with its oddly shaped holes waiting to be filled with corresponding plastic pieces. And all of it running against a timer. Once the clock started ticking, it was a frantic race to fit each object into its hole. At first it seemed okay. The pieces seemed to be going in smoothly. But when the fifteen-second point was reached and a pile of pieces still awaited placement, things reached fever pitch as you vainly attempted to squeeze everything into any available space. And then, inevitably, came the moment when the timer buzzed and the pieces were sent flying up into your face, an inescapable sign of failure and humiliation. Unable to attain perfection, we were forced back to less challenging games, and we never forgot it.

Then, just as it looked like we might escape our childhoods relatively intact, the video age dawned. I recall vividly the day my friend Paul got an Atari. It played only Pong, and we spent hours moving the little bar back and forth, watching delightedly as the ball pinged and ponged across his television screen. For a moment it seemed that games were fun again. My friends and I spent an inordinate amount of time in places like Chuck E. Cheese's, popping quarters into machines. Even the games where things had to be destroyed, like Centipede, were relatively harmless. When the centipede bit the dust, it simply exploded in a blast of brightly colored dots. No blood. No hearts. Just happy little pixels bursting across the screen in rainbow colors. And there was always another centipede right behind it.

But it wasn't to last. Pong gave way to harsher fare involving killing or being killed. Soon, two-player games were introduced, and the fight was really on. Now we could battle each other in real time through our Ataris. Sure, we'd played games like tag and hide-and-seek for years, and certainly capture the flag and kick the can were anything but cooperative. But now we could actually kill each other without legal retribution. Once we had the taste of blood, we became hooked. While knocking off aliens in Asteroids was fun, and even noble, knocking the crap out of our friends in Joust was completely gratuitous, and much more fun. It was a new era, and it resulted in things like investment bankers, studio moguls under thirty, and Steve Jobs.

I suspect there's about a twenty-year gap between the introduction of certain games and their direct results upon American society. In the '50s we had jacks and hopscotch — in the '70s we had Jimmy Carter and the

Carpenters. In the '60s we had Sit-and-Spin and Hippity Hop — in the '80s we had Duran Duran and *Dynasty*. In my time, the '70s, we had Operation and Don't Break the Ice! — in the '90s we have downsizing and Nirvana. No one can tell me these things are coincidental. I think it just takes that long for the effects of the games to manifest themselves. Those of my generation who mastered the labyrinthine rules of Dungeons & Dragons are busily paving the way to a new tomorrow; those of us who were never able to outsmart Simon sit stupefied as we gaze at our computers dully and wonder what went wrong. In fact, I think it's a safe bet that Courtney Love probably sucked at Ants in Your Pants and has been paying for it ever since.

It will be interesting to see where the Mortal Kombat Generation takes us. I'm not sure I want to know. Today's toys are downright scary. While games like Chutes & Ladders can still be found, more and more they're pushed out of the way by bigger, louder, more aggressive toys until all they can do is cower on upper shelves hoping some grandparent will rescue them from the jaws of the Street Shark action figures. Even Barbie and friends have had to butch it up, transforming themselves from empty-headed beach bimbos in brightly colored swimwear who cruised around in the camper into suit-wearing, briefcase-carrying Corporate Takeover Ken and the deadly Ninja Action Skipper.

As an experiment, I bought Candyland and took it to my friend Ellen's house one afternoon. Her eight-year-old daughter and six-year-old son were happily blasting away at each other with their Mighty Morphin Power Rangers laser guns. When I opened the game and started to set it up, they ran over to see what it was.

Encouraged, I quickly taught them the rules, and we started to play. Things went well for about five minutes. Then Sarah decided to push Morgan's little cardboard boy into Bubblegum Falls so she could sneak by him and get to the Gingerbread House first. He responded by knocking her solidly into the Lollipop Forest and kicking her under the table. From there it was all downhill. Snatching up their weapons, they went storming through the house with Sarah screaming, "I'm going to rip your head off, you twisted little freak!"

I'm a little frightened: She says she wants to run Disney when she grows up.

A Sporting Chance

Each morning from May through September, as my dog, Roger, and I go for our daily walk around the nearby public pond, we are treated to the spectacle of dozens of people standing on the shore staring blankly into the water's rippling surface. They wait, slack-jawed, for something to happen, looking suspiciously like the enraptured throngs who gather around religious icons that have been reported to weep real tears.

They are, of course, fishermen. And they are *always* men. Interestingly, I have never heard even the most ardent feminist demand that the word be changed to *fisherpeople*. This is because, with I'm sure some notable exceptions, generally only men are prone to this particular form of mental illness. Who else would get up before the sun for the sole purpose of standing around for hours doing absolutely nothing and calling it a sport? Can you blame anyone for choosing voluntary exclusion from such a group?

Because there are so many of them spaced at equal intervals around the pond like living garden gnomes, I have a lot of time, as Rog and I traverse the roughly mile-and-a-half path, to observe and think about what the fishermen as a race do. Normally I would be wary of such people, just as I tend to stay away from those who speak loudly or who insist on building their own patios. But for some reason I find the fishermen fascinating, much as I do those wonderful Discovery Channel programs about the tribes in the rain forests who manage to catch wild pigs using a length of twine and unusual berries. My daily exposure to these sad people has left me with some decided opinions about sportsmen in general, which I feel it is my duty to share, in the hopes that my revelations will prevent another generation of innocent young people from becoming trapped by this peculiar addiction.

If you ask me, fishing is not really a sport at all. The word *sport* implies the utilization of some kind of skill, such as coordination, strength, or speed. At the very least, a sport should involve jumping over something, running very quickly for some reasonable distance, or having to get an object from one side of a vast area to another while other people attempt to stop you. Where's the skill in throwing a hook loaded with tempting bait into the general vicinity of lots of perpetually hungry creatures with brains the size of mustard seeds? You might as well go to a playground, scatter M&M's around, and club to death the first four-year-old foolish enough to approach, believing innocently that such treats are readily available in nature. Yet not only do the fishermen actually club the four-year-olds; they then sit around and gut them while talking loudly to one another about how difficult it was to achieve such a feat, as though they had somehow used years of study to cunningly break through the elaborate security systems their prey had constructed to thwart them.

No, fishing is not a sport. Perhaps it could be if one of the aforementioned criteria were somehow incorporated. For example, if the fisherman had to run after the fish instead of merely reeling him in from the back of a boat, or if while a fisherman attempted to cast there were seven other fishermen hurling good-size rocks at his head. Then it might be interesting. But in its traditional form, it is merely stupid.

"But what about fly tying?" some of you might ask. Surely fly-fishing deserves some respect. After all, it's a centuries-old tradition, the secrets of which are handed down from practitioner to practitioner in hushed voices. Granted, there is something elegant about this oft-lauded trade, and I suppose it does involve some measure of coordination to bundle up a lot of bits of feather, fur, and sparkly things to make something a trout will eagerly want to give its life for. But given that the same men who boast proudly of their fly-tying accomplishments are often the first to go into shock at discovering their sons working up a smart beaded evening dress, I can't be all too enthusiastic about them. Besides, never have I seen a fisherman capable of performing a credible lip sync of "It's Raining Men" while wearing one of his own creations and flinging a boa seductively around his head.

No, fishing is not a true sport. Baseball, which is a real sport in my book, involves one team of players doing battle against another group of players with potentially the same level of intelligence. Even hockey, in which intelligence is not always assured, requires the players to balance on ice skates while smacking each other about. The fisherman, who even I will admit is probably smarter than the fish he chases after, needs only to stand there and wait. He can, in fact, even drink beer while waiting. In my opinion any activity during which you can enjoy a beverage is not a sport. It is a party.

This brings us quite naturally to hunting, which is simply fishing in the woods as far as I'm concerned. In fact, hunting may be even stupider than fishing, for while the fish are admittedly confined to a relatively limited area, at least they have the benefit of being hidden by water, making their capture dependent at least partially on luck. Animals in the woods have no such luxury, being generally larger and slower. And while fish actually have to bite a hook to be caught, thereby playing at least a small role in their own deaths, animals in the woods merely have to get in the way.

It has been explained to me that men enjoy fishing and hunting because it is a way for them to feel that they are (1) superior over animals and (2) that they have provided for their families and are therefore good men. My response to this is to point out that no man I know, no matter how facile his hunting skills, is in any way mentally superior to a dog who decides that 2 A. M. would be a wonderful time to go outside for a walk and manages to get his way. Just look at a sleepy-eyed owner, bathrobe askew, being dragged down the street by a wildly happy labrador who's gotten a bonus outing by whining continuously for three hours and tell me who's the smarter of the two.

And if men want to feel that they are good providers, why can't they learn to scour the aisles at A&P in search of groceries? Not only does that activity not take up an entire weekend but it seldom necessitates the purchase of a cabin in New Hampshire or the donning of truly offensive camouflage ensembles and hip boots. In addition, I think it is safe to say that successfully negotiating a store crammed with hostile shoppers and woefully unhelpful sales clerks, only to wind up in the one checkout line where the trainee needs to call for the key after every entry, takes far more patience and willpower than, say, blowing the head off of a grouse as it eats its breakfast.

My friend Bob, an avid fisherman, says that I am a hypocrite in this matter. He argues that there's no distinction between going out and catching a fish or hunting a deer and buying a salmon filet or package of 80 percent lean ground beef. In fact, he insists it's far more honest to kill something yourself than to pretend that somewhere in the world there exist cows that at a certain point magically disintegrate into hamburger patties and half-inch-thick London broils without the unpleasantness of slaughter.

I am a fair person, and I will concede that meat is meat and fish is fish, regardless of origin, and I probably wouldn't eat either one if I had to kill it myself. But I can't help but feel, however delusional it may be, that handing over ten dollars for a lovely piece of tuna ready for the grill is just a teeny bit more civilized than camping out for three days and peeing in the bushes to achieve the same thing. Besides, somehow paying for it makes it feel more like an honest trade, whereas just going out and killing the animal in its own home seems merely mean-spirited and hostile.

I have not come to my opinions on these issues easily, mind you. I grew up in an area of the country where fishing and hunting were not simply encouraged; they were mandatory. The opening days of both seasons saw the halls of my country high school empty as every able-bodied boy flocked to the river or the woods in search of blood. For weeks the lunchroom fairly bustled with boasting about rack size and fish weight, and woe unto the child who hadn't had his first kill by the time he was into grade school.

Of course, I suffered for my refusal to bring down a buck or land a bass. The butt of many jokes, I endured the taunts of my peers as I sat eating my peanut butter-and-jelly sandwiches while they feasted on roast venison and smoked trout they'd caught themselves on those days when they'd skipped class to hunt while I sat inside dutifully learning geometry. But I remained true to my convictions, insisting that my lunches tasted all the sweeter for being free from the taint of murder. My arguments convinced no one, but, like Gandhi, I kept on, knowing that one day I would be proven right.

In these more enlightened times, as vegetarianism and kindness toward all living things flourish, fishing and hunting seem to be declining in popularity. At the same time, I've begun to notice a strange new publicity campaign being waged for these pseudosports. This spin-doctoring, clearly brought to us by the same clever people who turned cotton candy into a health food by plastering "fat free" across the package, reaches out to a new audience and involves marketing fishing and hunting as meditation exercises. *Zen Fishing* proclaimed the cover of one book I spied at my local New Age store; *Hunting With the Inner Child* beckoned another.

Intrigued, I glanced inside and read for a bit. The essential premise of these books is that the hunting of animals, be they aquatic or earthbound, is really the physical acting-out of the search for inner peace. The animal, be it a trout, a bison, or a lion, is symbolic of our untamed nature. By tracking it down and killing it, we are facing our greatest challenge, and in winning over the animal, we win over our own fears and inhibitions. As such, diligent practice of either hunting or fishing can, in fact, lead to the attainment of enlightenment.

This is an interesting theory, and one I was willing to consider as part of my path to deeper understanding. After all, it is true that many of our daily activities are in some ways connected to our inner workings. My meditation practice had already proven that time and again. So on my next trip to the pond, I decided to do some searching of my own. Borrowing a fishing pole from my neighbor, I set out on a journey of discovery.

I approached a gentleman who was standing quietly near a tree, his eyes trained on a bright bobber some twenty feet away. I tried to imagine him as a Buddha focusing his mind on a single spot.

"Good morning," I said. "How goes the search?"

"Huh?" he said.

"Have you found your inner self?" I asked.

He stared at me blankly. "Are you a ranger?" he said.

"No," I reassured him. "I was just wondering if your daily communing with nature had yielded any revelations."

"I caught a perch yesterday," he said brightly. Then his face fell. "But nothing today."

Undaunted, I set myself up near a fallen log. Opening the plastic container of bologna I'd been assured by Bob was the favorite food of fish everywhere, I spiked the hook through a piece and prepared to cast. Roger looked on warily, I'm sure wondering why I was throwing a perfectly good piece of bologna into the pond.

After several failed attempts, I finally managed to get my hook and the accompanying bologna settled into an area near the fallen log. Holding my pole, I sat down and began to soak in the experience. I had to admit, it was peaceful sitting there with the sun shining down and the water gently lapping at the shore. Perhaps, I thought, I've been looking at this all wrong.

I felt a pull on my line. Suddenly, I was hit with a surge of adrenaline. The hunt was on. I jumped to my feet and began to crank the reel. It was me against the fish, and I was determined to win. I was gripped in the fist of raw nature, and it felt fine! Just like Hemingway's Old Man, I was coming face to face with my destiny. I turned and turned the reel, bringing the struggling fish closer and closer to me. Several times he rallied, pulling toward the middle of the pond, but again and again I brought him back. Finally, I pulled my prize, dripping and thrashing, from the water. It was, I think, a sunfish. Impaled on the hook, it nonetheless managed to perform an intricate series of gymnastic moves, flipping itself all over the bank of the pond. As Roger and I attempted to still it, I embraced for a moment the thrill of victory. I had, in fact, caught my inner fish.

I did eventually catch hold of the creature, primarily because Roger sat on it. Holding it up, I watched it attempting to breath, it's mouth opening and closing as it fought to stay alive in an unfamiliar element. Perhaps, I thought, in the fish's death I would come that much closer to my own enlightenment. Maybe what I gained would make up for the loss of its comparatively smaller life.

I tried to think of the fish as a teacher imparting an important lesson. I imagined it speaking to me of life and death and all of the things the author of *Zen Fishing* had written of. Just as a yogi imparted the secrets of the body or the tai chi master revealed the power of moving a single finger in a precise manner, I attempted to see the fish as another of my life's instructors. But try as I might, I had a difficult time picturing my meditation guide flopping around on his cushion gasping for air while I throttled him soundly and took one step nearer to nirvana.

Having learned his lesson, my inner child took the fish off the hook and threw it back.

Just One
of the Girls

My first summer living in New York, I couldn't wait for the annual Pride Weekend to come. I moved there in the spring, and as the days became warmer, I started counting down to the last weekend in June. After years of having no contact with a gay community, suddenly I was going to have a whole weekend devoted to all things queer. I scanned the *Pride Guide* carefully, making lists of things I thought would be fun to do. Parades. Rallies. Performances. Dances. They all went onto the list, and I was careful to balance the gratuitously decadent happenings with the more socially responsible events.

My guide that first summer was a lesbian friend from work named, appropriately, Mary. I knew very few gay men at that point, and Mary was hooked into the gay world in a way that I wasn't. She shepherded me around to the various events and made sure I saw everything. On Sunday she announced that we were going to what was supposed to be the crown jewel in the Pride Weekend crown — the annual dance on the Christopher Street pier. Mary was very much into dancing and the club scene, I was intrigued by the idea of mostly naked men, and she thought the pier dance would be a great way to indulge both our interests and allow us an opportunity to enjoy a couple of hours with our shared community.

Well, she was wrong. When we arrived at the dance, we discovered that Mary was one of only a handful of women present. Because the music sounded bearable, and because we had laid out twenty bucks apiece, we stayed. During the two or three hours we were there, my friend was treated to a continuous stream of hostile looks and sometimes outright abuse. More than once a dancing beauty would take a break from posing and come ask Mary if she was a "real" girl. Instead of feeling part of a community, she felt like an intruder. The only "pride" that seemed to be going around was in showing off the results of hours spent at the gym and under tanning lamps. The experience was ruined for both of us, and I vowed never to attend another dance.

The next year when Pride rolled around, I wasn't too enthusiastic. By then I'd had my fill of bars and clubs, one-night stands, and handsome men with empty minds. With just one rotation of the seasons, I'd decided that gay New York was a sorry place indeed. I decided that I'd sit Pride out and do something really fun, like sleep.

Then some friends invited me to join them at a women's dance that was being held as part of the Pride festivities. Now, it's a long-standing joke among my friends that I make a better lesbian than I do a gay man. I haven't seen *The Wizard of Oz* since I was four. I own every k.d. lang, Indigo Girls, and Melissa Ferrick album ever made. I even (and this frightens even my dykiest friends) know all the words and accompanying hand motions to "Filling Up and Spilling Over." I do not understand why John F. Kennedy Jr. is a sex symbol. I think Ann Richards should be pope.

Sitting at Henrietta Hudson's and looking at all of their expectant faces peering at me over mugs of Guinness, I was torn. I wanted very much to spend what amounts to the equivalent of Queer Christmas with my chosen family. But I still hadn't quite gotten rid of the bad aftertaste left by the miserable experience of the year before. Besides, I am also painfully aware that, compared with the number of men's spaces, there are very few places where women can go to be alone with other women. Reading *Our Bodies, Ourselves* in college will do that to a man.

But they worked on me the rest of the afternoon, and after three or four pints and an endless stream of pleading on their part, I found myself standing in Judith's Room in line to buy a ticket. I was, of course, the only man there, and I was convinced that everyone was looking at me with grim thoughts in their hearts. I sang along with the Ferron tape that was playing, just to let them know I was harmless. I heard whispering behind me. I sang louder and leafed through a copy of *Radical Chick,* hoping the newsprint wouldn't come off on my sweaty palms.

After what seemed like days, I finally made it to the counter and asked for a ticket. The woman, who sported a THELMA & LOUISE FOR PRESIDENT T-shirt, glanced at me, then looked back again. "Is this for you?" she demanded. Eyeing the wicked-looking labrys around her neck, I briefly considered lying and telling her it was for my friend whose double shift at the co-op/women's shelter prevented her from being there herself.

"Yes?" I finally said doubtfully, fully expecting her to send me packing.

To my surprise, she actually smiled. "Good," she said emphatically, handing me a ticket. "See you there."

Relieved to have passed the first test, I went home and got ready. As the time for the dance approached, I began to have second thoughts about the whole thing. The more I thought about it, the more it seemed what Pooh would call a Very Bad Idea. I called my friends several times, trying to get out of it with a variety of excuses.

"Look," Anne said firmly. "I know for a fact that you do not have to go to a twelve-step meeting for co-dependent pet owners tonight. Blaine is in that group, and she's all distraught because it was canceled for Pride. Apparently Gertrude and Simone have hidden under the bed and refuse to come out, even for liver snaps."

"Oh, please," said Katherine. "They are not going to make you recite Dorothy Allison poetry as proof of sisterhood. Besides, you know it all anyway. I saw that autographed copy on your shelf."

"You are not coming down with a temperature," said Emma, sighing. "Now get dressed and get your ass over there. We'll meet you at 9."

Finally, they all stopped answering their phones.

Knowing that what awaited me if I didn't show up was infinitely worse than anything that could happen at the dance, I dutifully walked over to the college where it was being held. Especially for the occasion I wore a T-shirt I had found that read LESBIAN TRAPPED IN A MAN'S BODY. It had seemed fun and carefree when I'd purchased it, but now I felt as though I was just asking for trouble. When I arrived at the school, I began to panic in earnest. There were about 2,000 women thronging the walkway. And me. I tried to be inconspicuous. But nothing could change the fact that I stand six foot two in my boots and am quite a bit hairier than most women. In short, I did not blend.

I half expected the women at the door to send me right home. But they took my ticket, stamped my hand, and let me in. I vaguely wondered if I had been given a blue ink stamp on purpose but decided not to worry about it. Even if I'd wanted to, there was no turning back against the incoming tide of bodies anyway. Once inside, my anxiety grew when I couldn't immediately find my friends and thought they'd abandoned me to a horrible fate. But after a few minutes of frantic searching, I discovered that they had very kindly situated themselves at the back of the room, forcing me to wade through swarms of dancing women to get to them. They thought it was funny.

"See any hot prospects?" one of them asked evilly.

"Just one," I shot back. "But it turns out she only likes butches."

We talked for a while, then hit the dance floor. I was so preoccupied with trying not to knock over anyone smaller than myself that I forgot about my shirt. Then just as I was finally relaxing, I noticed a woman pointing at me and laughing.

That's it, I thought. *They've figured it out, and they're going to make an example of me.*

The pointer worked her way over to me. In her fifties, she had a crew cut and wore a leather jacket with a skull painted on it. She reminded me of all the old-guard dykes I saw playing pool at the bar near my apartment, the kind who spoke fondly of the days when femmes were femmes. The Grim Reaper had come for me, and she was one butch number.

She stopped in front of me and looked me up and down, as though confirming that she would have no problem taking me down. I glanced around and saw that all of my friends had backed away. So much for family.

"I just want you to know," the Reaper said in a gravelly voice, "that I'm glad you're here. Thanks for coming — it means a lot." She gripped my hand in a viselike shake. Then she kissed me and disappeared back into the crowd.

I stood there for a minute, stunned, not knowing what to think. I wasn't sure if I was more surprised that I was still alive or that I'd just been kissed by a woman more masculine than any of my dates had ever been. Now that the tension I had been feeling was broken, I started to look around me. On the dance floor were women of all shapes, colors, and sizes. Their ages ranged from young teens to women well into their golden years. Women in Chanel suits danced alongside women in combat boots and flannel. I noticed five or six women in wheelchairs.

In some ways it was a complete parody of every lesbian stereotype. But it was also very real, and it suddenly occurred to me why everything felt different. It wasn't just that I was the only man around. I had attended dances before, but they had all been sponsored by and for men. At those dances, the groups were hardly what could be called mixed. The less-than-beautiful never belonged. Likewise the old, the disabled, women, or, for the most part, minorities. Sometimes someone from another group would manage to sneak in, but he usually spent his evening alone and ignored.

During the course of the evening, over a hundred women (I stopped counting at 136) came up and said something to me about my shirt. Countless others smiled or laughed without saying a word. It got to the point where I suddenly noticed my friends were being suspiciously silent.

"What's wrong?" I asked Anne, who was leaning against the wall sullenly.

She gave me a black look. "You're talking to more women than we are!" she wailed.

"Yeah," said Katherine. "I thought that cute woman in the leather mini and the Wonderbra was coming over to flirt with me, but all she wanted to do was hug *you*."

At one point someone grabbed my arm. "Hey," she demanded loudly, "are you a real girl?"

For a brief, horrible moment I was transported back to that first horrible pier dance, when my friend had been asked that same question. Only this time the question was meant in fun, posed by someone with no malice in her voice. Instead of questioning my right to be there, she asked me to slow dance. She led.

I suppose there were some women at the dance that night who objected to my being there. But if there were, they were kind enough not to let me know. Unlike other "community" events I have been to, the criteria for belonging were not physical beauty, political correctness, or a well-honed ability to make other people feel less than acceptable. Rather, the people at this dance were all there because we wanted to celebrate together what we spend so much of our time fighting for — the ability to be lesbian and gay people without having to live up to other people's standards.

Camille Paglia says that the lesbian and gay community will not advance until we learn to stop thinking in terms of gay and straight. I would add that we also must stop thinking in terms of women and men and start thinking in terms of people. We have enough other battles to fight with outside enemies; it's time to end the ones within our own family.

In the past I've noticed the relative invisibility of women at a lot of community events I have attended. But I never really thought about why it is that lesbians and gay men do so few things together. Now I know. Just like in junior high, when they suddenly grew six inches and developed breasts way before we needed to shave or wear jockstraps, the girls are still waiting for the boys to catch up.

I'm Not Saying
It's Wrong...

A few weeks ago, while vigorously avoiding doing any actual work, I flipped to C-SPAN. I like checking in with C-SPAN periodically because during the day they are prone to televising United States governmental hearings. The government, not surprisingly, is very fond of holding meetings. It has, in fact, perfected it to an art form, so that watching one of the hearings is much like watching a performance of *The Nutcracker* or *Aida* but without the dancing and singing or fun costumes. Fortunately for those of us who like this sort of thing, the government holds meetings about practically everything, from who's really to blame for the state of welfare to who's really to blame for the state of West Virginia. Twelve hours of watching reveals that no one wants to claim any knowledge of either one, but seeing democracy in action is a wonderful thing.

When I flipped to the channel, they were airing a congressional committee hearing about gay marriage. These are the best kinds of meetings to catch, because unlike standard procedural proceedings, they are controversial and involve far more yelling and tension than, say, deciding whether to add an amendment to Sen. Kennedy's harbor clean-up bill that says no Republicans have to give up their golfing allowances. It's sort of like the difference between a Rangers-Bruins face-off in the Stanley Cup finals and a predinner game of street hockey featuring the neighborhood kids. Both may have the same basic goal, but one is sure to be bloodier.

Now, to fully appreciate the enormous scope of this event, one must know that whenever some major subject is up for debate, Congress decides to hold a party. To this party they invite many people who are rumored to have interesting ideas about the subject at hand. This is all done in the name of making everyone informed, so that solid decisions about crucial issues can be made after hearing the facts from all the different angles.

What they don't tell you is that everyone invited to the party has already been screened, so that the panelists know exactly what they're going to say. They also don't tell you that normal people are never invited. You have to have written a book (not necessarily on the actual subject being discussed), taught a class at a prestigious university (again, subject matter is irrelevant), or once spoken to someone who did either of these things. If I were an unkind sort, I might even suggest that certain people are picked precisely because of what they're going to say on national television when cued by their respective sponsors. But we all know that doesn't happen in America, where we are fair to everyone, even when we don't agree with them.

All in all, these panels tend to be quite agreeable, especially if one watches them instead of writing the book one has promised one's editor will be finished and on her desk the next day. It was with this spirit that I watched part of the hearings. As I said, the subject was gay marriage. Specifically, as near as I could tell, the whole point of this hearing was to educate various government types about why gay people should or should not be allowed to marry, which of course is suddenly of utmost importance since all the fuss in Hawaii began. This is so that when the time comes for elected officials to decide whether they should support such legislation, these newly educated souls can claim to have done their research and then guiltlessly vote exactly the way they would have if they hadn't wasted six hours and millions of dollars on the hearings.

For this event, four people had been invited to share their views with the esteemed panel of congresspeople — two of them pro–gay marriage and two of them con. I have forgotten most of them, but they were all, I'm sure, very informed and very interesting, mainly because none of them was Ariana Huffington. I couldn't really tell, though, because I was having a hard time figuring out which ones supported and which ones did not support gay marriage. This is another fascinating aspect of congressional committee meetings: No one really knows who's on whose side, because everyone is from Harvard and uses enormously long words. By the time you've looked them up, they've moved on to someone else, because the speakers get only five minutes, and they're racing the clock. The representatives attending the meetings have large staffs of well-educated young people who flock about them like pigeons, whispering in their ears and translating what's being said by the speakers, so that their bosses know whether to smile or frown. Those of us at home have no such luxury and must muddle through as best we can.

The fourth person I do remember, however, because he did not use any long words. His name, as I recall, was Dennis Prager. From what I understand, Mr. Prager is the host of a popular radio talk show in California. My apologies to him for not knowing his work. I'm sure he is as unaware of me as I am of him, which I think makes us even. I'm sure he's very nice, though. He looked kind of like a big Phil Donahue, without the suspenders or Marlo Thomas.

Of all the panelists, Mr. Prager was the only one I thought truly deserved to be given air time. Now, just so you save a lot of time wondering, Mr. Prager is one of the people who does not like gay marriage. This, of course, makes him a little less nice than he might be. But I still found him fascinating, for unlike some of the other speakers, who didn't like gay marriage because it was "icky" and "wrong," Mr. Prager has a theory, which he stands behind 100 percent. According to Mr. Prager, his theory is based entirely on science. You can't argue with that.

Mr. Prager's theory is that everyone — himself included — is inherently bisexual. This, he says, is the fundamental nature of humankind. How we choose to act on this nature, however, is what concerns him. See, he thinks that expressing the homosexual aspect of sexuality is immoral. Why? Because the Judeo-Christian tradition (this is the new term for *Bible,* by the way) that we have adopted as our fundamental way of life in America says so. It also says that we should all get married as soon as possible and begin popping out Judeo-Christian children.

This is where the gay marriage part comes in and it all gets really good. What Mr. Prager believes is the correct thing to do is to suppress the homosexual aspects of our sexualities and allow the heterosexual aspects to flourish. According to his thinking, allowing gay people

187

to marry will send a message to young people that being gay is acceptable. Discovering that this is now an option to them, they would then cease to repress their homosexual sides and become born-again dykes and fags. He also fears that people who have already properly suppressed their homosexual sides and married will suddenly feel they have been given permission to abandon spouses and families to attend the Michigan Womyn's Music Festival and purchase condos in South Beach.

It is far better, he feels, to make homosexuality seem forbidden, so that no one will want to do it in the first place. This wonderful theory is based, according to Mr. Prager, on interviews he has conducted with "leading sex researchers." And he apparently knows a lot of them. Why they weren't invited to speak about their own views is something we did not have time to get into. Perhaps there was not enough room in the rotunda to hold them all.

Mr. Prager says he has no problem with gay people, which relieved those of us who were beginning to worry. Barney Frank, the openly gay representative from Massachusetts, asked Mr. Prager if he had a problem with Frank and his lover speaking to teenagers about being gay. Mr. Prager said he did not, because being gay is still seen as something freakish, and no self-respecting teenager would want to be freakish. Mr. Prager has apparently missed the proliferation of nose rings and tribal body art in the twelve-year-old set, or perhaps he is simply acquainted with a better class of young people than am I. At any rate he did not, he continued, think "legitimizing" Frank's relationship by allowing him to marry was a good idea, because then it would make kids want to be gay too. A more rational approach, he feels, is to create a society in which repressing homosexual feelings is considered a positive thing. I briefly wondered if he'd ever visited a single-sex junior high school during gym class.

Now, here's why Mr. Prager impressed me. With his simple statement, he launched a brilliant new campaign by the right wing. First, he admitted that homosexual tendencies are perfectly normal — we all have them. In this way he removed himself from the ultraconservative stance favored by people like Jesse Helms, whose supporters are easy to ridicule or to label hatemongers because they attempt to separate queers from everyone else as being somehow tainted. By becoming one of "us," at least theoretically, Prager became part of the family, albeit it a distant cousin.

Second, he then went on to say that, although these desires may be normal, ultimately any expression of them is harmful to society, which benefits from the coupling of two sexes together to form family units. Thus he brought back into his camp any of the anti–gay marriage people he might have lost with his earlier admission of homo leanings. Who isn't for anything pro-family?

In short, Mr. Prager admitted that although he might have inclinations to act a certain way, by using discretion and clearheaded thinking about what was best for everyone, he did not do so. This, by inference, makes him (and everyone like him who would love to suck cock or munch muff but is too afraid to and so doesn't) better people. They aren't hateful, or bigoted, or mean. They're patriotic. They are good citizens because they have sacrificed something that might have made them happy for the more important good of their neighbors, their children, their country. Homosexuals, in comparison, are not precisely wicked, just weak-willed, like people who gleefully inhale nicotine even though it's known to kill, in the process poisoning everyone around them with second-hand smoke just so they can fulfill their personal addiction. Apparently, those of us who "actively practice" homosexuality are guilty of throwing off second-hand queerness.

This is an absolutely flawless campaign. By admitting that you have the inclination to do something — say, commit murder — but then denying that you did it because it "just wouldn't be right," you allow yourself to be seen as someone who has clearly weighed all the options and chosen that which will benefit the most people. This allows others who might have previously felt guilty about having those same inclinations themselves to warm to you. "Of course I thought about murdering my wife. I even talked about it. But I could never actually do it." What a nice man. Of course we've all thought those things. Thank you for making us feel normal. Go home to Brentwood.

Now, no one was comparing being queer to murder, but you get the idea. If you buy Mr. Prager's arguments, everybody wins. Homophobes can feel better about themselves, because having queer thoughts is okay so long as you don't do anything about it. And actually being queer can reclaim some of the decadence it seems to have lost over the past decade or so. Instead of being freaks, we can see ourselves as flouting morals we simply don't agree with. Like the draft dodgers of old, we can rush up to Canada until the homophobes find something else to whine about. Chelsea Clinton, having followed in her father's footsteps, pardons us all and we're finally, if reluctantly, seen as the true rebels we always were, fighting for a just cause.

Or maybe not. Outwardly, Mr. Prager's five-minute speech was idiocy at its best. Kids won't want to do something because it's forbidden? We should all marry and pop out babies because it's what we've agreed to do as a society? Nonsense. This is pure right-wing conservatism masquerading as social conscience, and it's great fun to laugh at.

But therein lies the danger. People love idiots who seem like patriots, because they make the rest of us look good. I need only to point to the twelve years of presidents Reagan and Bush as proof. People like men with easy answers who make them feel good for having no idea what they really think. If Mr. Prager's way of thinking were to spread, queers would be seen as people who simply aren't willing to do enough for their country, while nonqueer people (in Mr. Prager's world no one is exactly straight) are simply doing what's right for everyone. It's the classic parental guilt statement: "I'm not saying what you did was wrong; I just said I was disappointed."

And Mr. Prager is disappointed. We in the queer community have failed him utterly. And if legal gay marriage becomes a reality in this country, we will have also failed both the suddenly unrepressed lesbians and gay men who will leave their hitherto happy families, as well as the many innocent children who will see us as people to emulate and who will undoubtedly trip merrily down the garden path in reckless defiance of Mr. Prager's Judeo-Christian vision of America. If he and his followers have their way, perhaps one day we'll wake up to find the streets plastered with posters like the ones minted during World War II urging Americans to be on the lookout for possible Nazis in their midst. A grim-faced Big Brother will be pointing a wary finger at two men or two women holding hands, while beneath his watchful gaze the words IT'S YOUR DUTY will appear in hellish red.

A Slightly Dented Childhood

If Jesus Loves Me, Why Hasn't He Called?

For many children in America, Sunday is a day of rest. It might involve a quick trip to Mass, or possibly a boring yet harmless trip to Grandma's for some pot roast and cheek pinching, but in general it is a day of sleeping in, of long hours spent doing nothing, of going to the beach or to the park for fun-filled picnics. Not for me. As a child, my Sundays were spent in Baptist Concentration Camp, a hideous den of horrors cleverly disguised with the innocent moniker Sunday School.

On the surface it all seemed harmless enough. Each Sunday morning, while our parents congregated in the sanctuary above us, fifteen or twenty freshly scrubbed youngsters would crowd into the Immanuel Baptist Church's gold-carpeted basement, where we would seat ourselves quietly on folding chairs and wait expectantly for the weekly ritual to begin. At precisely 9 o'clock, Mrs. Evans would come in, her polyester dress bouncing merrily about her large breasts and ample behind. Mrs. Evans was the commandant of Sunday School, and she took it very seriously. Childless herself due to an ovarian cyst (I heard my mother talking about it once), she had dedicated her life to nurturing the immortal souls of the young.

She took to it with unmatched fervor and over the years had honed her weekly routine into a spiritual workout guaranteed to make us tireless laborers for Jesus.

First came prayer. At Mrs. Evans's command, we stood and attempted to maintain our balance with our eyes closed while she recited the litany of things for which we should be thankful (our families, church, food, government) and things we should be concerned about (poor people, hungry people, people without governments, people who didn't have Sunday School). If there was something particular to the church family that needed attention, such as a sick child, a dying elder, or a new roof fund, that would get thrown in at the end. It all ended with a group "Amen!" said enthusiastically in the way that is bred into all Baptist children.

After the praying came the Sword Drill. According to Mrs. Evans, our greatest enemy in life was Satan. She never really explained exactly who he was, but we were led to believe that he was most definitely not someone who had attended Sunday School as a child and was therefore bad news. As such, we were instructed that we must be on constant guard for his tempting ways, although, again, what these ways were was never quite spelled out, leaving most of us with the firm impression that Satan was a cross between a used-car salesman and Farrah Fawcett, who in the 1970s was considered something of a tramp by good Baptist people.

Our weapon against Satan, explained Mrs. Evans, was the Bible, which we should always think of as a sword with which to slay him, should the need arise. Somehow this didn't seem as effective to me as a smart handgun would have, but Mrs. Evans was older and therefore knew better. The purpose of the Sword Drill was, essentially, to practice killing Satan. Holding our Bibles/swords at our sides, we would wait until Mrs. Evans called out a particular verse. Then we would draw our swords and flip frantically through the pages looking for the reference she'd given. Whoever found it first would begin to read it in a loud voice, thus scoring a direct hit on the Evil One. The rest of us, apparently, became casualties of friendly fire.

The Sword Drill lasted through five or six verses, until Mrs. Evans was assured that at least some of us had correctly memorized the order of the books of the Bible, or at least had the presence of mind to install clever little tabs with the names of the books printed on them, effectively creating the biblical equivalent of a semiautomatic weapon. Should we be particularly slow to use our swords, Mrs. Evans would shriek in a frantic voice, "Satan is getting closer! Satan is winning! Do you want Satan to beat you?" sending us into a panic as we scrambled for our ammunition.

Military maneuvers completed, it was then time for Flannelgraph. This seems to be an invention wholly original to Baptist Sunday School classrooms, which is really a pity, because in the right hands it could actually be quite fun. The Flannelgraph is a large board covered in black felt. Placed upon the board are paper dolls that have been backed with a flocked material that makes them stick to the felt. Using the paper dolls, a clever person can re-create an infinite variety of scenes. Handy books are provided filled with cut-out Jesuses, apostles, trees, farm animals, boats, food, demon-possessed vagrants, and anything else one might need for hours of Flannelgraph enjoyment. Like I said, it could be fun. But as with so many things, the Christian element makes it not as cheery as it might otherwise be, limiting it as it does to the retelling of Bible stories.

Mrs. Evans' favorite story in the Bible was, of course, the Crucifixion and Resurrection of Jesus Christ. She had told the story so often that she was able to maneuver the Flannelgraph figures about the board in such a way as to hold us captivated while she described the judgment, torture, and execution of our Lord.

Up went the Pontius Pilate paper doll, scorning the Jesus doll. "And they whipped him!" Mrs. Evans screeched, her meaty hands flailing in imitation of the lashes as she moved the paper Roman guard toward Jesus.

Then away they went, only to be replaced by Jesus, wearing a crown of thorns and carrying his paper cross on wounded shoulders while a paper crowd jeered cruelly, Mrs. Evans providing all of the taunting voices. Once at Calvary, up went Jesus and his cross, along with the two thieves crucified with him. A weeping paper Mary and the apostles brave enough to attend sat at the base.

"He hung there for three days!" Mrs. Evans said, her voice rising. "Three days! And on the third day, he died!" She let the last word hang in the air as we stared, wide-eyed, at the Flannelgraph. It was all very vivid, and by the time she rolled the paper stone away from the paper grave, we were beside ourselves.

There were, of course, other stories. And Mrs. Evans knew them all by heart. There was a paper Daniel in the lions' den, and Jesus walking on a paper sea. There were paper angels and paper clouds, and even a paper heaven with streets of gold. It was all glorious. Yet we were forbidden to actually touch the Flannelgraph materials ourselves.

Once, though, we did touch them. Mrs. Evans was out of the room, and the Flannelgraph was left unguarded. Scottie Hogan, who I can now only assume was under the influence of Satan, ran up and snatched a paper apostle Paul from the box. He then proceeded to reenact a scene from *Saturday Night Fever,* with Paul assuming the John Travolta role. The rest of us went wild, grabbing assorted figures and making them boogie-oogie-oogie along with Paul/John on the Flannelgraph disco floor. Somehow, we managed to put everything back in the box before Mrs. Evans returned, and if she ever wondered why we all were looking guiltily at our feet when she entered the room, she didn't let on.

The next item on the weekly agenda was arts and crafts. This gave us time to recover from the overwhelming influence of the Flannelgraph. Seated around conveniently child-sized tables, we would be instructed in any manner of Christian handiwork, all designed to further our love for Jesus and deepen our commitment to his work. A typical project would involve re-creating a biblical event (such as Noah's ark or the feeding of the 5,000) in Play-Doh or finger paints. Holiday-themed crafts were especially nice, as they generally involved the use of cotton balls, glue, glitter, and other exciting items that left us giddy with the creative spirit. On one memorable occasion, we cut Jesus's face out of a picture and decoupaged it onto Ivory soap, ensuring that every time we washed our hands we would be reminded of his cleansing love. My mother kept my soap in the guest bathroom, where for three years startled visitors left it untouched.

Lest things become too cheerful and lighthearted, crafts was followed by the weekly Missionary Report. Our class had "adopted" a missionary family. They lived

somewhere in Africa, where we were told they were saving the souls of the heathens, who we saw selfishly preferred tending their crops and worshiping ancestral
deities to holding Sword Drills and Flannelgraph. Slowly,
however, our missionary family was making inroads. We
knew this because they wrote us letters telling us how
many souls they had saved each month. We had a map of
their country, and for every ten souls, Mrs. Evans placed
another big gold star on the map.

Our job was to send money to the family. We had
each been given a bank in the shape of a globe. Each
week we were supposed to put as much money as we
could into the bank, then bring it to Sunday School.
There, at the appointed time, we would march to the
front of the room and empty our bank's contents into a
big bowl under the watchful eye of Mrs. Evans. If our
contribution was large, we were awarded with a beaming
smile and a card imprinted with an encouraging Bible
verse about people who supported missionaries getting
wonderful rewards in heaven.

If, however, our weekly earnings fell below an
acceptable level, we were told to stand before the class
and inform everyone what we had bought that week
with money that clearly could have been better used.
After one or two Sundays of having to look into the disappointed faces of your classmates and admit that you had
purchased one too many packages of gum or yet another *Star Wars* action figure, the lesson was learned: Our sin
was causing the Lord's work to suffer.

My favorite part of Sunday School was the song
period, simply because it was an excuse to stand up and
dance around a little bit, which normally Baptists do not
do. Certainly I didn't care for the music, finding it vulgar

and lacking in style. I don't know who wrote these songs, but in talking to other SS survivors, I have discovered that they are universally known. I can only suspect, then, that somewhere a secret agency is cranking out songbooks of unspeakable evil and whisking them off to churches around the world.

While most of the songs were generally cheerful and uplifting, if horribly awful, some were just plain bizarre. The worst of the lot was a song that cleverly combined knowledge of the alphabet with biblical tidbits. "A, B, C, D, E, F, G, Jesus died for you and me" went the first sing-song verse. "H, I, J, K, L, M, N, Jesus died for sinful men. Amen! O, P, Q, R, S, T, U, I believe God's word is true. U, V, W, God has promised you, X, Y, Z, a home eternally." At the time, I sang the song loudly and forcefully, proud to display my recently acquired alphabetical knowledge. Listening to it now, I get chills.

Singing marked the end of the Sunday School work-out. But on the first Sunday of each month, before sending us on our way, Mrs. Evans allowed us to partake of a junior version of the communion our parents and older siblings were receiving upstairs. Filing one by one to the front, we were presented with a Nilla Wafer and a small cup of Kool-Aid. The body and blood of Jesus Christ they weren't, but somehow we felt very grown-up and serious as we dutifully ate and drank, dreaming of the days when our cookies and fruit punch would be replaced by broken bits of cracker and grape juice doled out by the grim-faced deacons in their dark suits and greased-back hair.

Communion or not, each Sunday inevitably ended with a group sing-along of the old standby "Jesus Loves Me." Joining hands, we would sway from side to side, much like the joyous Hoos warbling away in *How the Grinch Stole Christmas*. Tiny voices raised in unison, we joined one another in the familiar words. "Yes, Jesus loves me!" we shouted. "Yes, Jesus loves me." We were one in our love for the savior and all he offered, and when it was over, we felt very good indeed.

Everything about Sunday School seemed fine for a while. In fact, for some time I felt very holy as I exited the church each Sunday, content in the knowledge that I had spent time with Jesus and done my Christian duty for yet another week. It felt good to be so much better than all of those African natives the missionaries were frantically trying to convert from their sinful ways.

Then one day, while sitting in the back seat on the ride home, things began to change. Maybe the sugar from the Nilla Wafer was too much, or maybe the heat in the basement had gone to my head. Maybe it was just that I was getting older and was starting to understand a few things I hadn't before. Whatever it was, the spell woven by Mrs. Evans, Flannelgraph, and the Kool-Aid wore off. Suddenly, my Sears three-piece suit seemed a little too warm, the clip-on tie a tad snug around my little throat. I was no longer the placid Christian child who had drawn his sword in victory. I looked down at the cross I'd made from popsicle sticks, and I started to wonder — what did it all mean?

The next week, right after Sword Drill, I raised my hand. When Mrs. Evans acknowledged me, I stood up. "I was just wondering," I said, "if Jesus loves me so much, how come he never calls or anything? My grandma loves me, and she calls every Tuesday night to tell me so."

Mrs. Evans's smile froze. She stared at me. Then she took a deep breath. "Well, Michael," she said, "Jesus isn't really a person like you are or like your grandmother is. He can't just pick up the phone and call. He talks to us in other ways."

There was rustling around me. This was the first any of us had ever heard about Jesus not being a person like we were. "What do you mean he isn't like us?" asked Janice Preston.

Mrs. Evans didn't look happy. "Jesus is God's son," she said. "He lives up in heaven."

"Why doesn't he come down here?" I asked. The others nodded.

Mrs. Evans sighed. "He is coming down," she said. "But not yet. It isn't time yet."

"When will it be time?" I asked.

"I don't know." The smile had left Mrs. Evans's face.

"Then how do you know he's there?" I pressed. "If he doesn't talk to you."

"I just do," Mrs. Evans hissed through clenched teeth. "Because the Bible says so."

We had her, and we knew it. Every child in that room had been given the "because I said so" answer, and we all knew what it meant: She didn't really have any answers. We moved in for the kill, and we were merciless.

"Who told the people who wrote the Bible what to say?" asked Janice.

"How do you know Jesus loves us?" queried Scottie.

"If Jesus can do anything, why can't he talk to us?" I tried again.

It was a mass epiphany, and I was the leader. It was as though, as one, we had broken free from the mindless obedience that had been drummed into our heads by group sing-alongs and Sword Drills. For the first time, we were thinking on our own, and we wanted answers. No longer willing to believe everything we were told, even if it was accompanied by Flannelgraph, we wanted proof. We were filled with the fire of emancipation, and we went wild.

"If you sin while you're falling out of a tree and you die when you hit the ground, will you still go to heaven?" John Carver asked.

"Why does God make the Africans go to hell if they've never heard of him?" wondered a boy who had never spoken a word as long as I'd been in Sunday School.

"How did Mary get pregnant if she wasn't married?" I asked. It was something that had bothered me for a long time, but I'd always been afraid to ask.

By the end of the hour, Mrs. Evans was near tears. Try as she might, she couldn't get us to stop our questioning. Flannelgraph didn't work. Arts and crafts were useless. We wanted nothing of singing. We all wanted to know just why it was that Jesus had never spoken to a single person in the room. When our parents finally came to retrieve us, Mrs. Evans pushed us into their arms and fled, crying, from the room.

"What was that all about?" my mother asked, helping me on with my coat.

I fixed her with a steely-eyed stare. "If Jesus loves me," I asked, settling in for a fight, "why hasn't he called?"

When I saw her face drain of color, I knew it was going to be a long ride home.

Confessions
of a Don't-Bee

As a preschooler, one of my great joys was sitting in my parents' big bed each morning and watching *Romper Room*. For those poor souls unacquainted with the joys of this now-defunct '70s-era children's television show, I will explain. Romper Room was an idyllic day-care center, where an audience of fifteen or so lucky four- and five-year-olds sang, danced, and experienced sheer joy in the company of the world's perkiest host, Miss Nancy. I understand that different cities had different hosts, but they all uncannily seemed to resemble Miss Nancy, as though some kind of government experiment in genetic cloning had gone horribly awry, resulting in an army of identical children's television personalities with permanent smiles and poor wardrobes. A sort of Kathie Lee for the preschool set, Miss Nancy doled out love to her assembled guests while the rest of us sat at home and watched, wondering what it was we had done so as not to be allowed to join the rabidly merry kids basking in her glow.

The premise of *Romper Room* was simple indeed. Miss Nancy sang and danced. We watched. In a time when, at least in my neighborhood, many mothers remained at home with their preschool children, it provided an hour of relief for parents who simply wanted to sit and drink their coffee in peace and quiet. Entranced by the fun taking place in Miss Nancy's room, those of us still young enough to find such things thrilling would stop everything to see what new song Miss Nancy would teach us today.

At some point in every *Romper Room* show, Miss Nancy would hold up her Magic Mirror. This clever prop was simply a hand mirror with the glass removed so that Miss Nancy's buoyant face could peer through. She would stare directly at the camera through the hole in the mirror and pretend to see all of the Friends at Home while she chattered on endlessly about all the fun she and her guests were having. This was supposed to make those of us alone in our rooms feel better about not being able to romp with the more fortunate children.

As much as I loved her, I thought Miss Nancy was full of crap when it came to the Magic Mirror. Even with my rudimentary knowledge of science, I knew she couldn't really see me at home, and I considered myself much more sophisticated than the obviously demented children in the *Romper Room* studio audience who shrieked with glee whenever Miss Nancy peered at them through the Magic Mirror and pretended to be looking across the airwaves. "I see Kathy," she'd say, and Kathy would squeal and clap her hands, in awe of Miss Nancy's mystical powers. Holding Kathy in contempt, I would sit in bed with arms folded, waiting for Miss Nancy to put down the Magic Mirror and move on to something more exciting, like a rousing group-sing of "Row, Row, Row Your Boat."

This all changed, however, the day Miss Nancy was discussing the crucial issue of color. I had always been

fond of color and was pleased that I was going to learn
something useful that I could share later on with my parents and friends. I watched carefully as Miss Nancy held
up circles of various colors and told us what they were
and how they could be put together to form new colors.
This impressed me greatly. After going over the relative
merits of red, blue, and green, she asked the children in
her studio audience what their favorite colors were.
"Blue!" they shouted, or "Yellow!"

Then Miss Nancy picked up the Magic Mirror and
held it in front of her face. "And what's your favorite
color, Friends at Home?" she asked cheerfully.

"Purple!" I screamed back. I knew that, in the
greater scheme of things, purple was a sissy color, but
what did I care? I was full of Froot Loops and feeling
fine. Purple was bold. It was different. And besides, Miss
Nancy couldn't hear me anyway. "Purple!" I screamed
again, giggling madly.

Suddenly, Miss Nancy's face inside the mirror broke
into a wide smile. "I heard a Friend at Home say purple!"
she chirped. "That's an *interesting* color to pick, isn't it boys
and girls?"

In that instant, my safe childhood world shattered
forever. Miss Nancy could hear me. Not only that but
she had announced to the world that a Friend at Home
actually preferred purple over blue or yellow. I stared at
the television in horror, waiting for all the children in
the *Romper Room* world to turn on me and begin
laughing derisively.

Then, just as the enormity of what had happened
began to sink in, another terrible thought entered my
four-year-old brain. If Miss Nancy could hear me, then
surely she could see me as well. Apparently, my knowl-

edge of how television worked was flawed in a fundamental way, resulting in my horrible admission of being
a boy who loved a color I thought only little girls were
supposed to favor. Who knew what else Miss Nancy
knew about me. She might have seen me engaging in my
favorite hobby of thumb sucking. Worse, she might actually be aware that on occasion I not only picked my nose
but actually ate what came out.

Unable to think clearly, I did what any reasonable
child would do: I hid under the bed. There, secure among
the dust bunnies, I peered out at Miss Nancy, watching
anxiously as she put down the Magic Mirror and moved
on to the next activity. I breathed a sigh of relief, thinking that maybe she had forgotten about me. The calm was
short-lived, however, when there was a knock on the
Romper Room door and Miss Nancy went to answer it.
Throwing wide the door, she turned to the camera and
beamed. "Hey, everyone, it's Do-Bee!" she cried.

Do-Bee was the *Romper Room* mascot and was, in
fact, a gigantic yellow and black bee, complete with
wings and bouncing antennae. Once every day, Do-Bee
would come into the room and greet all of the children.
He would buzz around, and the kids would go mad,
jumping up and down and pawing at Do-Bee's clever
costume. Invariably, Do-Bee would cover his mouth with
his hands and appear to giggle. Much later, I would realize that Do-Bee was, all along, a Queen Bee. At the time
I simply thought he was fabulous.

The purpose of Do-Bee was to teach us all the
things we should do or be. "We all want to be good Do-
Bees, don't we, boys and girls?" Miss Nancy would say
after a lesson on sharing or the importance of neatness,
and we would all nod agreeably. The opposite of a Do-

Bee was, of course, a Don't-Bee, a title no self-respecting child would claim. Satisfied that we were all normal and properly oriented, Do-Bee would then depart, antennae bouncing merrily, to pollinate the flowers or make honey or whatever he did in his off hours.

Normally, I welcomed the appearance of Do-Bee. I enjoyed his cheerful way of dancing from foot to foot and waving at the camera. But now everything had changed. If Miss Nancy could see me, so, of course, could Do-Bee. Suddenly, in a moment of sheer horror, it all came together in my mind. Do-Bee was Miss Nancy's henchman, the bee who carried out her dirty work. His brief appearance each day gave her the opportunity to point out the Friends at Home whose bad behavior she'd spied in the Magic Mirror. Thus identified as Don't-Bees, those children were then the targets of Do-Bee's wrath.

Clearly, after my declaration of purple-loving, I was now a Don't-Bee.

I scurried out from under the bed and turned off the television, severing the channel between me and Miss Nancy. But I feared it was too late. For the rest of the day, I walked around in terror, waiting for Do-Bee to come for me. I imagined him taking me away to wherever it was that children who didn't like normal colors like blue and yellow were kept. I pictured rows of cages holding children who, like me, had innocently admitted some terrible transgression. Perhaps they'd refused to smile at one of Miss Nancy's little jokes or been unable to keep up in Duck, Duck Goose. Maybe they'd sat sullenly while everyone else jumped rope, or, heaven forbid, colored outside the lines. Then, as they went about their days, they were suddenly plucked from their homes by Do-Bee and whisked away.

And if Miss Nancy was capable of such treachery, my feverish mind said, surely Captain Kangaroo was in on it as well. I thought of all the times I'd laughed innocently at Mr. Greenjeans's jokes, while in all likelihood he was watching my every move and taking notes, and I was filled with terror. By the end of the day, I'd developed a complete conspiracy theory that I was certain involved the core players of all major children's television programs. After gathering their information, Miss Nancy and the Captain would meet with Mr. Rogers, and possibly Bozo, at their secret headquarters. Together they would draw up a list of children who, for one reason or another, just did not fit in. Then, that night, Do-Bee would sweep through their homes like an angel of death, gathering up the wayward kids and taking them, I was certain, to Mr. Rogers's Kingdom of Make-Believe, where they would be held captive in Lady Elaine's merry-go-round. Lady Elaine, with her androgynous and slightly creepy appearance, had always frightened me in a vague way. Now I knew why — she was just waiting to get her twisted little puppet hands on me.

For the next week I slept fitfully, fearful that if I dozed off I'd next wake in some dank prison surrounded by other lovers of purple. My mother wondered why I didn't clamor any longer for my morning dose of *Romper Room,* preferring instead to actually play outdoors, constantly looking over my shoulder. "Don't you want to see *The Magic Toyshop?*" she asked, shaking her head in wonder when I turned pale and retreated to my room to build yet another Lego fortress. I avoided the television studiously, certain that now even Bobby and Cindy Brady weren't to be trusted. Surely they, too, were under the control of Miss Nancy and the evil children's television cabal.

Things went on in this way for some time. At first I could hardly walk outside my bedroom without fear of being ambushed. I jumped at the slightest sound and went to pieces at the merest hint of buzzing. I even tried to ward off Do-Bee by painting lots of pictures in bright, primary colors and hanging them on my bedroom wall. Perhaps, I thought, Miss Nancy would look into her Magic Mirror and see that I had changed. I hid my purple shirt and my purple bathrobe and my purple shorts and wore only blue or green things. I was determined to be normal, even if it made me miserable.

Then one day I was sent to a friend's house to stay while my mother did errands. Andy's mother sat us in the family room and turned on the television to *Sesame Street*. For some reason I cannot now imagine, I had never seen the show before. It was, however, Andy's favorite, and he immediately became engrossed in learning about the number *9* and the letter *q*. Terrified, I hid behind a bean-bag chair, waiting for the moment when yet another Big Brother figure would appear, pointing an accusing finger at the boy who admitted to a queer fondness for inappropriate shades.

When Big Bird came on, I trembled, watching his enormous, never-closing eyes for signs of spying. Even larger than Do-Bee, his huge feet and sharp beak looked capable of tearing a small boy to bits. I glanced at Andy, who was laughing at the deceptively affable bird's comic antics, and wondered if I should warn him about the danger he was exposing himself to. Doing so would be risking putting myself in further danger, especially since, like Miss Nancy, Big Bird had also said hello to the "friends at home." By now wise to the ways of the conspiracy, I knew that was a sign.

Andy was my friend, and I owed it to him to protect him from the clutches of Do-Bee and Big Bird. I had to speak out. But before I could utter a word of warning, Big Bird left and the scene switched to one featuring Bert and Ernie. Momentarily flustered by these new players in the game, I stayed in my hiding place and watched them for a minute to see what diabolical tricks they would try to use against me.

Despite my fears there was something about the on-screen pair that spoke to me, something I could relate to. Unlike the odd speechless rabbit of Captain Kangaroo, or Do-Bee's silent gesturing filled with ominous meanings, they were friendly and nonthreatening. Sure, Bert's single eyebrow was disconcerting, and he did look vaguely menacing. But Ernie's happy, smiling face reassured me. His sprightly tuft of hair made me laugh, and his gaily striped sweater looked like one I myself owned.

But more than that, there was something different about the way Bert and Ernie related to each other, something I had never seen before in all my hours of television watching. They joked amiably as they ate cookies together. They talked to each other about the things they liked. They went to sleep in their shared bedroom. They seemed to like each other in a way I could understand. On some deep level I didn't fully understand, I was certain that they too probably liked purple.

Eventually I came out from behind the beanbag chair, sat down, and watched some more. Soon I was laughing delightedly as Ernie counted sheep and Bert tossed restlessly beside him, all thoughts of Miss Nancy driven from my mind. While I wasn't entirely convinced that the menacing Do-Bee and his friends weren't still out there, waiting to pounce on children who didn't live up to their expectations, now I knew that I had friends on my side. There were others like me. Others who didn't quite fit in but who were nonetheless happy. That night, imagining Ernie asleep in a bed next to mine, I slept peacefully for the first time in days.

Packing for the Second Coming

When I was seven years old, I packed for the Second Coming of Jesus Christ, Our Savior. I did it in shoe boxes — seventeen of them — filled to near bursting with everything I thought I might need in the great hereafter. I even labeled them: PHOTOS, ART SUPPLIES, *STAR WARS* FIGURES. After watching my mother organize countless moves from house to house as our family trotted around the globe, I knew how it was done, and I was a model of efficiency. When I got to heaven, I would know exactly which box my toothbrush was in.

The hardest part was choosing which of my cherished items to leave behind. I knew from what my mother had told me about the streets being paved with gold that money was no good in heaven, so I left out my piggy bank. But being a veteran of school lunch-hour sandwich swaps, I had a vague suspicion that some form of barter was sure to exist behind the pearly gates, just as it did in the cafeteria of Westgate Elementary School. So in went the chrome-plated Collector's Series Hot Wheels cars my friend Mickey and I jealously collected. They were the rarest thing I owned, next to the shark tooth my grandmother had sent me from Florida, and I was sure they would come in handy.

Clothes were not a problem, since it had been made abundantly clear to me early on that everyone up there wore only shining gowns of whitest silk. Despite this fact, it was with some reluctance that I left my favorite item of clothing — my *Hee Haw* overalls — folded in the drawer. I assumed also that accessories would be thoughtfully provided, so I left my Captain Crunch Decoder Ring in its box, albeit wistfully. Since my mother had never been completely clear as to the status of pets in the afterlife, I threw in a stack of photos of the hamsters, the dogs, and the cat. Of these, the cat and one of the hamsters had already preceded me into the beyond, and I half believed I would find them waiting when I arrived. But being a sensible child, I figured it couldn't hurt to prepare for the worst. Photos of my family remained behind, as I innocently expected them all to be there with me.

The remainder of the boxes housed my extensive collection of *Charlie's Angels* trading cards. I couldn't really think of what I would do with them once I arrived in my lord's bosom, but I had put more effort into collecting and organizing them than I had into anything else I'd ever done in my short life, and I wasn't leaving them behind. Secretly, I hoped that one of the rewards awaiting me (and I was positive there were rewards) was the hard-to-find card featuring Kelly in hot pants that had long eluded me.

Two things were responsible for this frenzy of packing. One was the approaching American bicentennial celebration of 1976. For months I'd heard about this wondrous time, and although I had no idea what it actually was, I figured anything that could inspire both a newly minted quarter and a series of McDonald's commemorative jelly glasses must be of some significance.

The only thing I could conceive of being worthy of such honors was the return of Jesus, which both the pastor of our church and my mother insisted would happen soon but, when pressed, could not put an exact date on. Putting two and two together, I thought myself very clever indeed for unraveling the mystery that had puzzled biblical scholars for centuries.

The second, and probably most influential, thing was a charming little song called "I Wish We'd All Been Ready," which I'd recently heard one of my sisters playing on her stereo. It was sung by a Christian rock singer named Larry Norman, and it was all about the unbelievers who were left behind when Jesus came to sweep up his chosen people before the world was burned up in the end times. For whatever reason it had gained some amount of popularity among the teenage Christian set that summer and was quickly replacing Ocean's "Put Your Hand in the Hand" as the anthem of socially conscious American youth.

It says something about the nature of Norman's cheery ditty that I can still remember most of it today. It isn't hard, really, because essentially each verse was a mini-horror movie about another unfortunate soul shocked into awareness of his or her sinful existence by the sudden disappearance of a more pious friend or loved one during the rapture. Take, for instance, my personal favorite line: "A man and wife asleep in bed, she hears a noise and turns her head [dramatic pause] he's gone." Just in case the message was somehow lost, the chorus nailed it home. "I wish we'd all been ready. There's no time to change your mind; the son has come, and you've been left behind."

Children, they say, are visual creatures to begin with. In my little, and admittedly overactive, mind, I saw a woman rolling over in bed, only to find it empty because her husband (who of course had begged her for years to accept Christ in preparation for just this kind of thing) had flown up to heaven, leaving her to face the tortures of Armageddon, not to mention the bills and hungry pets, all by herself. From there it was but a small leap to picturing myself waking up one sunny morning and going in search of my family, only to find the house empty and Satan himself knocking at the front door.

I decided that the Fourth of July would be The Day. I knew that the Fourth was the special occasion everyone was waiting for, and I was certain Jesus would want to make a big entrance. It made sense (to me, anyway) that he would surprise everyone by showing up in time for the fireworks and picnics I was told were in the planning. Having determined that the time was upon us, I prepared accordingly. When I'd packed everything and sealed it tightly with tape, I arranged the boxes in a pile. Then I attended to my traveling wardrobe. According to my mother, what one wore for a trip was of utmost importance, especially if traveling long distances. I had no idea how far heaven was from Virginia, but since John Denver swore that West Virginia was "almost heaven," I assumed it was probably somewhere above Route 19, perhaps near Gaithersburg. I'd been there once, and I recalled that the ride back featured only one pit stop at Dairy Queen, which meant it wasn't too far.

Opening my closet, I thought about what outfit would be most fetching in the eyes of the Lord, Our God. While I knew that shortly after arrival I would be shedding my earthly clothes for those of heavenly design, I wanted to make a good first impression. After pausing briefly at my green polyester three-piece suit purchased especially for Easter, I decided instead on an ensemble of shorts and a shirt, which the attached raccoon Garanimal tags assured me were perfectly suited for each other in both color and form. They were lightweight — which I was certain would be an advantage when being lifted up to God — and sporty.

After dressing, I sat on my bed and waited. I wasn't entirely sure what I was waiting for, but I did it patiently and expectantly. No one had ever explained to me exactly what would happen when the rapture occurred, but I had some ideas. Drawing from a variety of sources, I had determined that there would probably not be much warning and that it would all be over rather quickly. Those who were left on Earth would suddenly discover themselves riding in cars without drivers, talking to companions who were no longer there, and becoming tangled in jump ropes as the turners on either side were whisked away to the great reward.

I confess I was secretly thrilled by the idea of unmanned cars skidding around the roads while the sinners inside screamed, and I hoped I'd get to see it. I also allowed myself to wonder, momentarily and a little guiltily, if all of my family members would really be joining me on the trip. It strikes me odd now that I didn't tell any of them of my plans. I like to think that I was just preoccupied with the preparations and that there was no malice of forethought in my secrecy.

As for myself, I suppose I expected the heavens to open up and to feel myself being raised gently into the skies like a kite, or like the revolving swing ride at the annual state fair, giving me a good view of all the doubters below crying out for forgiveness as I hovered, saved, above their heads. I wondered if it would feel like being in an airplane, which I was by then a veteran of due to many trips overseas. I hoped someone would present me with a plastic pin commemorating the event, as a friendly pilot had once done on a Pan American flight my family took from Africa back to America.

And so I sat and waited. After a few minutes, when everything seemed to be going on just as it had before I'd packed, I started to wonder if maybe something was a little off in my timing. I tried to remember whether Norman had specified precisely what time the Son was coming. I thought about going downstairs and getting my sister's record of the song and checking the liner notes for clues, but I feared that being separated from my belongings when the blessed event occurred would be a tactical error similar to attempting to check through nine pieces of luggage and two pets at Heathrow while changing planes for Venice. My father had done this once, and we'd arrived in Italy with three cats and six bags, none of which were our own, while our two Irish setters and my favorite shirt made their way to Rome. While I knew it was not a charitable thought, I didn't want another Christian to arrive in the Lord's presence with my trading cards.

After an hour had gone by with not the slightest hint of a rapture, I decided that I'd been had. Jesus wasn't coming. I got up and looked out the window. Outside, kids were running up and down the street playing kick the can in the afternoon light. None of them seemed worried in the slightest about missing Act 2 of the earth's destruction (Act 1 being the flood Noah escaped from). They were laughing and having a good time while I sat inside waiting for someone who clearly had no intention of keeping our date.

Suddenly, the skies clouded over with angry gray. There was a rumble of thunder, followed by a crack of lightning, and it began to pour. The kids scattered as the rain descended in sheets, and darkness fell over the neighborhood. The whole world seemed to be surrounded by the storm. It certainly wasn't what I'd expected the rapture to look like. I'd thought it would be more like *The Sonny and Cher Comedy Hour,* with bright lights and maybe some lively music.

Then a horrible thought entered my mind: What if this wasn't the rapture but the beginning of Armageddon? Every good Baptist child knew that after the beauty of the rapture was the horror of Armageddon, the final battle in which Satan's demons warred with the troops of heaven. It was, we were told, a terrible time, filled with death and fire and long lines at the supermarkets, where only those whose foreheads were branded with 666 — the mark of the beast — would be allowed to buy food. The branding itself might not be so bad, but the trade-off was that, once marked as Satan's plaything, a person would never be allowed into heaven. Being faced with the choice of either starvation or eternal damnation was not something I was keen to have happen.

What if Jesus had already come while I was packing, and now the storm was heralding the imminent arrival of the seven-headed beast with the whore of Babylon astride its back? Oblivious to the departure of the saved, I could have missed the whole thing, and now the apocalypse was upon me. I reeled at the thought that somewhere along the line I'd skipped a step in the process of salvation, and now I was doomed to burn with all the other sinners. Maybe Jesus had sensed my earlier gleeful musings on viewing the punishment of the wicked and decided to leave me behind.

Filled with terror I ran from my room screaming. I half expected the halls of my house to be overrun with lurching demons reaching out to drag me into hell. Holding my arms in front of my face as protection, I dashed into the living room, wailing, "No, Jesus! I didn't mean it! Please, come back! Whatever I did, I'm sorry!"

Sitting on the couch were two women I had never seen before. They looked at me, pieces of cake paused in midair in front of their open mouths. I stopped, gasping in huge breaths, and stared at their anxious faces. They didn't look like demons to me, but I couldn't be sure. I knew the devil and his ways well enough to know his minions appeared in many forms, even as cake-eating middle-aged ladies. "Be gone!" I shouted forcefully, dragging up from my subconscious the words our pastor claimed Jesus used to vanquish the evil ones. I pointed my finger at them defiantly. "In the name of Jesus Christ, go back to hell!"

The ladies looked at me, panting and wild-eyed before them. Then they screamed. Then I screamed. Then I fainted.

The next thing I knew, I was lying in my bed with my mother looking down at me worriedly. "Is this heaven?" I asked hopefully, thinking maybe Jesus, impressed by my stand against the demons, had decided to come back for me after all.

"What?" she said.

"Where are the demons?" I asked.

"What demons?" she said. "What are you talking about? And why did you interrupt my garden-club

meeting? You scared Mrs. Whitley and Mrs. Hogan half
to death."

Garden club? Then it wasn't really the apocalypse
after all. I breathed a sigh of relief. I started to get out
of bed.

"Oh no you don't!" my mother said. "You stay right
there and take a nap. I think you have a fever."

She left, shutting the door behind her. I looked out
the window. It was still raining, but the world wasn't ending. Larry Norman was a big, fat liar. I wasn't sure at first
if I was comforted or saddened by this thought. On the
one hand, it would have been fun to have seen heaven
and found out once and for all what it was really like.
Never having met anyone who'd been there, all I had to
go on were second-hand descriptions. I wanted to see it
for myself. And I had done such a nice job of packing. It
was a shame to see it all go to waste.

Then again, there were a few things to look forward
to right here on earth. It was summer. I'd just gotten a
skateboard and new sneakers I hadn't even worn yet. My
father had promised to take me and my friend Stephanie
to *Star Wars* for the ninth time. My birthday was coming
up, and I'd been hinting around for a bike. Besides, it was
the Fourth of July, and I knew there were sparklers in my
future when the rain stopped. There was a lot left to do;
maybe heaven could wait a while. Satisfied that I wasn't
quite ready for Jesus to come back after all, I settled into
the pillows and closed my eyes.

Before I drifted off, I looked at the stack of boxes
next to the bed. Half asleep, I picked up the box with my
favorite *Charlie's Angels* cards in it and tucked it behind
my pillow. Just in case.

The Crown of Heaven

The clearest memory I have from my eighth summer is of kneeling behind a station wagon in Mickey Whitlow's driveway and saving the soul of a girl named Susan. I have forgotten Susan's last name — or likely never knew it — but I do remember that she had a pinched face, startling green eyes, and frizzy red hair. We were frequent playmates and usually spent the long July afternoons racing our Big Wheels up and down the street in mad delight.

That summer I was spending several mornings a week attending Vacation Bible School at our church. Vacation Bible School is the Baptist version of summer camp, but without the fun or the mosquitoes. It consisted of sitting on the scratchy-carpeted floor of the basement of Immanuel Baptist Church and listening to our teacher, Nancy Higgins, tell us about Jesus. Nancy Higgins was a college student home on break for the summer. Before assuming the role of teacher, she had been known to the neighborhood kids simply as Fat Nancy, an unkind but completely appropriate appellation. Now, placed in a position of authority, she was determined to get her revenge for our years of torture.

On the first day of Vacation Bible School, Fat Nancy suggested that we each pledge to win over a soul to

Christ by summer's end. Should we fail to accomplish this goal, we would disappoint Jesus in some fundamental way that, she implied, would result in his not liking us very much. She did not quite say that we wouldn't be allowed into heaven, but somehow we were nevertheless left with this impression.

Deciding that I might as well get it over with as quickly as possible, I decided that the most logical choice for my conversion subject was Susan. On the day in question, I took it upon myself to take her down not the road upon which our Big Wheels raced but the much more exciting road to heaven. Fat Nancy had been very explicit in her instructions for soul-saving, and I had memorized the required steps thoroughly.

"You have to pray to Jesus," I told Susan as we knelt on the scratchy asphalt, the tar warm under my bare knees. She looked at me and blinked. "Like this," I said. I folded my hands and tried to appear as earnest as possible. "Dear Jesus," I intoned solemnly, "please forgive me for all of my sins and come into my heart."

Susan repeated my plea in a quiet voice. When she was done, she frowned. "I don't feel any different," she said. "If he's in my heart, shouldn't I feel it or something?"

I nodded. "You won't for a while," I reassured her. "But he's there. Now, no matter what you do, you won't go to hell."

We had spent a long time on hell before getting to the actual moment of salvation. I had described it for Susan in the fullest and grimmest of terms — all fire and burning and endless centuries of torment. I assured her that without Jesus, she was headed there immediately, should she suddenly be struck down by a car while riding her bike or choke to death while downing the contents of a Jumbo Pixi Stik from the 7-Eleven. That, in fact, was what finally sold her on the Son of God and all he had to offer. That, and the fact that I told her that her dog would be waiting for her in heaven when she got there.

"Is that it?" she asked, picking absentmindedly at a scab on her elbow. She seemed to be expecting some big finale, like a musical number or something.

I thought for a minute, staring at our distorted reflections in the slightly rusted chrome of the station wagon's bumper. I didn't want her to go away thinking she'd been cheated. "Now we sing," I offered.

Her face brightened. "What do we sing?"

I chose at random a song I had heard my sisters playing on the stereo. "Don't stop thinking about tomorrow," I warbled. Susan joined in, her thin voice mingling with mine as we chanted the familiar chorus together. "Don't stop, it will soon be here." Thus sanctifying our act with the words of Christine McVie and Lindsey Buckingham, I declared her born again.

That night, during dinner, I told my mother what I'd done. She beamed at me over her meat loaf. "You'll get a jewel in your crown for that," she said as she spooned peas onto my plate.

This was the first I'd heard about jewels, or crowns. All Fat Nancy ever talked about was making Jesus happy. "What kind of jewel?" I asked. I had visions of something vaguely tiaralike, similar to what Miss America wore on her runway walk, or perhaps something more reminiscent of the crown the Burger King wore in the television commercials for his restaurant.

"Was Susan Catholic?" my mother asked.

I looked at her blankly. I really had no idea.

"Was she Jewish, then?" my mother suggested hopefully.

"I don't know," I said finally.

My mother sighed. "You really must find out," she said. "It's important."

"Why?" I asked. Quite honestly, I didn't really know there was a difference. I'd just assumed there were Baptists, like us, and then a general multitude of sinners. Until her salvation by my forceful message of grace, Susan, I had believed, was simply one of the latter. Now, if I was hearing correctly, there were actually categories of the unsaved. Secretly, the thought delighted me no end.

"It's important," my mother explained, "because when you get to heaven, you will get a crown covered with jewels, one for each soul you've saved while you're here as God's messenger. You get different kinds of jewels for different kinds of souls. For Catholics you get sapphires. For Lutherans you get emeralds. For all of those Eastern types like Buddhists and Hindus and whatnot, you get rubies. And for Jews," she said triumphantly, "you get diamonds, which are the best of all. That's because the Jews killed Jesus, and winning one back is very special."

"I think she was Catholic before," I said doubtfully. Although Jews were clearly the bigger prize, to my mind sapphires seemed somehow much more festive than diamonds.

My mother smiled. "That's fine," she said, seemingly satisfied with my achievement. "There are so many of them; it's good when we can show one of them the right way."

I sat through the remainder of dinner contemplating this new information. If my mother was right — and I had no reason to believe she was not — the choice of which souls to lead to salvation held far greater importance than merely swelling the ranks of Christ's army. Where once I had thought it enough simply to snatch my peers away from Satan's fiery grasp, now I understood more clearly what was really at stake in the cosmic battle between good and evil.

As I thoughtfully consumed my meat loaf, I envisioned the crown I would one day wear in glory, the construction of which would be my life's work from that moment on. Now that I knew the rules, I feverishly designed in my mind the exact pattern of jewels I would work toward. Not to be satisfied with any old hodgepodge of gems, I was determined to meet my Lord dressed in a smartly encrusted crown of diamonds and sapphires, with perhaps a hint or two of emerald, if I could scare up a few Lutherans.

Later that night, alone in my room, I took a piece of yellow construction paper and cut it into two strips, which I taped together to form a crown. Using the blue crayon from my Crayola 48 set, I drew a sapphire onto the paper. Placing the crown on my head, I gazed at myself in the mirror over my dresser. Although admittedly only a poor copy of the real crown I was sure was being forged for me up in heaven, it looked very nice indeed, if a bit bare. It was time to get started on filling up the empty space with jewels.

I took out the school annual and found the picture of my class. I ran my finger down the list of names, counting the numbers of souls waiting for the deliverance I, with the helping hand of Christ, could offer them. With a red felt-tip pen, I carefully wrote in *c*'s next to those students I felt must surely be Catholic and *j*'s next to the ones who seemed, by whatever vague criteria I was using, to be Jewish. Those I was unsure of, such as Annie Chang, received question marks. When I was finished, I had a list of nine Catholics, five Jews, and four question marks. Folding it neatly, I stuck it into my notebook, where I could easily find it when the appropriate time came. Putting my crown on top of my bedside table, I went to sleep.

I dreamt that night of Jesus. He came to me in a long white robe, his face rosy with celestial delight. I approached, and he beamed, his mouth curling into a beatific smile. In his hands he held a crown — my crown — only now it was glittering with blue and white, the accumulated reward of a life spent in faithful service. As I stood before him, holding my breath, he placed it on my head. I felt its weight settle around me and looked up into my Lord's adoring eyes. As the heavenly host broke forth in song around us, he leaned down, bathing me in all his glory.

"Fabulous," he whispered in my ear. "Absolutely fabulous."

The next day my salvation campaign began in earnest. No longer motivated simply by the fear of Fat Nancy's veiled threats, I now had a real reason to spread the word of God throughout my neighborhood. Armed with my notebook and list of names, and fueled by my dream of the night before, I marched straight over to the house of the first kid on my list — Wayne Lerner.

I knew Wayne was Jewish, because the previous Christmas our teacher had given us a brief description of Hanukkah to explain that not everyone sang carols and waited for Santa to come down their chimneys. At the time I had felt sorry for Wayne because he didn't get to have Christmas. Now that I knew Jesus was also absent from his life, I considered it my duty to attend to his salvation as quickly as possible. Besides, I remembered what my mother had said about Jews being worth diamonds. Winning them over to the Lord might be tough, but I was experienced. With my easy conquest of Susan under my belt, I felt no need to warm up by practicing on a few Lutherans first. Ringing the Lerners' bell, I waited patiently until Wayne appeared.

"Hi, Wayne," I said cheerfully.

"Hi," he said. "I'm watching cartoons. What do you want?"

"Want to hear about Jesus?" I asked hopefully, visions of sparkling diamonds floating through my head.

"Jesus?" he said, his face wrinkling into a bewildered look. "There's no such thing as Jesus."

I stared at him, my mouth hanging open. No such thing as Jesus? I couldn't believe what I was hearing. Perhaps, I thought, this wasn't going to be so easy after all.

"But Jesus died for you," I said. "He died for your sins. You have to believe in him or you'll go to hell." Hell had worked wonders on Susan; I hoped it would do the same for Wayne.

"There's no such thing as hell either," Wayne said. This time he seemed very pleased with himself, as though he knew something I didn't.

"There is too a hell!" I yelled, determined to make my point. "And there is too Jesus! You take that back."

Wayne held his ground. "No, there isn't. Jesus is all made up. So is hell. My dad said so."

He had me there. He had his father's word behind him. The only authority I had to back up my claims was Fat Nancy and my mother, and I knew their names carried no weight with Wayne. Frustrated, I resorted to the only weapon I had left in my arsenal. Recalling what my mother had said about Jews, I gave him a menacing look.

"Killer!" I said forcefully, pointing at him. "Murderer! You killed Jesus!"

The next thing I knew, Wayne was flying down the steps. He tackled me, and we fell to the ground, shouting, punching, and kicking. We rolled around in the grass for a minute, both of us yelling our heads off. Then Wayne's mother appeared and managed to pull us apart.

"What's going on here?" she demanded.

Wayne and I scowled at each other. "I was trying to save him from hell," I explained, sure that any intelligent adult would see the reasonableness of this. "I was trying to tell him about Jesus."

"He said I killed Jesus," Wayne said sullenly. "He said I *killed* him."

With Wayne and I in tow, Wayne's mother marched over to our house, where she told my mother what had happened. "He said that Wayne killed Jesus," she said. I hung back, silent, knowing that my mother would side with me.

Instead, she grabbed me by the arm. "Apologize," she said, thrusting me toward Wayne. "Go on — tell Wayne you're sorry."

"No," I said. "I won't. He killed Jesus." Fat Nancy had told us several grim stories about missionaries being persecuted by the very people they were trying to save, and she assured us that suffering for Jesus was just as good as actually saving souls. "Besides, you said...," I began.

My mother pinched me hard. "Say you're sorry," she hissed through clenched teeth. Then she leaned down and whispered in my ear, "If you do you can watch an extra hour of television tonight."

I was confused. My mother was actually encouraging me to lie. It didn't make any sense. Why didn't she want me to stand up for Jesus? Just last night she had told me that the Jews killed Jesus. Now here she was making me apologize for saying so. Wayne and his mother were both staring at me, waiting for me to say something. My mind raced as I tried to decide what to do. I weighed the possibility of an extra hour of television against the reward I might get for standing my ground for Jesus. Then I remembered that *The Love Boat* was on that night. I'd never been allowed to see it before because it was on past my bedtime. I caved in.

"I'm sorry," I said sweetly.

Wayne's mother smiled. Wayne made a face at me. My mother said, "Honestly, I don't know where he comes up with these things." Then the two of them left. Afraid that my mother would revoke her promise if questioned too heavily about it, I left her to her gardening and spent the rest of the day in my room.

That night, after a blissful hour spent watching Gopher and Isaac laugh it up with Charo and Robert Wagner, I went to bed. Again I had a dream where I was wearing a jewel-studded crown. Just as before, I saw Jesus approach me, and I waited to feel his forgiving hand on my shoulder. I knew he would understand why I had done what I'd done. Who could stand firm against the temptation of Charo?

Just before he reached me, Jesus was transformed into the glowering figure of Fat Nancy. She stood over me, her terrible eyes flashing, as she snatched the crown from my head.

"You've disappointed Jesus," she said venomously. "And you lied. He's taking back your crown, and you're going to hell!" The ground beneath my feet opened up, and I felt myself falling into a pit of flames. Above me, Fat Nancy held up my crown and cackled triumphantly as I screamed "I'm sorry!" and plunged to my doom.

Just before I hit the flames, I woke up. I looked around my dark room for the horrible spectre of Fat Nancy as my heart raced wildly. Finding myself alone, I turned on my light. The crown was still on my bedside table. Picking it up, I tentatively placed it on my head. I knew the dream was a warning. I'd been forgiven once, but I couldn't fail a second time. I had to make it up to Jesus.

Opening my notebook, I looked at the next name on my list — So Yung Kwan. Afraid to go back to sleep and encounter Fat Nancy again, I leaned back against the pillows and went over and over in my head exactly what I would say to So Yung the next day when I rang her bell.

The Theory of Relativity

As queer people we seldom have the advantage, when we are very young, of having role models to guide us in the ways of being successful dykes and queens. Rarely does anyone point out the "spinster" aunt and suggest that the girls of the family emulate her ways, and "bachelor" uncles with their hosts of amusing, witty friends are almost never invited to spend time with their nephews, teaching them the finer points of homosexuality. Still, I've discovered that most of my friends did have at least one family member who, however unknowingly, provided a few hints as to what might be in store for them later in life.

In my family that person is my Aunt Betty. Aunt Betty is my father's sister, the only girl in a family of four boys. Since before I was born, she has lived with her "friend" Doreen in a little house right up the road from my father and his brothers. The house is surrounded by concrete lawn ornaments including, but not limited to, dwarves, frogs, deer, little boys peeing into the air, and even a life-size burro being led by a life-size Mexican man in a sombrero, who long ago was christened "Pedro Pulling His Donkey" by my ribald cousins. Aunt Betty herself is slightly shorter than Pedro and a little taller than his donkey. Her hair has always been cut very,

very short, and she wears cat-eye glasses trimmed in rhinestones.

Doreen looks exactly like Roy Orbison, the singer who sang "Pretty Woman." She wears brown tinted glasses and lots of turquoise jewelry, and she smokes long, brown cigarettes that look like sticks hanging out of her mouth. Because she's smoked so much for so long, her voice is very low and throaty, and she follows almost everything she says with a drawn-out cough. For years she drove a small orange pickup truck, to the hood of which she had affixed one of the small metal bulldogs that adorn the hoods of Mack truck tractor trailers.

When I was younger I liked to visit Aunt Betty and Doreen not because they provided me with any clues to my future but simply because their house is fascinating. See, they collect things. Not the usual stuff, like comic books or baseball cards, or even dead bugs or seashells. Weird stuff. And their collection spans more than five decades. The whole barn behind their house is crammed with plastic model horses, old aftershave bottles shaped like boats and trains, garage calendars from the '50s that have frisky paintings of naked women on them, '60s psychedelic memorabilia, and license plates from every state except Idaho, which Doreen says she finds disturbing because of its fascination with potatoes. The walls are plastered with posters of Farrah Fawcett, Shaun Cassidy, Erik Estrada, and other '70s icons.

The house itself is even more crowded. Over the years the two women have amassed an intriguing assortment of oddities, all of which are prominently displayed. Doreen is the keeper of the museum and delights in showing visitors around. She proudly points out the pictures of dogs playing poker and will wax eloquent about the *Star Trek* memorial plates that line an entire wall. There are boxes of playing cards decorated with film stars of the '40s, Barbies of every shape and size, and even a cabinet filled to overflowing with all manner of Trolls, those big-bellied, genderless, plastic figurines sporting shockingly bright tufts of hair.

But the thing Doreen loves most is her collection of Elvis spoons. She has a whole rack of them that hangs in the living room next to the plate commemorating the wedding of Prince Charles and Princess Diana. Every time anyone comes to visit, she has to drag the person in to see the Elvis spoons. "Look," she says, holding them like they were the frozen embryos of extinct animals, "this is The King when he was thin."

If she's really on a roll, Doreen will take down every one of her twenty-two spoons and explain where she was when she got it, what The King is doing on it, and how much it's worth (not that she'd ever sell). Sometimes she puts on Elvis records and sings along, twisting around the room belting out "Heartbreak Hotel" in her raspy voice while the long brown cigarette smokes away and her turquoise earrings glitter in the lights.

The saddest moment in both Aunt Betty's and Doreen's lives was when The King died. They had tickets to the concert he was to perform the next night. Now framed, these tickets hang in a place of prominence over the fireplace, and every so often during a visit one or the other of the women will touch them gently and begin to cry. "It's so tragic," she'll say before moving on.

When I was a child, my favorite thing to do when visiting Aunt Betty and Doreen was to sit at the giant player piano on the screened-in porch and work the ped-als that made it turn. Aunt Betty had found somewhere an enormous stash of music for the piano, and I would spend hours fitting the punched-paper cylinders into the playing mechanism and listening to the songs. My favorite was "Talk to the Animals," from *Doctor Doolittle*, and I practically wore it out playing it repeatedly, pumping the pedals faster or slower to see what effect it had on the melody, until inevitably one of the adults would come out and ask if didn't I maybe want to stop now and do something else. Years later, when I first saw a bunch of queens sitting around a piano singing show tunes, I would have flashbacks to those days on the patio and wonder if it was entirely coincidental that songs like "Oklahoma" and "Over the Rainbow" had been left out on the bench before I came by.

Along with the curiosities, Aunt Betty and Doreen also collected small dogs. In particular, they were very fond of Pomeranians. When I was little they had two Poms. One was large and white and called Honeybun; the other was small and orange and called Dee-Gee. I adored Dee-Gee and Honeybun, but they hated me unequivocally. Clever little beasts, they'd developed a system to their torture so that no one suspected their malice toward me. When I would arrive they would be all happy barks and wagging tails, and it was always suggested that I sit in the living room with them while the adults had coffee. But the minute I was left alone with the pair, they chased me up onto the plastic-covered sofa, where I would stand, looking down at them, as they bared their sharp little teeth and growled as only small, incredibly fuzzy dogs can do.

Things picked up slightly when Doreen brought home another dog, a pug that was christened Jada. Jada was as friendly as Dee-Gee and Honeybun were terrifying. She snorted and licked her way around the house, bullying the Poms and getting into everything. I loved her pushed-in face and curled tail and took to her immediately. I was not, however, allowed to pick her up. According to Aunt Betty, if I did, her little bug-eyes would immediately pop out of her head. The vet, she said, had shown her how to pop them back in, but she didn't want to take any chances. Horrified at the thought of an eyeless Pug and two little eyeballs rolling about on the kitchen linoleum, I restricted my affections for Jada to petting.

But the greatest curiosity in Aunt Betty and Doreen's house at that time wasn't the dogs, or even the player piano, but Doreen's aged mother. Mrs. C, as she was called, came to live with her daughter after she drove her car into a pond and it was decided she was no longer able to take care of herself. Thus she was packed off to the palace of lawn ornaments and small dogs, where she was installed in the guest bedroom.

If I was afraid of Dee-Gee, Honeybun, and Jada's unpredictable eyes, I was positively terrified of Mrs. C. She had been born and raised in England and had about her a decidedly regal air. Combined with the fact that she had long ago become irretrievably insane, she was formidable indeed, especially to a very small boy. She insisted, for instance, on being served afternoon tea, complete with sandwiches and a steaming pot of Earl Grey, every single day. The rest of her time was spent sitting in her room, watching game shows and waiting for visitors who never came.

My one vivid memory of Mrs. C occurred on a day when I had decided once and for all to see what would happen if I did indeed pick up Jada. I had begun to suspect that the popping-eye story was not entirely true, and when I was left alone with the dog while Doreen and Aunt Betty went into the garden for a minute, I saw my chance to put it to the test. Gripping Jada firmly around the middle, I began to lift her off the floor. I did it slowly, with the idea that if her eyes did begin to slip out of her head, I could probably put her down again before they tumbled out completely. I had lifted her front feet off the floor with no ill effects when suddenly I heard a shrill voice behind me.

"You there, boy. What are you doing?"

I dropped Jada and whirled around. Standing in the doorway to the kitchen was Mrs. C, clutching a handbag. Her hair had been put up in a rapidly falling pile, and her cheeks were rouged the color of cotton candy. Other than that, she was stark naked. All I could do was look at her wrinkled body in sheer terror.

"The queen," she announced loudly, stepping into the kitchen and pointing a long, thin finger at me. "The queen will be here in fifteen minutes."

With that, she squatted on the floor and released a small stream of urine, which pooled under her. She then stood up, turned, and went back to her room. When Aunt Betty and Doreen returned a few minutes later, I was still standing there, mouth open, staring at the puddle on the floor.

"What's that?" Doreen said suspiciously, eyeing Jada, who was hiding under the table.

I couldn't speak. I didn't know how to tell her that her mother had just made wee on the floor.

"Um, I don't know," I said. "It just sort of…happened." It sounded completely unconvincing, even to me.

Doreen grabbed a wad of paper towels and began to wipe up the mess. She never mentioned the incident again, but I had the distinct impression that whenever I went over there she kept one eye on me at all times.

It never occurred to me, when I was young, that Doreen and Aunt Betty were lesbians, mainly because I didn't think much about the subject at all. But even if I didn't know about Aunt Betty, she certainly knew about me. One afternoon, when I was about twelve, I was alone with her in the kitchen. She was washing dishes, and I was playing with Jada. For no apparent reason she turned to me and said, "I just want you to know that life is very hard for people like us." I nodded, unsure of exactly what she meant, and she went back to washing dishes. Like the puddle of pee, we never spoke of it again.

It took me many years to realize that while I found them delightful and fun, other people in the family thought Aunt Betty and Doreen were just plain strange. They came to all the family events and were even included in the annual Christmas Secret Santa swap, where everyone drew names out of my Uncle Dick's John Deere cap and bought gifts for whomever they picked. But slowly I began to notice that when they were spoken of, it was with a tone of faint puzzlement, as though no one could quite figure them out. Their relationship to each other was never discussed, even though my father and uncles had themselves built the bedroom addition onto the house and installed in it the single big bed the two women shared. Nor did anyone ever really answer when I asked, as I did several times, why Aunt Betty had never married.

My mother in particular had a strong dislike for the couple, especially for Doreen, whom she found positively frightening. She refused to go to their house and

avoided them at family functions after saying a quick
hello. The year she drew Aunt Betty's name for her Secret
Santa, she made my father switch names with her. Once,
when during a heated argument my sister said, "You
know, I'm starting to think Aunt Betty is the only normal one in this whole family," my mother began to sob
uncontrollably and ran from the room. At the time, I
couldn't understand why.

Many years later, when I was old enough to know
about both Aunt Betty and about myself, I would discover that my mother's stepbrother was also gay. When
my mother's mother died, David and his lover, George,
attended the funeral. At the house after the service, my
mother stood tensely in the living room while David and
George took over the kitchen and organized the cleaning up. I knew she was upset at having two of "them" (my
grandmother had adored the men, by the way) in her
mother's kitchen, but she couldn't do anything about it. I
desperately wanted to go in and talk to them, but I was
too frightened.

As we stood there, my mother wishing David and
George would leave and me wishing they'd take me with
them, my mother looked across the room at my grandfather's sister, who was talking forcefully about politics as
her daughter sat meekly by her side. "I don't know why
she has to be so loud," my mother said irritably. "I don't
know what her problem is."

Just then, Aunt Betty came up to us. Overhearing my
mother's comment, she snorted. "Her?" she said. "I'll tell
you what her problem is — she's a goddamned dyke. She
tried to pick me up at the service."

For my mother this was a moment of pure horror.
For me it was a wonderful revelation. We were every-

where. As my mother quickly left to get away from the growing number of queers in her midst, Aunt Betty turned to me and laughed. "She had that coming," she said simply and took a bite of her Jell-O salad. I went home that night pleased beyond words. For the first time I understood just why those old garage calendars and Elvis spoons had made me feel right at home all those years. I thought about my own fascination with things like old cigarette advertisements featuring film stars and statues of the saints, and it all started to make sense.

Unfortunately, David and George were both killed in a car accident a few years later, before I ever had a chance to ask them everything I wanted to. As for Aunt Betty, she still lives in the little house with the lawn ornaments. The dogs are long gone, as is Mrs. C, but the Elvis spoons remain, and Doreen continues to polish them regularly. Whenever I go home, I can be sure that when I drive by, the two of them will be sitting on the porch smoking their long, brown cigarettes.

Sometimes I think about what my life would have been like if I hadn't had Aunt Betty's peculiar presence in my life to, knowingly or not, reassure me that being different from everyone else around me was okay after all. And sometimes I think about her and her strange house and strange lover of almost forty years, and I wonder about the possibility that it runs in the family. My nephew is showing a decidedly queer bent these days, and he spends a lot of time at that old player piano. Is it a sign? I sure hope so. After all, someone has to inherit the Elvis spoons.

Saying Good-bye
to Grandma

My grandmother took a long time to die. Bred from hearty Irish stock, she survived a succession of strokes, heart failures, and other maladies that would have felled a rhino, despite the fact that she was barely four feet tall, weighed no more than sixty pounds, and subsisted almost entirely on a diet of Mountain Dew and Girl Scout cookies. Although doctor after doctor assured her children that she couldn't possibly make it through another year, she refused to pass on, outliving even the miniature dachshund my aunt bought to comfort Grandmother in her last days.

When she finally started to go, she required almost constant care, a task no one in my father's family was eager to take on, having already endured her for nearly eighty years. Finally, it was my mother who volunteered for death watch, and she devoted much of her time to attending to the old woman in the last months of her life. None of us really knew why she did it. Maybe it was because, under the numbing influences of the painkillers they gave her to quiet the angry voice of the cancer inside her, my grandmother finally became the mother-in-law my mother had wanted in the first place: one who wasn't able to harangue her with a steady stream of complaints and accusations. More likely it was simply that my mother enjoyed the opportunity to have her enemy just where she wanted her for a couple of hours a day — flat on her back and incapable of getting away. I have happy, if unfounded, visions of her leaning over the recumbent figure of the old woman and whispering in her ear, "Let's see you criticize the way I baste a turkey now, you miserable witch," before dancing gaily about the room.

Whatever her reasons, when the end came my mother spent many hours with the woman who bore my father, I suspect asking her what she had done to make him the way he was. She administered medications, gave sponge baths, and sometimes just read to grandmother from the endless stream of religious tracts left by the local clergyman who, tipsy from his lunchtime "tea break," would frequently spend a hazy hour or so with my grandmother talking about how wonderful it would be for her to finally see her Lord. Somewhere along the line, my Irish-Catholic grandmother (she had been sent to a convent at a young age but somehow managed to be impregnated by my English grandfather while still behind its walls) had switched her allegiance to the Baptist church, which was also my mother's denomination of choice. I think my mother always felt slightly offended by this, as though Grandma were trying to horn in on yet another area of her life, and secretly hoped there would be a mix-up in the heavenly paperwork that would prevent her quarrelsome in-law from ever achieving eternal rest.

Still, my mother went every day. Usually she would go over sometime in the early afternoon to the house where my grandmother was playing out her last dramatic scenes, returning around suppertime with updates on the death watch. Generally there was nothing much to report. But one night when she came home, my mother had an unusually chipper air about her. She whistled as she came in the door and greeted us with unusual warmth.

"Oh, lord," my father said instantly. "She died, didn't she?"

My mother laughed lightly. "No, not yet." She removed a piece of paper from her pocket and waved it at us. "However, we did discuss the imminent event in detail this afternoon."

"That looks like a napkin," my father said, squinting.

My mother unfolded the paper, which we saw was decorated with festive red and green poinsettias. "It is a napkin," she said. "It's all I had to write on when she started talking."

"Talking about what?" I asked.

My mother smoothed out the wrinkled napkin and smiled. "Her funeral plans," she said. "She decided this afternoon to arrange her funeral, and she asked me to write it out for her so that everyone would know what she wanted."

"You're kidding," my father said, shocked but obviously impressed by his mother's unfailing ability to organize everything around her even as she stood with one foot in the grave and the other on rapidly eroding ground.

"No, I'm not," my mother answered. "It's all here in black and white. Well, red and white anyway. All I had in my purse was a marker."

"What does she want?" my father asked.

My mother fair near radiated joy as she looked at us and delivered her pronouncement. "She wants to be buried in the pet cemetery."

"The what?" my father asked, incredulous.

"The pet cemetery," my mother repeated. "You know, the one behind Dick's house."

My Uncle Dick had, in fact, created quite an extensive burial ground in the wide grassy field behind his tool shed. Presided over by a lovely cement replica of St. Francis of Assisi, who according to Catholic legend (despite their mother's conversion, the children, with the exception of my father, were all staunchly Catholic) had done something miraculous involving swarms of animals, the graveyard was a repository for all of the deceased family pets. As each one died, Uncle Dick fashioned for it a cunning tombstone, which he spent days carving by hand and inscribing with the dead pet's name, dates of birth and death, and sometimes a clever saying. My family was quite fond of pets, and over the years there had been quite a number of dogs, cats, birds, assorted rodents, and even the odd snake and frog that had gone to their rewards. Each one rested now in the pet cemetery, immortalized by epitaphs such as MUFFIN 1960–1966: CATS HAVE NINE LIVES; HE GAVE UP AFTER SIX or AMY 1970–1984: A FAST DOG, BUT THE CAR WAS FASTER.

"She wants to be buried in the pet cemetery?" I said, both shocked and secretly thrilled.

My mother nodded firmly. "She says the dogs were the only ones who ever loved her, and she wants to be surrounded by them forever." I could tell she was trying not to laugh.

"She's nuts," my father said simply. "She's just nuts."

"That's not all," my mother continued. "She says that she wants to be cremated—"

"What's so odd about that?" my father interrupted.

"—and she wants the ashes placed in her garden gnome," my mother finished.

My father looked at her blankly. My mother, no longer able to contain herself, was shaking with laughter as tears streamed down her face. The garden gnome had long been a sore spot in family history. It had originally been given to my grandmother by my Aunt Betty one Christmas. Approximately three feet tall, it looked like any other concrete garden gnome commonly found in the gardens of people — like my relatives — for whom that sort of thing is of ceaseless interest.

Except that his particular gnome had been painted to resemble turquoise-colored marble. It's wizened little features had been glazed an unearthly blue-green and then streaked with black to create the ultimate specimen of white-trash high art. The gnome was holding in its stunted arms a small flowerpot, in which it was expected that one would plant geraniums or pansies or some other cheerful flower. It was into this pot that my grandmother wished her earthly remains to be placed.

The garden gnome had caused trouble from the moment it came on the scene, topped with a bright red bow and waiting under the tree during the annual holiday gift exchange. My father, thinking it a joke, had made some unkind comment about it looking a bit like a midget with an advanced case of blue balls. My aunt, who had spent many hours at Mimi's Ceramics Studio achieving the marbled finish, burst into tears. It had been a tense moment and one that was not spoken of again, for fear of bringing up even more bad feelings. My grandmother, for her part, had placed the gnome in a position of honor in her yard, where it had remained until she became ill, at which point my father wrapped it in burlap and hid it in the darkest recesses of the barn. Now, with her final death wish, my grandmother threatened to reopen old wounds.

Still, the idea of my grandmother being forever embraced by the arms of her beloved gnome and resting among a bevy of dead pets was funny. I started to laugh along with my mother, who was by now too far gone to stop. Even my father cracked a smile. "Of course she can't do that," he said, vainly trying to appear genuinely astounded.

My mother gave a great heaving sigh and wiped her eyes. "And why not? It's her last wish — I think we should respect it."

Ultimately, the issue of the gnome was put to a family vote, and in the end my mother stood alone against the assembled aunts and uncles, all of whom found the idea absolutely appalling. When my grandmother died a few weeks later, she was indeed cremated, but the ashes were then buried with great ceremony alongside her husband, whom she had never really liked, in the family plot. There was no statue of St. Francis, no merry little headstone with a witty epitaph, no garden gnome. But the relatives were happy. It was probably the one and only time they had ever dared defy her.

Later that day, during the immense feast that inevitably accompanied any family event, whether it be a birth, wedding, or death, my mother took me aside and showed me a small jelly jar filled with dust. "It's some of her ashes," she said, shaking it for effect. "I took them from the box this morning when no one was looking. Come on."

While the rest of the family sat inside enjoying their pasta salad and reminiscing about Grandma, we crept out to the barn. Heaving the gnome into a wheelbarrow, we wheeled it out to the old pet cemetery and placed it among the deceased pets, between an ancient setter and a guinea pig. My mother took the jar and put it in the gnome's flowerpot.

I looked at the gnome's hideous grinning face. "He looks demented," I said.

My mother laughed. "Give him a week with her," she said. "He'll be certifiable."

If you have lived in other cultures, *Screams in the Desert* will have you screaming with laughter. Sue will also sometimes leave you silently screaming in conviction by her equally powerful insights and applications of scripture to daily life in a cross-cultural setting.

Jeff Adams, Ph.D., Senior Pastor, KCBT

Awesome! Truly funny. Totally real. Hit my missionary funny bone. I laughed, I cried. Sue's eyes and ears were open to the daily delights and despairs of living overseas. Her observations and skillful writing style will help many cross-cultural workers.

Fran Love, editor of <u>Longing to Call Them Sisters</u>, Frontiers

---

As a missionary of 25 years, I wish I had something like this book as a resource to encourage my heart and process my experiences alongside of Scripture. I highly recommend this book for any missionary at any stage of their missionary career.

Sterling O'Neill, Women's Ministry Coordinator, CrossWorld Mission

Screams in the Desert howls with humble, humorous, honest humanity. It's a devotional, biography, team workbook, and testimonial to the faithfulness of God, and of His ambassadors around the world who endure much difficulty to His glory.

Johnny V. Miller, Senior Pastor, Calvary Church, Lancaster, PA

Women in missions—both married and single—will benefit from these transparent, down-to-earth, humorous, and above all Jesus-centered devotionals based on the author's life and ministry.

Kyeong-Sook Park, Professor of World Missions and Evangelism, Moody Bible Institute

---

Sue has written a personal, yet universal book about the issues of life. Practical, challenging and encouraging, this book will truly assist women in their spiritual growth. Enjoy!

Deborah K. Hinkel, Assistant Professor, Church and Ministry Leadership, Lancaster Bible College

Screams in the Desert

Hope and Humor for Women in Cross-Cultural Ministry

WILLIAM CAREY
LIBRARY

Cover Design: Jon Pon
Typesetting: Joanne Kay, Amanda Valloza
Editing: Beth Barron

Published by William Carey Library
1605 E. Elizabeth Street
Pasadena, CA 91104
www.missionbooks.org

William Carey Library is a ministry of the
U.S. Center for World Mission, Pasadena, CA
www.uscwm.org

Printed in the United States of America

Library of Congress Cataloging-in-Publication Data

Eenigenburg, Susan K.
  Screams in the desert / Sue Eenigenburg.
     p. cm.
  ISBN 978-0-87808-517-0
  1. Devotional exercises. I. Title.
  BV4832.3.E37 2007
  242--dc22
                              2007027353

To my husband Don
Who has loved me through every scream
And encourages me to follow our Savior
wholeheartedly.

To our children –
Stephen, Michael, Kristi and Katie
Who have brought joy to my heart
And for whom I daily thank God.

To our teammates who loved me unconditionally
While working together to plant churches
For the glory of God.

Table of Contents

Foreword   xi

Preface   xiii

1. Great Expectations   1

2. Diarrhea and Team Life   5

3. Terrorists and Chocolate Cake   11

4. Culture Shock Without Electricity   15

5. Maybe Normal, Maybe Different...   19
   Definitely His

6. Getting Into Hot Water   25

7. Flesh or Spirit?   29

8. Survival in a New City   33

9. Reverse Psychology and God   37

10. Suicide and Laundry   41

11. Jesus Loves Me   47

12. Facing Change...Almost Fearlessly   53

13. Let Me Show You   59

14. Listen, God, I'm Speaking   65

15. Language Learning Made Difficult   69

16. Pursuing God   73

17. If I Were a Warthog   77

18. Little Shoe in a Big City...   81
     Little Faith in a Big God

19. It's Me Again, Lord, and I Need   85
     Your Help

20. A Mother's Prayer Journal   93

21. A Godly Car?   97

22. In Appreciation of My Thyroid   101

23. Eternity In and Out of My Home   107

24. Creative Outlooks   113

25. I Gave God My Life,   117
     But Not My Toothbrush

26. Running Away From Home   121

27. Third Culture Kids, Peanut Butter   125
     and GI Joe

28. To Hide or to Confess,   131
     That is the Question

29. Eight Hours and a Camel   137

30. Faithfulness, Perseverance and   143
     Trusting in God

31. Balconies, Jump Ropes and Little Girls   147

32. Saying Good-bye Twice   151

33. Thoughts About Underwear,   155
     Police and Uncertainty

34. Jesus is Always Undisturbed   161

35. Barb's Legacy   165

36. An M Is Better When Followed   167
    by "&M"

37. Of Headaches and Hospitality   175

38. The Totaled Woman's Rest in   179
    His Everlasting Arms

39. A Daughter's Tears   183

40. Becoming a Mother-in-law   189

41. Who Will Pack My Computer?   193

42. Time and a Changing Perspective   199

43. Loneliness and a   205
    Swiss Mountain Man

44. The Power of Words   209

45. Unexpected Opportunities   213
    Meet Faith

46. Welcoming a New Neighbor…   219
    or Not

47. God's Will is Better Than Life   223

48. Praying For Safety   227

49. Why Am I Still in Culture Shock?   233

50. Forgiving Dirty Old   237
    (and Young) Men

51. To Adapt or Not to Adapt,   243
    That is the Question

52. Do the Possible…   249
    Trust God for the Impossible…
    Don't Confuse the Two

Foreword

I first met Sue in her home in Dallas where we had lunch together. Straddling her second son on her hip, she was a young mother and seminary wife, trying to adapt to the idea of a future serving God cross-culturally. Our lives intersected again several years later in the Middle East. By then she was a mother of four, as well as a language student and team leader's wife. Lightly seasoned in missionary challenges, her humor began to intrigue me. By the time she and her family arrived in another Middle Eastern city to join our team, our friendship included a long-term commitment to work together as wives, mothers and ministry partners seeing least-reached women and missionary women draw close to the Savior. When she and her husband joined us again in mission administration some years later, it was to complement each other's gifts in Women's Ministry.

Over the years I've seen Sue grow into the person she had desired to be. She listens to God and talks with Him about everything. Surviving motherhood and illness, harassment from Middle Eastern men, culture shock and lost shoes – nothing is too small to share with her Lord. She tackles marriage, grand parenting and a master's degree in leadership as she does each article in this devotional, with diligence and a giggle. Humor wins over the fear of criticism, circumstances, seasons of life or even a night in jail with dirty underwear. While writing and speaking now fill her days, memories of homesickness and small children with diarrhea connect her with young women fearful of taking that next step in obedience. Now able to travel more as her nest is emptying, Sue challenges men and women with the importance of woman to woman ministry in church planting.

Of course, when you work together desk-to-desk for eight years developing Women's Ministry at Christar as Sue and I did, you share more than ideas and editorial tidbits. We passed Elizabeth Peters' Egyptian mysteries back and forth, shared chocolate, e-mail humor and foibles in our children's lives. We traveled to Mesa, Atlanta, St. David's and Fort Worth together to help facilitate consultations on ministry with Muslim women. And we've broken the same finger in the same game of volleyball with our teammates.

For all women who think *being super* would delight the heart of God, Sue brings perspective by just being herself. As you enjoy her trip through tuna fish and team life, reflect on what you can learn from each hilarious story and do what you need to do to turn your *screams* into sounds of praise, worship and repentance. Your present desert will blossom again.

Mary Ann Cate
Christar
May 1, 2007

Preface

Screams in the Desert: A one-year weekly devotional combining humor, experience and scripture for women in cross-cultural ministry.

Cross-cultural work can be gloriously exhilarating. It can be scary and unpredictable. Cross-cultural work is rarely boring! You have followed God's call on your life. He will lead you step by step on your adventurous journey into a new culture, a new language, and new home.

May you learn as I share personal experiences with you in this book. More importantly, may you rely on the Word of God as you follow his leading and call on your life. As you seek to share the good news with new friends far away from your old ones, know that prayer is foundational for life and ministry. Know and accept who you are. Continually give who you are to God. He will mold you, sometimes gently and sometimes quite roughly, into the person he wants you to be. He will give you opportunities to serve him that are beyond and different from your own expectations.

As you allow God to work and rule in your life as you follow him overseas, you will encounter many unexpected events. You will laugh. You will cry. You will be embarrassed. You will have questions where you previously thought you had the answers. You will make mistakes. You will serve the Lord. You will rejoice. You will grow. You will tire. You will be energized. You will succeed. You will fail. You will feel like giving up. You will persevere. You are not alone. Others have gone before you. More will come after you.

As God works in you and through you, your life will touch others … and could help change the eternal destiny of the souls of the men and women you come to know and love.

May we all live and work for His glory.

Directions as you begin:

- Read the story and the scriptural passage written below it.
- At the end of each story are some questions for you to answer and space in which to write out your thoughts in light of the scripture read and your own cross-cultural experiences.
- There is an action point and prayer for each section. Please follow through on the action point presented or else determine another action point more specific to your situation each week.

Chapter 1
Great Expectations

A sick feeling stole into the pit of my stomach as we neared New Personnel Orientation back in 1985. What was I doing? I had always been willing to work overseas; I just never thought I actually would. I didn't attend any of those pizza suppers where recruiters talked about working in a different country. Yet here I was, along with my husband and two little boys, on the way to prepare for life overseas.

I read many books about famous people who lived and worked overseas—people who did amazing things, faithful men and women who served God. These people had books written about them. They had deep sayings that people quoted; they seemed like super-saints to me. How in the world was I ever going to fit into this same mold? Did the ones who had gone before me ever struggle with having their quiet times consistently? Were they ever afraid? Did they ever doubt their calling? How did they balance their work and their family? Were they always such spiritual giants? Did they ever sin? Did they ever crave chocolate?

My expectations for myself soared as I officially became a worker overseas. I should be able to do it all—keep a clean house, have long quiet times, raise near–perfect children, be near perfect myself, be a loving wife, lead thousands, well, at least hundreds, to truth, keep up with all correspondence, cook healthy foods, do laundry in such a way that the colors remained vibrant and the whites would dazzle the eyes!

I knew I couldn't do this in my own country—I just hoped something magical or even better, something supernatural, would happen to me as I crossed the ocean for my new vocation.

It didn't.

I was still me. As we settled in, I felt even more was expected of me—learning the language and culture well, attending and participating in team meetings, hospitality, fearlessness, boldness, visiting neighbors, and the list continues.

I admit that I put many of these pressures on myself. I wanted to be super spiritual so that I could be like those who had gone before me. Wouldn't it be neat if people wrote books about me? (*Sue Eenigenburg's Spiritual Secret* or *My Utmost Isn't Much but It's Still for His Highest*). I would love it if someone quoted me because of something really deep that I had said.

Eventually, God broke through my day dreaming of greatness, as well as through my guilt of not being as great as I wanted to be. I could never do all I wanted to do or be all that I wanted to be. Most of my great expectations were self–focused, self–propelled, and self–gratifying. It didn't matter if anyone ever wrote a book about me; I was still loved and valued by God. He wanted me to be me—to love him, walk with him, be faithful to him, serve him. He is the One who matters. His is the name I should want to honor.

The main reason I had that sick feeling back in 1985 is that I, unknowingly, felt the whole process and end results of my life and work were up to me. They're not.

You can quote me on that.

Read Matthew 22:34–40

When the Pharisees heard how he had bested the
Sadducees, they gathered their forces for an assault.
One of their religion scholars spoke for them, posing a
question they hoped would show him up: "Teacher,
which command in God's Law is the most important?"
(vv. 34–36).

Jesus said, "'Love the Lord your God with all your
passion and prayer and intelligence.' This is the most
important, the first on any list. But there is a second to
set alongside it: 'Love others as well as you love
yourself.' These two commands are pegs; everything in
God's Law and the Prophets hangs from them." (vv.
37–40).

Questions

1.   Take a minute to evaluate whether you have
been basing your value on what you do rather
who you are. When do you feel good about
yourself? When do you feel bad about yourself?

2.   How are these feelings linked to behavior?

3.   Recognizing God's love for you, how have you
responded to him this week?

4.   Write down expectations that you had of
        yourself, your team and God. How have these
        been met or remained unfulfilled?

5.   According to Matthew 22:34–40, what are the
        most important things to do in life?

Action
Sing a love song to God.

Prayer
Father, this life is all about you.
Help me to not depend or focus only on myself.
May I seek to love you above all else.
May I love others in word and deed.
May my passion for ministry never exceed my passion for
you.
Glorify your name through me. Amen.

Chapter 2
Diarrhea and Team Life

I had been on a basketball team, Bible quiz team and volleyball team. However, nothing had quite adequately prepared me for being part of a church-planting team. When we had been in the Middle East only a short time, I came down with "King Tut's Revenge." During our weekly team meeting, we had a time for sharing prayer requests. I wanted to share as delicately as I could about my "diarrhea," so I merely asked for prayer concerning stomach problems. Suddenly the team bombarded me with questions, "Do you have diarrhea?" "What color is it?" "Is there any blood?" "Does it smell really bad?" "Is there mucus?" "Is it all liquid?" Was *nothing* private? Did these people have to know what color it was?

I slowly began to realize these people wanted to help. Because of their experience in this area, they knew what kinds of medicine would be best for what symptoms. They weren't embarrassed. I didn't have to be embarrassed. We were a team—all for one and one for all.

As time went on, I realized that a team is not just a group of people that hang out together and work together; it is a group of individuals who are deeply committed to each other and to the Lord. They want to know (and often need to know) details of how my life is going—even to know the color of my "King Tut's Revenge"! They can and want to help.

Once I was so angry with my husband over an issue that I didn't sit next to him at our team meeting as I usually did.

A friend asked me, "Did you and your husband have a disagreement?" Amazed, I told her, "Yes," and wondered how she could tell so easily. She exhorted me to get it fixed right away. I was not angry at her for interfering in what could be considered "my business." I knew that my business, especially if it were a growing root of bitterness, would affect my life, team life and ministry. I heeded her advice and soon my husband and I were sitting together again.

Relating as teammates doesn't only involve confrontation. It includes encouragement. At one team meeting, a person took one look at me and said, "It is obvious that God has done something special in your life this week. Would you please tell me about it?" I shared how God delivered me from the sin of reading novels that were too sexually explicit. I had been trapped and unwilling to give up this habit of reading books that were unsuitable for me. The Holy Spirit gave me victory as I yielded this area of my life to him. As a result, the light that had been hidden in my life was finally revealed. A team member noticed the change and we glorified God together.

Being a part of a team involves carrying responsibilities. We seek the best for each other. In fact, we are committed as a body to carry each other along. When I am in trouble, a team member is there for me. When a team member is in trouble, I try to be there for her. As we share the burden together, the load is lighter and the love we have for each other thrives.

Before we left for the field, no one told me how hard it would be to be a part of a team. No one explained that it would take so much work, time and understanding. No one told me of the great joy of deep friendships in team life. Who could have told me of the pain that comes from caring enough to be involved in each other's lives and the forgiveness that is constantly in evidence? I need to love each team member enough to prayerfully "interfere" when necessary. I must also be prayerfully ready for people to interfere in my life. It can hurt. It isn't always fun. Nevertheless, our love for each other also deepens and strengthens our relationship with God.

Today, at team meetings and during prayer requests if I hear someone new mention a stomach problem, I can hardly believe my ears as I ask them, "Do you have diarrhea?" "What color is it?"

Isn't team life grand?

Read Romans 12:9–21

> Love from the center of who you are; don't fake it. Run for dear life from evil; hold on for dear life to good. Be good friends who love deeply; practice playing second fiddle. (vv. 9–10)

> Don't burn out; keep yourselves fueled and aflame. Be alert servants of the Master, cheerfully expectant. Don't quit in hard times; pray all the harder. Help needy Christians; be inventive in hospitality. (vv. 11–13)

> Bless your enemies; no cursing under your breath. Laugh with your happy friends when they're happy; share tears when they're down. Get along with each other; don't be stuck-up. Make friends with nobodies; don't be the great somebody. (vv. 14–16)

> Don't hit back; discover beauty in everyone. If you've got it in you, get along with everybody. Don't insist on getting even; that's not for you to do. "I'll do the judging," says God. "I'll take care of it." (vv. 17–19)

> Our Scriptures tell us that if you see your enemy hungry, go buy that person lunch, or if he's thirsty, get him a drink. Your generosity will surprise him with goodness. Don't let evil get the best of you; get the best of evil by doing good. (vv. 20–21)

Questions

1.   What do you appreciate about your team?

2.   What has been hard about being on your team?

3.   Why is being part of team good? How does God use teams?

4.   Who are some people who formed teams in Scripture?

5.   What are some commands in Romans 12:9–21 that when obeyed will help build team relationships?

Action

Pray for each of your teammates as well as your role as a team member.

Prayer

Lord, you were a team leader.
There were arguments, disagreements, questions and different personalities on your team.

Yet, you loved them and were committed to developing them for your Father's glory.
Help me be a team player and to commit myself to loving my teammates. Amen

Chapter 3
Terrorists and Chocolate Cake

I guess every family has a grapevine. When we told my husband's mom about our desire to go to least-reached people, she shared this information with other family members. As it went from one member to another, the wording of the information changed. When we went to visit my sister-in-law, we were sitting at the table and she told me how much she admired us for what we were going to do and where we were going to go. She looked so sincere that I was startled. I asked her, "Where are we going?" She replied, "You are going where no white man has ever gone before!"

We have had many responses to our desire to go to the Middle East and share Christ with the least-reached. Here are some examples: "How could you take your children so far away and expose them to such danger?" "Aren't you afraid of terrorists?" "I would never go there." "I am surprised that you would go to people who kill children." "It is so dangerous there. How can you go?"

We were bold in telling people how we trusted God to take care of us. Our security does not depend upon circumstances or location, but rests in the loving hands of our heavenly Father. Since God had called us to this task, would he forsake us? Is he not present in other countries? Could he not protect our children there, as well as in our home country?

When we make decisions based on fear, we limit God. It isn't as if we are going out alone and depending solely on our own resources. Wherever we live, our security doesn't lie in our situation, good or bad. Our security lies in knowing that God is sovereign and lovingly in control of everything that goes on in our lives. We use common sense and walk wisely, but we do not walk in fear.

When we arrived overseas, our breast-fed daughter, who had yet to eat any solid food, was five months old. We stayed in a room of a small house. As I lay down to take a nap, I made a comfortable, little pallet on the floor next to me where our daughter could sleep. When I awoke, she was gone! I looked under the bed, outside with my husband, under the wardrobe and under the bed again. She was nowhere to be found. "Oh, no! Some terrorist has kidnapped my baby," I thought, as I remembered people's concerns. I began frantically to search for her throughout the house and finally found her in the back room. A sweet national lady was feeding her chocolate cake which she was enjoying very much. It was so easy to forget His loving hands and remember instead fear-filled preconceived notions about this foreign land.

Time passed and we enjoyed making friends in our new home. Our national friends asked us where we were from. Don answered, "Chicago." These were some of the responses we heard: "Chicago! We could never live in Chicago." "It is too dangerous to live there!" "We know it is impossible to open a store there without gangsters coming in to steal and kill." "I would be afraid to live in Chicago."

It is all a matter of perspective, isn't it?

Read Psalm 56:8–13

> You've kept track of my every toss and turn through
>   the sleepless nights,
> Each tear entered in your ledger,
>   each ache written in your book. (v. 8)
>
> If my enemies run away,
>   turn tail when I yell at them,

Then I'll know
that God is on my side. (v. 9)

I'm proud to praise God,
proud to praise GOD.
Fearless now, I trust in God;
what can mere mortals do to me? (vv. 10–11)

God, you did everything you promised,
and I'm thanking you with all my heart.
You pulled me from the brink of death,
my feet from the cliff-edge of doom.
Now I stroll at leisure with God
in the sunlit fields of life. (vv. 12–13)

Read Proverbs 3:25–26

No need to panic over alarms or surprises,
or predictions that doomsday's just around the corner,
Because GOD will be right there with you;
he'll keep you safe and sound. (vv. 25–26)

Questions

1.   Describe when you were last fearful.

2.   Think back to a time in your life when you were
afraid. Write down how God comforted you
and helped you.

3.   Can a person live in faith and fear at the same
time? Why or why not?

4.   Doubt is not the opposite of faith. Fear is. List your fears, give them to God and determine to walk by faith, trusting in Him.

5.   Rewrite Proverbs 3:25–26 in your own words.

Action
Memorize Psalm 56:12–13

Prayer
Lord, sometimes I am afraid.
Help me not to let fear rule in my heart and determine my future course of action.
May I walk by faith, trusting you to hold my hand and guide me. Amen.

Chapter 4
Culture Shock Without Electricity

After my husband Don finished carrying and moving our fourteen trunks about fifteen times, we finally arrived at our destination! It was 115 degrees that day in the Middle East and we were quite warm as our taxi deposited us at our new home. The gardener had just watered the dirt, and after Don finished arguing with the taxi driver about the fare, he left the kids and me in the courtyard to wait while he walked several blocks to get the key. Before he got back, three of my four kids had fallen in the mud. The fourth one had tried to eat it.

As my husband was walking, someone pick-pocketed him and took all the money he had just exchanged. Don got the key and came back. We washed up the kids, put our stuff inside and left to go eat with our new friends. As he closed the door, we realized the key was still inside. We slept at a hotel that night.

The next morning, my husband broke into our haven so we could begin life in our new home. Our first week there, my older son got an intestinal bacterial infection and had a temperature of 103 degrees. My baby also had diarrhea. My husband was sick.

At night, we tried not using the air conditioner, but we were swimming in our sweat. I got up, closed the windows, and turned on the air conditioner. The electricity went out. I got up, opened the windows, nursed the baby, and again lay down in more sweat. My son was calling to me *again*—he couldn't make it to the bathroom. I cleaned up the mess on the floor and around the bathroom *again* and got him back to bed. I used all of the paper towels. The toilet paper was all gone. When did the tissues disappear? The electricity came back on. I got up, closed the windows and turned on the air conditioner. The baby cried and wanted to nurse. I finally fell asleep after changing her diaper. It was the last diaper.

When we woke up, the baby had another dirty diaper. We had no more diapers, no toilet paper, no paper towels, no tissues—just a naked baby, a sick boy, a sick dad, a tired mom and two more hungry kids. Someone had to go to the store. I elected my husband. As he slowly got ready to leave with the list of much needed supplies, I burst into tears at the door. "What is the matter?" he asked. "It's your birthday and I forgot to get you a present," I replied. "It will be a happy birthday if we make it through this day!" he said.

As he walked out the door, I felt the need for a little emotional release. I cried and cried and cried—without tissues, which made it even worse! I couldn't figure out why God had brought us here if it was going to be so terrible. I turned to Psalm 73:25–28 and felt the comfort and peace of God flow through me. I knew God was with me even in circumstances like these!

One night, as my husband and I snuggled in bed (when the air conditioner was on), we were discouraged about living out of trunks, getting cheated by almost everyone, getting stared at by everyone else, and fighting the dirt, the bugs and the traffic. I asked him if we could go home. He said that we could, as long as I was the one who repacked everything and carried the trunks.

I decided we could stick it out a while longer!

Read Psalm 73:21–28

> When I was beleaguered and bitter,
> totally consumed by envy,
> I was totally ignorant, a dumb ox
> in your very presence.
> I'm still in your presence,
> but you've taken my hand.
> You wisely and tenderly lead me,
> and then you bless me. (vv. 21–24)

You're all I want in heaven!
You're all I want on earth!
When my skin sags and my bones get brittle,
GOD is rock-firm and faithful.
Look! Those who left you are falling apart!
Deserters, they'll never be heard from again.
But I'm in the very presence of GOD—
oh, how refreshing it is!
I've made Lord GOD my home.
GOD, I'm telling the world what you do! (vv. 25–28)

Questions

1.   What is the worst culture shock you have experienced so far?

2.   How could you have prepared better for culture shock? Share your answer with your sending agency to help others.

3.   How does Psalm 73:21–28 comfort you?

4.   What is one thing that someone could do that would help you deal with culture shock?

5.   Ask a more experienced team member about their worst culture shock experience.

Action
Be on the lookout for a worker newer than you are. Share
your story with her. Pray with her and remind her that Jesus
is worth it all!

Prayer
You are worthy, Lord.
I know that what I'm going through today will enable me to
serve you more effectively in the future. This is hard, though.
Life feels miserable to me at times. Why am I here?
Sometimes I lose sight that you are the reason.
You are worthy. Amen

Chapter 5
Maybe Normal,
Maybe Different. . .
Definitely His

It was six weeks before my wedding. I had just finished
reading the story of Joni Erickson Tada and was thinking how
neat it would be to become "different" so that God could use
me in a great way. I was swinging on the playground behind
my church going higher and higher as I prayed to God and
committed my future plans to him. I had just finished telling
him how impressed I was with Joni and how I, too, was
willing to be a quadriplegic so that I could serve him
uniquely. I was dreaming about how that might be when I
heard a snap, started to fall, and landed with a thud. The
chain had rusted through on the swing. I lay there unable to
move and barely able to breathe, unable to call for help,
feeling paralyzed with pain and fear.

"Lord, maybe becoming like Joni wasn't such a good idea!" I
thought. No one was around and as I lay on the ground, I felt
like an idiot for being willing and even anxious for God to do
this to me. "Help!" I yelled as loudly as I could, but it came
out only as a whimper.

In time, I was able to crawl, then lift myself and limp into the
church to ask someone to call my parents. After my dad
carried me to the car, my parents took me to the hospital.

I was almost 21 years old and felt embarrassed as I explained
to the admitting nurse what had happened. How I longed to

say that I was skydiving, rock climbing—anything more exotic than, "I was swinging on the playground and fell."

My hands were scraped, my posterior felt numb, and my legs ached. As they took X-rays and examined me, I thought that although being a quadriplegic may sound exciting in a book, in reality it would be a terribly difficult thing. I was relieved to hear that I was fine!

Throughout my life, I have thought of how helpful it would be for ministry if I were "different" from seemingly normal people. I would be more useful to God. If only I had this person's great singing ability or spiritual gift or that person's physical disability, if only I would stick out from the crowd, I knew that I would be more dedicated to God; my service would be so much more effective for him.

Moving overseas, I became different overnight. I was taller, thinner, and fairer than most people around me were. I talked differently, walked differently, dressed differently and thought differently. When going places, I was gawked at, touched and sometimes ridiculed by others who looked at me and thought, "She is different from us. She is foreign."

When people wanted to get to know me, I was never sure if it was because of my supposed influence at the embassy (could she get me a green card?) or because they wanted me as a friend. People sometimes made snap judgments about me, "Oh, she is western. She must be immoral." When I was ignorant of a custom, they could have easily thought I was just being rude. When our family went to the zoo, as the only foreigners there, we quickly became an exhibit ourselves. Being different wasn't easy and it didn't automatically make my ministry more effective.

Many years have passed since my fall from the swing. I have been seen as normal and different. I have read about and seen how God has worked through Christians as they gave themselves to him. It didn't matter whether they were blind, deaf, burned, suffering loss, near death, physically challenged, struggling with addictions, or normal. The key was not their uniqueness, but that they put their trust in Christ and gave their lives to him.

I will admit I am still sometimes tempted to think, "If only I was different like this person or that person, God could use me more!" Then I remember Joni and the swing (more accurately, I remember my fall) and am content, not only in my own circumstances, but also with whom God has made me to be. Daily I will trust him and continue to give him my life, letting him take care of the details and place me in situations where he would like to use me.

Normal or not, I am his!

Read Psalm 139:13–18

Oh yes, you shaped me first inside, then out;
you formed me in my mother's womb.
I thank you, High God—you're breathtaking!
Body and soul, I am marvelously made!
I worship in adoration—what a creation!
You know me inside and out,
you know every bone in my body;
You know exactly how I was made, bit by bit,
how I was sculpted from nothing into something.
Like an open book, you watched me grow from
conception to birth;
all the stages of my life were spread out before you,
The days of my life all prepared
before I'd even lived one day. (vv. 13–16)

Your thoughts—how rare, how beautiful!
God, I'll never comprehend them!
I couldn't even begin to count them—
any more than I could count the sand of the sea.
Oh, let me rise in the morning and live always with you!
(vv. 17–18)

Read Jeremiah 1:4–5

This is what God said:
Before I shaped you in the womb,
I knew all about you.
Before you saw the light of day,
I had holy plans for you:
A prophet to the nations—
that's what I had in mind for you. (v. 5)

Questions

1.   How have you wished you were different?

2.   What is different about how people perceive you where you live now compared to how people perceived you in your home country? How have these perceptions affected you?

3.   How does Psalm 139:13–18 affect you as you think of God intentionally forming you in your mother's womb?

4.   How did God affirm and help Jeremiah in Jeremiah 1:4–5?

5.   In your host country, when have you been surprised by your mistaken perceptions of others?

Action

Thank God for making you the way you are. Renew your commitment to his plans for you.

Prayer

You have made me.
You know my insecurities
and my desire to serve you in spite of them.

Thank you for how you have made me.
I am open to your plan for me.
Help me not be caught up with my own plans for my life.
I am yours. Amen.

Chapter 6
Getting into Hot Water

One benefit of living overseas is that household help is affordable. For a small fee, a helper will clean your house, wash your dishes, and even do laundry or cleaning. Our maid, Umu Hana', came every Sunday and Wednesday to clean. I enjoyed getting to know this pleasant person and I appreciated her work. I would wait for her to arrive as the kids were going off to school. Then I would take my morning shower while she started cleaning.

A problem soon developed. While I was in the shower, Umu Hana' would start to wash the breakfast dishes. The hot water would leave the shower and go to the kitchen for the dishes. I was left standing half-soaped with only cold water to use for rinsing! Brrrr.

One morning I told her, "Umu Hana', I am going to take a shower now. Would you please clean the living room until I am done?" She gave a knowing smile and went to clean the living room. That worked so well that it became a habit to tell her each morning that she came, "I am going to take a shower." She would always smile and work elsewhere until I was done.

I was quite happy with this arrangement. She always smiled brightly in response, so I knew the arrangement was okay with her, too.

Several months later, I was at our ladies' monthly get-together. As we were discussing cultural differences, a more experienced worker said that Arab men and women don't usually shower daily as Americans often do. However, whenever a woman takes a morning shower, people know she has been with her husband the night before!

Suddenly it hit me. My face grew warm. It wasn't that my maid was simply a pleasant person with a ready smile. She wasn't smiling to show she understood my Arabic. She smiled because she knew that I was "busy" with my husband every Saturday and Tuesday night!

Read 1 Corinthians 9:19–23

Even though I am free of the demands and expectations of everyone, I have voluntarily become a servant to any and all in order to reach a wide range of people: religious, nonreligious, meticulous moralists, loose-living immoralists, the defeated, the demoralized—whoever. I didn't take on their way of life. I kept my bearings in Christ—but I entered their world and tried to experience things from their point of view. I've become just about every sort of servant there is in my attempts to lead those I meet into a God-saved life. I did all this because of the Message. I didn't just want to talk about it; I wanted to be *in* on it! (vv. 19–23)

Questions

1.   Write about an embarrassing cultural mistake you have made.

2.   Laugh about it. Write what you learned through it.

3.   How do Paul's words in 1 Corinthians encourage you to learn more about your host culture?

4.   What is the ultimate purpose of adapting to a new culture?

5.   Commit to continue learning more about the culture in which you live, even if you make more mistakes. What are some ways you can adapt to the culture of your new home (as long as it is within biblical guidelines) and keep learning?

Action

Identify a cultural practice that you may not understand, and consider how your interaction with that practice may be misunderstood by members of your host culture.
Determine if any of the misunderstandings should be avoided, and how you will go about addressing them.

Prayer

Lord, help me learn more and more about this culture.
Help me to adapt so that more doors will open where I can share the Gospel more effectively.
Give me wisdom as I determine when to adapt and when not to adapt to this new culture.
May all I do bring honor to Jesus' name. Amen.

Chapter 7
Flesh or Spirit?

We had been overseas for a little over two years. The language was harder than I expected. The children were having a hard time adjusting, but an easy time getting sick. My husband seemed to expect a clean house and even cleaner laundry. I only wanted to be a perfect wife, perfect mother, glorious soul winner and homemaker—all the things I had never been in the States, but longed to be! I was feeling totally unappreciated for what I did manage to do. No one said thank you to me for all those mundane tasks—laundry, dishes, cooking, cleaning—that I hated to do, but did anyway because they had to be done. I felt overworked, underpaid and unloved.

What had happened to our marriage? People used to admire how much in love we were. We had always been so happy together. Now there were complaints that socks were missing, the house was a mess, and there were no clean shirts. I wanted respect, appreciation for my "finer qualities," and to be told that life would be unbearable without me!

What had happened to our children? They used to be so cute and easily entertained. They obeyed and thought I was an okay mom. They seemed happily well adjusted. Now there were complaints, "I hate you" spoken in anger, threats to run away, crying, not wanting to go to school, disobedience, so many troubles! People no longer seemed to look at me and say, "Oh, she is such a good mom with her little angels." I felt they were saying, "She doesn't know how to control her kids. She's a terrible mom."

I didn't see any spiritual fruit around me. No one appreciated me. No one was meeting my needs! I wanted to escape.

One morning I read in Galatians 5 about the deeds of the flesh and the fruit of the Spirit—what a contrast! The Holy Spirit convicted me that morning that I had been living in the flesh. All I had been doing, I was doing for me. I was being a wife so that my husband would thank me and love me. I was trying to raise well-behaved children so that others would think I was a good mom. Stricken, I realized that part of me was being a missionary so that others would respect me and talk about me: "She is amazing—imagine being busy at home and still leading thousands of women to the Lord!" Me! I was depending on and living for myself.

But as I read about the fruit of the Spirit—love, joy, peace, patience, kindness, goodness, faithfulness, gentleness and self control—I realized these only come about when you live to give and not to gain. It was painful to see the ways I was living for me. I felt so ashamed. I confessed my sins of selfishness and pride and asked the Holy Spirit to fill me and enable me to live as God would want me to live. The Lord began a liberating process in my life that morning that is continuing through today.

I don't think circumstances have totally changed. My husband sometimes still searches for his socks. My kids can still act up in public and make me "look bad." I am still not a great soul winner or homemaker. However, now I know that I do not have to worry about what others may say or think about me. I do not have to meet my own unrealistic expectations. I am free to give, to love, to serve, because I am not living for me. I can live to give because of the Lord.

Read Galatians 5:16-24

My counsel is this: Live freely, animated and motivated by God's Spirit. Then you won't feed the compulsions of selfishness. For there is a root of sinful self-interest in us that is at odds with a free spirit, just as the free spirit is incompatible with selfishness. These two ways of life are antithetical, so that you cannot live at times one way and at times another way according to how you feel on any given day. Why don't you choose to be led by the Spirit and so escape the erratic compulsions of a law-dominated existence? (vv. 16-18)

It is obvious what kind of life develops out of trying to get your own way all the time: repetitive, loveless, cheap sex; a stinking accumulation of mental and emotional garbage; frenzied and joyless grabs for happiness; trinket gods; magic-show religion; paranoid loneliness; cutthroat competition; all-consuming-yet-never-satisfied wants; a brutal temper; an impotence to love or be loved; divided homes and divided lives; small-minded and lopsided pursuits; the vicious habit of depersonalizing everyone into a rival; uncontrolled and uncontrollable addictions; ugly parodies of community. I could go on.

This isn't the first time I have warned you, you know. If you use your freedom this way, you will not inherit God's kingdom. (vv. 19-21)

But what happens when we live God's way? He brings gifts into our lives, much the same way that fruit appears in an orchard—things like affection for others, exuberance about life, serenity. We develop a willingness to stick with things, a sense of compassion in the heart, and a conviction that a basic holiness permeates things and people. We find ourselves involved in loyal commitments, not needing to force our way in life, able to marshal and direct our energies wisely. (vv. 22-23)

Legalism is helpless in bringing this about; it only gets in the way. Among those who belong to Christ, everything connected with getting our own way and mindlessly responding to what everyone else calls necessities is killed off for good—crucified. (vv.23-24).

Questions
1.   List the relational stresses you are experiencing.

2.   Contrast the deeds of the flesh with the fruit of the Spirit in Galatians.

3.   Which characteristics do you want others to see in your life? How would they be evident?

4.   Pray through your list of relational stresses and evaluate your life. Ask God to show you what you need to do in order to improve these relationships.

5.   How can a person tell if they are working in their own strength as opposed to depending on God?

Action

Sometimes it helps to get away for a while. Take a day off this week to relax. Do something you really enjoy doing.

Prayer

Forgive me, Lord, for sometimes caring too much about what people think of me.
Forgive me for depending on my own strength and for having selfish motives.
May your Holy Spirit fill me and produce his fruit in my life.
I choose to live for you, not me.
Empower me by your Spirit. I live for an audience of one.
Amen.

Chapter 8
Survival in a New City

Soon after our arrival in a new country, we moved into our apartment. We needed to unpack, buy necessary supplies, find schooling and/or childcare for our kids, and begin language study within a week or so. We decided to divide responsibilities. I would stay home with the children and unpack; Don would go out to buy supplies.

I worked at unpacking, keeping track of the kids, and cleaning the apartment. Don was out scouring the marketplace for our much-needed supplies. I had given him a long list of things we needed and was waiting expectantly for his return.

I heard him at the front door and went to help him carry in all the stuff I had requested. I saw him enter with a mop and bucket. To be honest, those two things were not high on my priority list. (I rarely use them.) Where were all my other direly needed things? As I began complaining about him not getting more items on my list, he quietly suggested that if I was dissatisfied with how he was doing things, then I should go out to buy supplies and he would gladly stay home with the kids. As I looked at the grim look on his face and the tiredness that seemed to ooze from his very being, I listened. He told me how hard it was to find things and how many miles he had to walk up and down the steep, hilly streets in the scorching heat. I realized how very fortunate I was to own a mop and bucket!

As we ate tuna for every meal those first few days—we couldn't find the butcher—and began slowly settling in, I grew tired. I had to find a new way to cook. There were no canned soups for casseroles and no cake mixes.

I started language school. My mouth made sounds it seemed never designed to make; my brain grew weary with verb conjugations and new vocabulary; my body dragged as I did my normal daily chores, played with the kids and put them to bed at night.

Exhausted and just wanting to sleep, each night I would get ready to go to bed …with or without my husband. I had little extra energy for romance and almost no desire for physical intimacy. I was simply trying to survive. "Help me make it through the day and leave me alone at night," was my battle cry! Don, on the other hand, seemed to thrive and had lots of energy and desire for amorous activities, but by the time he got to bed after turning off the light, I would be snoring and he would be disappointed. If we ate by candlelight, it was because the electricity was out, not because of romance. If I closed my eyes when he came near me, he thought it was time for a kiss. Actually, I was just falling asleep.

As time passed, surviving became easier. I was learning the language, feeling more at home, and dealing with all the "normal" stresses in a cross-cultural worker's life. I talked with Don about my struggles. When I was worn out and feeling guilty because I couldn't do it all, Don encouraged me to get house help so that I wouldn't feel so frazzled. (Someone finally got to use that mop and bucket!) We were going to make it. Our relationship had survived the onslaught of stress from first-time culture shock.

I had more energy … Don had more fun … and we had another baby on the way.

Read James 5:7–11

Meanwhile, friends, wait patiently for the Master's Arrival. You see farmers do this all the time, waiting for their valuable crops to mature, patiently letting the rain do its slow but sure work. Be patient like that. Stay steady and strong. The Master could arrive at any time. (vv. 7–8)

Friends, don't complain about each other. A far greater complaint could be lodged against you, you know. The Judge is standing just around the corner. (v. 9)

Take the old prophets as your mentors. They put up with anything, went through everything, and never once quit, all the time honoring God. What a gift life is to those who stay the course! You've heard, of course, of Job's staying power, and you know how God brought it all together for him at the end. That's because God cares, cares right down to the last detail. (vv. 10-11)

Questions

1. What do these verses in James say to you about perseverance?

2. What effect has cultural stress had on your relationships?

3. What are the top three cultural adjustments you have had to make?

4. What has been your biggest stress point?

5. How have you been coping with cultural stress?

Action

Get together with your husband or a trusted friend to talk about cultural stress points and how you are dealing with them. Allow yourself to vent. Accept feedback in case you need help developing more strategies to work through cultural adjustments.

Prayer

Lord, sometimes I hate this culture. I dislike the people.
I don't even like myself and the feelings I am having.
I feel foreign and unwanted.
I want to do things right, but it is hard when
I don't know what is appropriate in this culture.
I get tired of being a learner.
Help me to be willing to keep learning.
Forgive me for my unloving attitude.
I know that I need your grace, compassion and love
in order to survive.
I look to you for help.
Help me gain a clearer perspective of the stresses I am experiencing.
Thank you that you are here with me and I am not alone.
Amen.

Chapter 9
Reverse Psychology and God

From the time I was young, I heard about people who would say, "Anywhere but Africa." Of course, they always ended up in Africa. The point is that we should be willing to serve the Lord anywhere. If we have any reservations, God may put us there just to help us learn to trust him and let him be the leader, not us.

So, when my husband and I were considering work overseas, I was careful to be open to any place God might lead us. I had doubts as to whether I could handle certain fields, but I tried to remain open to them. As we felt God calling us to the Middle East, I was excited about going there.

We arrived in our host country and God provided all that we needed. We knew that through good times and bad, he was our leader and we were following him. I must admit, though, that when times became extremely stressful, I was desperate for a new strategy that would direct us to an easier ministry. I told the Lord I was willing to go anywhere but Hawaii.

Please note: reverse psychology does not work with God.

As the years flew by, I grew more comfortable in our new home. However, a growing attitude that I never expressed, but felt deeply, took me unaware. My attitude was becoming, "Lord, I will serve you anywhere but America. I want to be where the action is, on the cutting edge, on the field."

Needless to say, several years after that attitude had time to become entrenched, we were moving back to the States. I doubt that the reason we moved is because I told God,

"Anywhere but America." Yet I do think that God delights in helping us recognize that he is the leader, not us. When we follow him, we are blessed wherever we serve him.

So, as his followers our attitude shouldn't be, "Lord, send my anywhere but …" Rather it should be, "Anywhere you send me, Lord." He will bless us and our ministries when we follow him no matter where he might lead—even Hawaii. I really am open to serving him in Hawaii!

Read Matthew 4:18–22

Walking along the beach of Lake Galilee, Jesus saw two brothers: Simon (later called Peter) and Andrew. They were fishing, throwing their nets into the lake. It was their regular work. Jesus said to them, "Come with me. I'll make a new kind of fisherman out of you. I'll show you how to catch men and women instead of perch and bass." They didn't ask questions, but simply dropped their nets and followed. (vv. 18–20)

A short distance down the beach they came upon another pair of brothers, James and John, Zebedee's sons. These two were sitting in a boat with their father, Zebedee, mending their fish nets. Jesus made the same offer to them, and they were just as quick to follow, abandoning boat and father. (vv. 21–22)

Questions

1.   What is hard about following someone?

2.   Why is trust important in a follower/leader relationship?

3.   When have you been tempted to try reverse psychology on God?

4.   What are other ways people might try to
manipulate God to do what they want?

5.   Do you trust God? Write yes or no. If yes, tell him
why. If no, tell him why.

Action

1.   List some of the ramifications for Peter, Andrew,
John and James when they followed Jesus.

2.   Write how they compare with what happened to
you when you decided to follow Jesus.

Prayer

You are sovereign and good, O Lord.
Sometimes I think I know more than you know.
I try to get you to do what I want
rather than trusting you to do what is best for me.
Thank you that you cannot be manipulated,
that you see motives and fears that I am not even aware of.
Your love for me never increases or decreases,
even when I mess up or think you have made a mistake.
I am secure in you and in your plans for me.
I determine in my heart to keep trusting in you. Amen.

Chapter 10
Suicide and Laundry

I have never considered myself a suicidal person. I really do enjoy life: I love to laugh and have a good time; I have a wonderful husband and four adorable children; I have fellowship with the creator of the universe through my risen Savior; his Spirit is living inside of me. Why in the world would I even think of jumping off the balcony of our fourth floor apartment while hanging out the laundry? Was it all the laundry I did day in and day out? Was it a bad day with my adorable children? Was it that my husband was busy and we were going to have company again that night? Why would a sane, mature, stable, easygoing, sensible young woman ponder the idea of jumping?

Looking back, I can see that I was tired. The children were ages eight, six, four and two. We were in a fairly new culture and a different home in a huge foreign city. We were struggling with stress, culture shock, family relationships, and high expectations with few realizations. The children were attending a new school for the third time in three years and I was trying to be super-mom, super-worker, super-team member, super-language learner, and super-wife all at the same time! There was always laundry to do, children to discipline, homework to do, children to play with, meals to cook, language to study, and more laundry to do. I was tired and could see no relief in sight.

My children seemed to be rebelling; my husband seemed disapproving of all my efforts. It seemed so easy to think about jumping four stories to end it all. Then my husband could find a wife who could do all the things I could not, the kids would have a mother who knew what she was doing, and, more importantly, someone else would have to do the laundry!

Why didn't I jump? First of all, I learned to laugh. So I would laugh when I felt the pressure mounting. What can you do while waiting an hour and a half with six kids for a taxi to take you home? (Would you be brave enough to pick us up?) What can you do when, no matter how hard you try to find missing socks, they have actually disappeared? Sure, I cry. Sometimes I get mad. But laughing, maybe after the fact, has helped me more than anything.

Second, I talked. I told God as well as fellow team members when I was struggling. Do you know my teammates could relate? They did not judge or discourage me. They prayed for me, encouraged me and listened to me. It helped to tell people that I didn't have my act together, to let my guard down and let them see the real me. I found out that they struggle, too. I even found out that everyone has disappearing socks!

Third, I discovered that in time things got better. Our family adjusted. We learned that nothing happens instantaneously. Many of my expectations were too high. I hadn't taken into account the new culture, new adjustments and new responsibilities. It takes time. We continued to learn and continued to adjust.

Finally, I realized that if I jumped and didn't die, my clothes would get dirty on the way down through the trees and on the ground. Then I would have even more laundry to do!

**see note at end of the prayer*

Read Psalm 42 meditate especially on verse 5
A psalm of the sons of Korah
A white-tailed deer drinks from the creek;
I want to drink God,
deep draughts of God.
I'm thirsty for God-alive.
I wonder, "Will I ever make it—
arrive and drink in God's presence?"

I'm on a diet of tears—
tears for breakfast, tears for supper.
All day long
people knock at my door,
Pestering,
"Where is this God of yours?" (vv. 1–3)

These are the things I go over and over,
emptying out the pockets of my life.
I was always at the head of the worshiping crowd,
right out in front,
Leading them all,
eager to arrive and worship,
Shouting praises, singing thanksgiving—
celebrating, all of us, God's feast! (v. 4)

Why are you down in the dumps, dear soul?
Why are you crying the blues?
Fix my eyes on God—
soon I'll be praising again.
He puts a smile on my face.
He's my God. (v. 5)

When my soul is in the dumps, I rehearse
everything I know of you,
From Jordan depths to Hermon heights,
including Mount Mizar.
Chaos calls to chaos,
to the tune of whitewater rapids.
Your breaking surf, your thundering breakers
crash and crush me.
Then GOD promises to love me all day,
sing songs all through the night!
My life is God's prayer. (vv. 6–8)

Sometimes I ask God, my rock-solid God,
"Why did you let me down?
Why am I walking around in tears,
harassed by enemies?"
They're out for the kill, these
tormentors with their obscenities,
Taunting day after day,
"Where is this God of yours?" (vv. 9–10)

Why are you down in the dumps, dear soul?
Why are you crying the blues?
Fix my eyes on God—
soon I'll be praising again.
He puts a smile on my face.
He's my God. (v. 11)

Questions

1.   List your pressure points for this week.

2.   Describe a situation when it has helped to laugh.

3.   Share your pressure points and your feelings with
        a trusted friend.

4.   Write down the questions in Psalm 42:5a and fill in
        your answers to them.

5.   How does his presence help you in your current
        situation?

Action

Take an extra day off this week. Maybe make it a long
weekend to get away for a bit and relax.

Prayer

Lord, you know I get tired and there is always so much to do.
Help me to realign my expectations of myself with what you
want me to do.
Help me to keep up with the things I need to do in my home
and please restore my vision for the nations
in the midst of my daily life.
Thank you for laughter.
May I not take myself too seriously.
Thank you for listening to me at any time of the day or night.
Amen.

***Note: If you stay depressed, lose your appetite or your friend
thinks you need more help, please make an appointment with a
physician and/or counselor. You are not alone. If thoughts of suicide
persist, you may need medication or professional help.*

Chapter 11
Jesus Loves Me

I am a born people pleaser. For years, if I felt other people were happy with me, I was happy with myself. If I felt that others were angry with me or thought I was wrong, I felt badly about myself. I based my self-image on what I thought others thought of me.

This continued until I realized that I could not continually please other people. My husband and I are different. If I like a tie, he doesn't. If he likes a tie, I don't. Our ideas of what makes a clean house differ dramatically. I saw a plaque recently that described me correctly when it said, "My idea of cleaning is sweeping the room with a glance!" If someone says that I did a good job, I feel good about myself. If a person questions me or says something negative, I immediately feel pressure to do what will make that person happy with me.

If we listen only to other people to gain our sense of worth, our feeling of value will increase or decrease depending on how we think others see us. For years, I tried to shape myself so that other people would feel happy with me, so that I could feel happy with myself. As time went on, I began to feel totally unacceptable, because I couldn't do enough to make everyone happy with me all of the time.

Several years ago, when a virus caused me to have a very low energy level, I could do nothing. After taking a shower, I would have to rest before I could dry my hair. After drying my hair, I would have to rest again. I couldn't go out and play with my children as I saw my husband heading out the door to go for a walk with them. My mother did the laundry, the cooking and the cleaning for all six of us. I remember sitting in church, tears streaming down my face, as I could only whisper the words of a hymn that others could stand and sing. I could do nothing to make others like me or to try to feel worthy of God's love. I felt guilty that we couldn't return overseas at the appointed time because of my illness. If I couldn't be a cross-cultural worker, how could I define who I was? Wasn't my worth dependent on what I could do and how others perceived me to be?

The answer is a resounding, "No!" My self-worth is not dependent upon what others think of me. My value as a person is not based upon what I do, how I act or how others perceive me. My value is based on God's opinion of me. He is my judge. Though I am a sinner, he mercifully considered me worthy to die for and to redeem. He loves me unconditionally. Whether I do good or bad, whether I am having a good hair day or a bad one, his love for me never increases or decreases. I am a treasure in his eyes.

Because I am secure in him, other people's opinions of me shouldn't affect how I view my value as a person. I can accept others' encouragement without being dependent on their opinion of me to confirm my worth in God's eyes. I can accept criticism and repent when necessary without giving way to despair or feeling like a failure.

Of course, it is easier to remember my value when I receive positive feedback ... so if you like this devotional, let me know. If you don't—and you must let me know—I'll read this devotional again to reaffirm that my value to God isn't based on what I do!

Read Romans 5:1-11 especially note verse 8

Developing Patience
By entering through faith into what God has always wanted to do for us—set us right with him, make us fit for him—we have it all together with God because of

our Master Jesus. And that's not all: We throw open our doors to God and discover at the same moment that he has already thrown open his door to us. We find ourselves standing where we always hoped we might stand—out in the wide open spaces of God's grace and glory, standing tall and shouting our praise. (vv. 1–2)

There's more to come: We continue to shout our praise even when we're hemmed in with troubles, because we know how troubles can develop passionate patience in us, and how that patience in turn forges the tempered steel of virtue, keeping us alert for whatever God will do next. In alert expectancy such as this, we're never left feeling shortchanged. Quite the contrary—we can't round up enough containers to hold everything God generously pours into our lives through the Holy Spirit! (vv. 3–5)

Christ arrives right on time to make this happen. He didn't, and doesn't, wait for us to get ready. He presented himself for this sacrificial death when we were far too weak and rebellious to do anything to get ourselves ready. And even if we hadn't been so weak, we wouldn't have known what to do anyway. We can understand someone dying for a person worth dying for, and we can understand how someone good and noble could inspire us to selfless sacrifice. But God put his love on the line for us by offering his Son in sacrificial death while we were of no use whatever to him. (vv. 6-8)

Now that we are set right with God by means of this sacrificial death, the consummate blood sacrifice, there is no longer a question of being at odds with God in any way. If, when we were at our worst, we were put on friendly terms with God by the sacrificial death of his Son, now that we're at our best, just think of how our lives will expand and deepen by means of his resurrection life! Now that we have actually received this amazing friendship with God, we are no longer content to simply say it in plodding prose. We sing and shout our praises to God through Jesus, the Messiah! (vv. 9–11)

Questions

1.   Can you ever do anything that could make God love you more or less? Why or why not?

2.   List some of the truths you see in Romans 5.

3.   How do you know that God loves you?

4.   Describe a time when you were overly sensitive to another person's comments. How did it make you feel about yourself and how did it affect your relationship?

5.   On what do you normally base your value? What changes would you like to make in this area?

Action

From Romans 5, list the ways that God shows His love for you. Revel for a minute that God's love for you never changes.

Prayer

Lord God, your love for me never fails.
Even when I fail, your love never wavers.
Thank you for that security.
Help me to keep separate my value to you and the work that I do.
Help me to grow in confidence that what other people think does not have an effect on my value as a person.
You treasure me … and that knowledge is my treasure!
Amen.

Chapter 12
Facing Change
... Almost Fearlessly

While some people fall into ruts. I jump into them. I like routine. I enjoy knowing what the plan is and how things are going to come together. I usually don't like surprises—unless it is my birthday party, because that implies gifts!

I tend to be fearful of new situations and new opportunities. My husband likes using different routes to get to the same places, for the sake of variety. I like finding one way, no matter whether it is longer or shorter, and feeling secure in my surroundings and unable to get lost.

Raising children involves constant change. As soon as I begin to enjoy the stage my children are in, they are moving onto another. Thankfully, we have four children so I am becoming familiar with many of the stages and can feel at home with whichever stage they are in at the moment!

Different life stages also bring changes and opportunities. I put off going back to school to complete my degree because I was afraid of driving the two-hour round trip, and was fearful of whether or not I could still study and do well in school. What would people think if I failed? What if I started and couldn't keep going? How would it work to study, take care of my family and keep up with my responsibilities at work? These things scared me.

Life even ends with the unknown. I am not afraid of death. I am afraid of the dying process. Trying new things has always been hard for me, but once I find out how to do something, I'm okay with it. However, you can't practice dying and you can't learn from others to see how they did it. They are not here to ask and their bodies all end up the same way.

People fear lots of things. Some personalities seem braver than others. There are those who love challenges, are always ready to blaze new trails and try new foods. They may look at those of us who are a bit more cautious with something akin to disdain.

Because I recognize my limitations and fearful tendencies, I make it a goal to do at least one new thing a year. (If I do it in January, I have it easy the rest of the year!) I will talk myself into going a new way to a familiar place; or I may buy a totally different style of shoes to wear; or brainstorm about new things to cook and go for it. To be really daring, I sometimes try pushing keys on the computer rather than asking someone to help me. The possibilities are endless! I must make an intentional effort to break out of my comfortable ruts and zestfully forge ahead to new territory.

If I make even a little headway, choose a few changes, and deny fear when it tries to hold my life in its grip, I feel better and do more. I feel brave and am ready to tackle more new things. Fear loses its tenacity and I find myself worrying less about getting lost, people's opinions or my own security. I am busy looking ahead choosing new paths, tackling new projects and making new friends.

I am ready to take on the world, one step at a time . . .

Read Judges 4:1–16

The People of Israel kept right on doing evil in GOD's sight. With Ehud dead, GOD sold them off to Jabin king of Canaan who ruled from Hazor. Sisera, who lived in Harosheth Haggoyim, was the commander of his army. The People of Israel cried out to GOD because he had cruelly oppressed them with his nine hundred iron chariots for twenty years. (vv. 1–3)

Deborah was a prophet, the wife of Lappidoth. She was judge over Israel at that time. She held court under Deborah's Palm between Ramah and Bethel in the hills of Ephraim. The People of Israel went to her in matters of justice. (vv. 4–5)

She sent for Barak son of Abinoam from Kedesh in Naphtali and said to him, "It has become clear that GOD, the God of Israel, commands you: Go to Mount Tabor and prepare for battle. Take ten companies of soldiers from Naphtali and Zebulun. I'll take care of getting Sisera, the leader of Jabin's army, to the Kishon River with all his chariots and troops. And I'll make sure you win the battle." (vv. 6–7)

Barak said, "If you go with me, I'll go. But if you don't go with me, I won't go." (v. 8)

She said, "Of course I'll go with you. But understand that with an attitude like that, there'll be no glory in it for you. GOD will use a woman's hand to take care of Sisera." Deborah got ready and went with Barak to Kedesh. Barak called Zebulun and Naphtali together at Kedesh. Ten companies of men followed him. And Deborah was with him. (vv. 9–10)

It happened that Heber the Kenite had parted company with the other Kenites, the descendants of Hobab, Moses' in-law. He was now living at Zaanannim Oak near Kedesh. They told Sisera that Barak son of Abinoam had gone up to Mount Tabor. Sisera immediately called up all his chariots to the Kishon River—nine hundred iron chariots!—along with all his troops who were with him at Harosheth Haggoyim. (vv. 11–13)

Deborah said to Barak, "Charge! This very day GOD has given you victory over Sisera. Isn't GOD marching before you?" Barak charged down the slopes of Mount Tabor, his ten companies following him. (v. 14)

GOD routed Sisera—all those chariots, all those troops!—before Barak. Sisera jumped out of his chariot and ran. Barak chased the chariots and troops all the way to Harosheth Haggoyim. Sisera's entire fighting force was killed—not one man left. (vv. 15–16)

Questions

1. Do you prefer routine or adventure? Why?

2. What situation is tempting you to feel unsettled or afraid?

3. What scares you about your situation as you live in a cross-cultural setting?

4. Read Judges 4. Why was Barak afraid to obey God's command?

5. Note Judges 4:14. What does Deborah say to Barak to encourage him to go? How does that affect you and your situation?

Action

List the situations you are going to face today. Think about God going before you. Thank him for never sending you where he has not already been.

Prayer

You always go before me.
The way is forever clear to you because you know the end
and the beginning.
I do not have to fear the future because you are not limited by
time and have already been there.
You have promised to show me the way
and I will follow you.
Lead on, Lord. Amen.

Chapter 13
Let Me Show You

When I was a little girl, I saw my mom and grandma sitting on the front porch. My grandma had some sort of silver utensil in her hand that I had never seen before, and when I asked her what it was, she replied, "Tweezers." I asked her what they were for and she told me to come near her so that she could show me. Trustingly I moved forward and she proceeded to pluck a hair from my eyebrow. I was stunned—not so much by the sharp stab of pain, but by the fact that my grandmother had caused it! (I am often glad she wasn't holding a gun or knife!)

I heard in an education class that "more is caught than taught." I don't ever remember my grandma sitting down with me and saying, "Now, this is how you love your husband." She never held a class for my cousins or me on how to parent or grandparent. She simply showed us the way by living it.

I watched her and my grandpa love each other. Grandma would get up earlier than my grandpa to fix him biscuits and eggs for breakfast. She told me recently that she will never understand "women's lib"—imagine women not being willing to rise at 4:00 a.m. to give their husbands a good breakfast. She would go to the store with us every Thursday to buy groceries and purchase Lorna Doone cookies because he liked them.

When Grandpa was healthy, she stood by him through good times and bad. Together they handled their infant son's death; together they cared for my Aunt Linda during her fight and ultimate loss to diabetes. When Grandpa was sick, she took care of him. They got married when she was fifteen and he was seventeen. They did not know teen marriages aren't supposed to last. They were together for fifty-four years until God called my grandpa home.

I watch Grandma love her family. No one ever has to guess what kind of mood she will be in when we visit. She is always warm and kind. My parents, aunts and uncles, cousins, sister and I always find love and acceptance at Grandma's house. When I was little, my dad had the movie camera out and I wanted Grandma in the movie. She was being shy, so I remember dragging her through the house by the feet so he could film her. She laughed, or at least I think she was laughing. How many grandmas would let their granddaughters do that? I guess she could ask how many granddaughters would do such a thing! Anyway, Grandma played with us and I felt comfortable acting playful with her.

Grandma loves cooking our favorite foods and baking her famous biscuits and rolls for us. She will sit and chat or do a task to help us. She is love in action, continually giving and serving. My children have the privilege of knowing and being loved by their great-grandma. They love it when she visits and they can simply enjoy being near her. When one of my girls was little, we were talking about Great Grandma and she said, "Oh, may she live forever!"

She is a great-great-grandma now and another generation has the opportunity and privilege to be mentored by my grandma. She didn't finish high school. She has never been to college. She hates to be in the public eye. She has only flown once (she said that was enough)— to attend my wedding. She has not written a book, given a speech or traveled extensively. Yet, her influence extends far beyond what she can imagine. She has had eight children, sixteen grandchildren, at least twenty-seven great-grandchildren and three great-great-grandchildren. Her life has touched each one of these intimately and through them has touched people she has never met on more than four continents of the world.

My grandma is a mentor. She probably didn't intend to be and possibly doesn't really know or care what a mentor is. She lives and loves, and from her example, we learn how to live and love as well.

As our granddaughter, Sophie, grows older, and if perhaps she sees me with a pair of tweezers and asks me what they are, I will simply say, "Come here, sweetie, and I will show you."

Read Luke 1:26-56

In the sixth month of Elizabeth's pregnancy, God sent the angel Gabriel to the Galilean village of Nazareth to a virgin engaged to be married to a man descended from David. His name was Joseph, and the virgin's name, Mary. Upon entering, Gabriel greeted her:
Good morning!
You're beautiful with God's beauty,
Beautiful inside and out!
God be with you. (vv. 26–28)

She was thoroughly shaken, wondering what was behind a greeting like that. But the angel assured her, "Mary, you have nothing to fear. God has a surprise for you: You will become pregnant and give birth to a son and call his name Jesus.

He will be great,
be called 'Son of the Highest.'
The Lord God will give him
the throne of his father David;
He will rule Jacob's house forever—
no end, ever, to his kingdom." (vv. 29–33)

Mary said to the angel, "But how? I've never slept with a man." (v. 34)

The angel answered,

The Holy Spirit will come upon you,
the power of the Highest hover over you;

Therefore, the child you bring to birth
will be called Holy, Son of God. (v. 35)

"And did you know that your cousin Elizabeth
conceived a son, old as she is? Everyone called her
barren, and here she is six months pregnant! Nothing,
you see, is impossible with God."

And Mary said,

Yes, I see it all now:
I'm the Lord's maid, ready to serve.
Let it be with me
just as you say.

Then the angel left her. (vv.36–38)

Blessed Among Women

Mary didn't waste a minute. She got up and traveled
to a town in Judah in the hill country, straight to
Zachariah's house, and greeted Elizabeth. When
Elizabeth heard Mary's greeting, the baby in her womb
leaped. She was filled with the Holy Spirit, and sang
out exuberantly,

You're so blessed among women,
and the babe in your womb, also blessed!
And why am I so blessed that
the mother of my Lord visits me?
The moment the sound of your
greeting entered my ears,
The babe in my womb
skipped like a lamb for sheer joy.
Blessed woman, who believed what God said,
believed every word would come true! (vv. 39–45)

Mary stayed with Elizabeth for three months and then went back to her own home. (v. 56)

Questions

1. Describe a past mentoring relationship in which you have been involved. What made it successful or unsuccessful?

2. From reading Luke 1, how do you think Elizabeth may have mentored Mary during their time together?

3. Is there a mentoring relationship that would help you as you live cross-culturally in which you could be involved, whether local or through long distance?

4. What are some qualities of a good mentor?

5. List the benefits of mentoring and being mentored.

Action

Write a thank you note and send it to someone who has mentored you.

Prayer

Lord, thank you for the mentors in my life.
Thank you for the examples of godly men and women that
I can follow.
Please use me to be a mentor to someone else.
May my life be one that will honor you.
May it encourage and be a model for those around me.
Amen.

Chapter 14
Listen, God, I'm Speaking

One Sunday I was teaching a group of four and five-year-olds about Samuel. Samuel was a young boy who was sleeping when he heard a voice call his name. He thought it was Eli, the priest, but Eli told him it was God and that he should reply, "Speak, Lord, I'm listening." I asked the children questions and they knew the story pretty well, so I decided it was time to act out the story to reinforce the importance of listening to God.

One little boy was excited, yet a little nervous to portray Samuel. After some encouragement, he was ready to begin. He heard his name called out and ran to "Eli" and then went back to answer God. He heard his name being called again and in his nervousness called out, "Listen, God, I'm speaking!" His little face looked up at me and he said, "That wasn't right, was it?"

No, it wasn't correct in the story, but I wonder if it is a more accurate description of how I sometimes perceive my time with God. I come to him with my needs and wants, and of course, I try to remember to praise him and thank him following the ACTS strategy for prayer. I must admit that I can tend to hurry through the first three (adoration, confession and thanksgiving) so that I can get down to real business of asking God for the things I need (supplication). It is so easy to have a list of what I require, what I want to do, and then ask him to bless my efforts. I tell him where I want to go and ask him to go with me. I look at what I see is needed in my family and I present those needs to God, offering suggestions for how he may want to meet those needs. I have my vision, dreams, and goals and I use my common sense to determine if I can accomplish any or all of them.

I think my vision, my dreams, and my goals must seem puny to God. If I plan and do not take into account his omnipotence, his omniscience, and his benevolence, I am left relying on my own human ingenuity and knowledge. Everyone knows how limited we humans are! It is more exciting to come to God ready to listen. I must choose to step off my self-god soapbox where I expound on all I would like to see happen and when or how it should happen. Instead of praying like that little boy who said, "Listen, Lord, I'm speaking," I must choose to humbly kneel and cry out, "Speak, Lord, I'm listening." This is not only a choice, but also a learned discipline.

I want to be able to say, "Listen Lord, I'm *not* talking ... I'm listening!" and then quietly listen ... and wait ... and listen more as he unveils his plan, his resources and his divine wisdom.

Read 1 Samuel 3:1–10

The boy Samuel was serving GOD under Eli's direction. This was at a time when the revelation of GOD was rarely heard or seen. One night Eli was sound asleep (his eyesight was very bad—he could hardly see). It was well before dawn; the sanctuary lamp was still burning. Samuel was still in bed in the Temple of GOD, where the Chest of God rested. (vv. 1–3)

Then GOD called out, "Samuel, Samuel!" Samuel answered, "Yes? I'm here." Then he ran to Eli saying, "I heard you call. Here I am." Eli said, "I didn't call you. Go back to bed." And so he did. (vv. 4–5)

GOD called again, "Samuel, Samuel!" Samuel got up and went to Eli, "I heard you call. Here I am." Again Eli said, "Son, I didn't call you. Go back to bed." (This all happened before Samuel knew GOD for himself. It was before the revelation of GOD had been given to him personally.) (vv. 6–7)

GOD called again, "Samuel!"—the third time! Yet again Samuel got up and went to Eli, "Yes? I heard you call me. Here I am." That's when it dawned on Eli that GOD was calling the boy. So Eli directed Samuel, "Go back and lie down. If the voice calls again, say, 'Speak, GOD. I'm your servant, ready to listen.'" Samuel returned to his bed. (vv. 8–9)

Then GOD came and stood before him exactly as before, calling out, "Samuel! Samuel!" Samuel answered, "Speak. I'm your servant, ready to listen." (v. 10)

Questions

1. How does a person listen to God?

2. How can a person determine if it is God speaking?

3. Evaluate your prayer life. Is there adequate time spent in praise, worship, confession? Is there a time set aside for listening to God? What changes would you like to make?

4.   At the end of this section set a timer for five minutes. Spend that time listening for God to speak to you.

5.   How do you think Samuel felt as he realized God was speaking to him?

Action

Choose a day this week where you ask nothing of God, only give thanks and worship him for who he is.

Prayer

I am sorry that I come into your presence so busy speaking that I leave little time to listen to you.
Tune my ear to your voice as I spend these next five minutes listening to what you say.
Speak, Lord. I am listening. Amen.

Chapter 13
Language Learning
Made Difficult

Before we started studying the Arabic language, I had heard and seen how difficult it would be to learn. I guess I still thought it would come easily, so I was totally distressed when, on our first test in language school, I missed every single word. I knew I had to do something desperate—like study!

I began slowly but surely picking up new words and phrases, making an effort to study hard. Teachers stressed the importance of using every social activity as an opportunity for learning the language better, so that became my goal. Going to the doctor, going to the store, going to church, watching TV, or visiting friends were all opportunities to try to learn and reproduce the sounds and words I heard.

In the early days of our language study, I attended the funeral of our landlady's mother. Entering a room filled with women, I felt alienated from the others. It was hard being in a room full of people, able to sense their loss, but unable to communicate with them or understand what they were saying to each other. I felt like such an outsider, the foreigner who was intruding. I was unable to offer comfort or say even a simple sentence to communicate correctly or effectively the hope found only in Jesus.

As I silently sat there, I decided to use this as an opportunity to learn some Arabic. I remember telling myself something like this: "Now listen, Sue, and see if you can pick up just one new word tonight. In time, you will be able to tell these people about Christ. You will be able to offer comfort and hope, and even be able to ask where the bathroom is! Don't feel lonely. Jesus is here with you. Just follow the conversation and pick out a new word. This isn't a waste of time; use it as an opportunity to learn Arabic."

I began to get excited. I kept hearing one word again and again. I knew it must be important. I went over it time after time in my mind. I rehearsed how to say it exactly as I heard it. A new word! I was so proud, I didn't just sit and feel lonely and sorry for myself. I used the time profitably—my vocabulary was expanding. I would be able to use this new word to communicate with people. In time, I would become fluent!

I wanted to start using my new word in sentences. As I left the funeral, I asked the landlady's daughter about this word. "I kept hearing one word many times when the women were talking. Can you tell me what *hadadeen* is?" She looked at me and said, "Oh that is my family name."

Well, I don't use that word frequently, but it is one Arabic name that I can pronounce correctly and will never forget!

Read Acts 2:5-11

> There were many Jews staying in Jerusalem just then, devout pilgrims from all over the world. When they heard the sound, they came on the run. Then when they heard, one after another, their own mother tongues being spoken, they were thunderstruck. They couldn't for the life of them figure out what was going on, and kept saying, "Aren't these all Galileans? How come we're hearing them talk in our various mother tongues?
>
> Parthians, Medes, and Elamites;
> Visitors from Mesopotamia, Judea, and Cappadocia,

Pontus and Asia, Phrygia and Pamphylia,
Egypt and the parts of Libya belonging to Cyrene;
Immigrants from Rome, both Jews and proselytes;
Even Cretans and Arabs!
"They're speaking our languages, describing God's
mighty works!" (vv. 5–11)

Questions

1. What is your biggest frustration in language study right now?

2. Describe a recent victory in language efforts.

3. Think back to your language learning classes. List some new ideas that you could try this week to learn the language.

4. Plan a time to put into practice a new language learning idea.

5. Pretend you were one of the foreigners in Acts 2. Describe how you would have felt hearing "the mighty deeds of God" in your own language.

Action

Make an appointment to talk with a veteran missionary
about their language learning process.
Ask questions. Learn from them.

Prayer

May I be disciplined in my language study.
May I be bold enough to make mistakes in my new
language and learn from them.
Oh God, you know all the languages there are.
Would you enable me to persevere and learn this language
well so that one day I can clearly communicate your
mighty deeds to my new friends? Amen.

Chapter 16
Pursuing God

Years ago when I was young and wrinkle free, I remember thinking, "When I grow up I know having my quiet time will be easier!" I was struggling to either get up early or stay up late to spend time alone with God. When I was in college, I thought, "Once I am out of college and married I will have more time." After I was married and working, I longed for the future when I could stay home with kids and have more free time. (Ha!) When the kids were little, I just knew it would be a breeze to set aside time with God after they were all in school. Well, they are all in school. Reality set in recently as I met an eighty-year-old believer and asked her when it would become easy to set aside time to spend with God. She said that as far as she knew it must be sometime after eighty!

Why is it so hard to do the most necessary thing as a believer? Sure, I know I am in a spiritual battle. But maybe I think I don't really need that time alone with God. I seem to be doing fine on my own. It is so easy to see what needs to be done all around me: parenting, laundry, cleaning, cooking, ironing, visiting, studying, and shopping. However, it is often difficult to see the spiritual neediness in my own heart and in the lives of those around me. Even when I am involved in ministry, that same ministry can keep me so preoccupied that I don't take time to more intimately get to know the one I serve.

I don't think it is just me. Many believers live day to day on past victories, infrequent quiet times, and stale prayer lives. It isn't enough to merely preserve my spiritual life, I must actively pursue spiritual growth. In order to prosper spiritually—or even survive—I must spend time with him regularly. I must make this relationship a top priority.

How this works out in my life varies. Depending on my "season in life," I have had my quiet time at different times—mornings, afternoons, and bedtime. I have had "loud times" with God when my children were little, because if it was ever quiet, I would fall asleep! I have planned this time with God for every day, every other day, or five days a week. I have used Bible study books, done word studies, read through books of the Bible or used devotional guides. I have kept prayer journals, prayer lists, or prayed while taking a shower—aloud or silently. I have gone through dry times when I was simply being obedient and wet times when things were so meaningful I could only sit and cry.

Pursuing God will be a lifelong process. Wherever we are in the midst of life, we must make the time to spend with God. Whether we are young or old, we must work at setting this time aside. The only difference is how wrinkled we are as we struggle to do it!

Read Psalm 63

A David Psalm, When He Was out in the Judean Wilderness
God—you're my God! I can't get enough of you!
I've worked up such hunger and thirst for God,
traveling across dry and weary deserts. (v. 1)

So here I am in the place of worship, eyes open,
drinking in your strength and glory.
In your generous love I am really living at last!
My lips brim praises like fountains.
I bless you every time I take a breath;
My arms wave like banners of praise to you. (vv. 2–4)

I eat my fill of prime rib and gravy;
I smack my lips. It's time to shout praises!
If I'm sleepless at midnight,
I spend the hours in grateful reflection.
Because you've always stood up for me,
I'm free to run and play.
I hold on to you for dear life,
and you hold me steady as a post. (vv. 5–8)

Those who are out to get me are marked for doom,
marked for death, bound for hell.
They'll die violent deaths;
jackals will tear them limb from limb.
But the king is glad in God;
his true friends spread the joy,
While small-minded gossips
are gagged for good. (vv. 9–11)

Questions

1.   What could you do to improve your pursuit of
     God?

2.   List some creative methods for Bible study and
     prayer. Choose two that you would
     like to try.

3.   List the benefits of spending time with God and
     the detriments of not making that time.

4.   How has living cross-culturally affected your pursuit of God, either positively or negatively?

5.   What inspires you from Psalm 63 to know God better?

Action

Think about the last time you were really thirsty and a drink of cold water refreshed you. Ask God to give you a heart that thirsts after him and that you would regularly seek refreshment from him.

Prayer

Sometimes I act as if I can get along without you, Lord.
I know it isn't true.
I understand that I need you and I must spend time with you to thrive in my soul.
I am sorry for neglecting you.
You are my life.
May my life and the time I spend with you reflect my dependence on you. Amen.

Chapter 17
If I Were a Warthog

While we were on our family vacation in Washington, DC, we decided to visit the zoo. It was fun to relax, hang out with different family members and see the wild animals. As we came to one exhibition, we noticed a scale. If a person stood on it, the scale would tell him/her what animal in the zoo weighs the same as he/she does. I didn't see many people clamoring to get on it, but I thought it would be fun. I stood on the scale and cringed as it said that I weighed the same as a female warthog.

What kind of person even chooses a warthog to compare to another human being? Have you seen a picture of a warthog? They could have chosen a gazelle, a zebra, a bear—anything but a warthog! What can possibly be good about a warthog? Well, I decided I would have to do some research.

Did you know . . .

- A female warthog travels in a group called a sounder. A female warthog has the support of friends to help her and her young. She doesn't have to walk, live, or die alone.
- The male warthog has more marked warts than sows do. So that is good—there is always someone with more warts! However, these warts are mainly used to protect the face during fights, so it is good to remember that some warts are actually good to have!

- Warthogs don't like to dig, but use burrows other animals have dug for shelter. When entering, they back in. This enables them to defend themselves. When they wake up, the warthogs burst out of their burrows as fast as they can so that they can get a running start on any enemies that may be waiting. Talk about using what is available, knowing how to defend oneself, and how to always be prepared!

I am beginning to admire the female warthog.

Despite their fierce appearance, warthogs try to avoid confrontation. However, if forced to, they fight aggressively. I also don't like to fight. But if the issue is important, I can be like the warthog and get in there and fight for what is right or important to me.

And read this—warthogs allow birds to eat the parasites that live on their bodies. This lets the birds eat well and enables the warthogs to get rid of pests that bother them. Give and take—sharing is what warthogs and people can do to make relationships work well.

One article described the warthog, "Neither graceful nor beautiful, warthogs are nonetheless remarkable animals." So all in all, I guess it isn't so bad to be compared to a female warthog. They have some very admirable and useful traits. They have friends, are resourceful, get along well with others, protect their young, utilize their strengths, and build on them.

And my husband, ever the optimist, reminded me that it could have been worse: I could have weighed the same as a male warthog.

Read 1 Corinthians 6:19–20

Or didn't you realize that your body is a sacred place, the place of the Holy Spirit? Don't you see that you can't live however you please, squandering what God paid such a high price for? The physical part of you is not some piece of property belonging to the spiritual part of you. God owns the whole works. So let people see God in and through your body.

Read 1 Peter 1:17–21 focusing on verses 18–19

You call out to God for help and he helps–he's a good Father that way. But don't forget, he's also a responsible Father, and won't let you get by with sloppy living. (v. 17)

Your life is a journey you must travel with a deep consciousness of God. It cost God plenty to get you out of that dead-end, empty-headed life you grew up in. He paid with Christ's sacred blood, you know. He died like an unblemished, sacrificial lamb. And this was no afterthought. Even though it has only lately—at the end of the ages—become public knowledge, God always knew he was going to do this for you. It's because of this sacrificed Messiah, whom God then raised from the dead and glorified, that you trust God, that you know you have a future in God. (vv. 18–21)

Questions

1.   Personalize I Corinthians 6:19-20 as you write it in your own words.

2.   From the two scripture passages, how does God show how special you are to him?

3.   How has your self-image been affected by living in a different country?

4.   Look in the mirror (go on, find one) and say,
      "You are special to God."

5.   Recognizing your value to God, how can you
      serve God in a new way today?

Action
Write a brief summary of how God has made you and one
way you can honor him today.

Prayer
You made warthogs with abilities and strengths.
You made me with abilities and strengths, as well.
I trust you that you made me exactly the way you wanted
me.
May I develop my strengths and recognize my
weaknesses. Thank you for making me.
Use me to honor you, my creator. Amen.

Chapter 18
Little Shoe in a Big City . . .
Little Faith in a Big God

We were riding in one of the thousands of taxis in the capital city of our new host country. My youngest daughter had just gotten a brand new pair of shoes from her grandma. They looked so cute on her little feet. When we arrived at our destination, I got out of the taxi, paid the driver, and went on my way carrying Katie. As we were walking into the store, I noticed that one of her new shoes was missing. It had fallen off her foot in the taxi. I ran outside, but I was too late. The taxi was already gone.

I was so sad. We had just received those shoes as a gift from my mom and I had liked them. I thought about praying for that shoe; but I realized that with all of the taxis in the city, it would be impossible for that shoe to find its way back to us, so I dismissed the idea of praying and accepted the inevitable loss of one cute shoe. She would probably lose the other one soon and then her feet would match again!

I saw some co-workers that day and told them of this minor loss, but I couldn't help feeling a major disappointment. It was the first time she had ever worn them—too bad we would never see that shoe again. She had only gotten to wear them for fifteen minutes or so.

Later that day, our teammate, Mark, was riding in a taxi talking to the driver. The driver asked him where he was from and Mark said, "America." The driver was impressed with Mark's Arabic and told him of an American woman who had ridden in his taxi that morning. She had also spoken Arabic. He then proceeded to hold up the shoe that she had left in the taxi. Mark looked at the shoe and told him he knew that American woman and the shoe belonged to her daughter! The driver asked him where she lived.

A little later, I heard a knock at the door. I went to open it and there was this man holding out my daughter's shoe to me. I was speechless. I took the shoe and my husband came to the door with me to thank the driver.

Impossible. Too hard. Why even pray about it? It could never happen. All of a sudden, I became aware of the limitations I had put on God. He was showing me that nothing is impossible for him. Finding a tiny shoe in a city of eighteen million people—that's about thirty-six million shoes—and having this one little shoe brought back to me in my own home was a simple thing for God. He merely arranged a few taxi rides.

Why did he do this? Was it that he liked the shoe, too? I think God wanted to change my viewpoint. He was disappointed in my estimation of him. I had little faith and saw a huge impossibility in one tiny shoe. God wanted to renew my vision, to see that I can trust him. If I can look to him to take care of little details like this, I can trust him even more with the important things in life!

The next time you are tempted to think, "Oh, that's impossible!" remember a little shoe in a big city that came home to a woman of little faith who had a big God!

Read Matthew 19:23–26

> As he watched him go, Jesus told his disciples, "Do you have any idea how difficult it is for the rich to enter God's kingdom? Let me tell you, it's easier to gallop a camel through a needle's eye than for the rich to enter God's kingdom." (vv. 23–24)

> The disciples were staggered. "Then who has any chance at all?" (v. 25)

Jesus looked hard at them and said, "No chance at all if you think you can pull it off yourself. Every chance in the world if you trust God to do it." (v. 26)

Read Luke 1:36–38

"And did you know that your cousin Elizabeth conceived a son, old as she is? Everyone called her barren, and here she is six months pregnant! Nothing, you see, is impossible with God."

And Mary said,
Yes, I see it all now:
I'm the Lord's maid, ready to serve.
Let it be with me
just as you say.

Then the angel left her. (vv. 36–38)

Questions

1.   What looks impossible to you right now?

2.   What is God bigger than? What is bigger than God?

3.   Write down an event in the past when God did something that you thought was impossible.

4.   How does a person limit God or put him in a box without even knowing it?

5.   How do you think Mary felt as she responded to the angel in Luke 1:37-38?

Action
Write out your list of impossibilities. After each one write, "God is able!"

Prayer
Lord, I know that you can do the impossible.
Sometimes I get so focused on what needs to be done or the difficulty that I am facing that it appears bigger than you do.
Enable me to focus on you and not my circumstances,
to begin with knowing who you are and then together we can face any obstacle. Amen.

Chapter 19
It's Me Again, Lord, and I Need Your Help

I went to Bible school. I attended church faithfully. I went
to a women's Bible study. I had my time with the Lord. I
took courses in everything I could to be ready for cross-
cultural work: apologetics, theology, and education
classes. But sometimes, no matter how hard I trained, how
much I prepared, it all came down to, "It's me again, Lord,
and I need your help."

Who could prepare for locking themselves out of an
apartment for two hours? I had just stepped outside to tell
the boys not to yell on the stairs when the wind blew the
door shut, trapping my two little daughters inside. My
youngest was sick with roseola and had been sleeping in
her crib. My two-and-a-half-year-old was walking around
giving me updates through the key hole. She told me that
the baby was now crying in her crib and said, "Don't
worry. I gave her a toy to play with." Did she throw it in
bed with her? What toy was it? Was it heavy? Did it hit
her? Was she bleeding? Was it so small that she could
choke on it? I wished I had thought to get training as a
locksmith or a firefighter so I could find and use an axe to
chop down the door. "It's me, Lord and I need your help!"
I prayed, as I waited impatiently for a locksmith to come.

Who could be ready for two small children getting lost in a
city of 18 million people? We had just moved into an

apartment and I was home with the baby. The three older children had walked to a nearby store, located on a circle. My oldest left the store, sure that his eight-year-old brother and five-year-old sister would know the way home. They didn't. My husband wasn't home. It was getting dark, so I left the baby with my ten-year-old and went to search. The man at the store said that they had left. As I walked, I asked strangers, "Have you seen two foreign children?" "Yes, they were walking and crying as they came down this street." I kept walking and asking until further down that street no one had seen them. I went home to call Don so we could drive the car and search the streets more quickly and thoroughly. I returned home to find that our phone wasn't working. "It's me again, Lord, and I need your help!"

As I went to use our neighbor's phone, I heard the pitter-patter of little feet coming up the stairs. I saw my children's tear-streaked faces. They told me how they had gotten confused with the circle and weren't sure on which street our home was located. However, my son knew the way from a major road, so he had hailed a taxi, paid a pittance to the driver—God bless him—and rode to the major street. From there they then found their way home. I wished I had trained as a detective, or at least been blessed with omniscience, so I could have known where they were and found them.

There were no classes in matchmaking to enable me to help national friends find spouses from the same background who shared their new faith. I don't remember a class in how not to feel stupid after making major language and culture mistakes. In the midst of cross-cultural counseling, there would be a key word I didn't know and once again it came down to, "Lord, it's me again and I need your help."

Because I wanted and needed more training, I went back to school to finish my degree. I desired to be as effective as possible in my work for God. I had to study and work hard, but in all my endeavors, I must remember that it is God who will see me through situations for which no one could even think to be prepared.

Two planes exploded into the World Trade Center. The tall buildings collapsed. Fear was rampant. Threats seemed widespread.

"Lord, it's me again and I need your help."

Read Psalm 37

A David Psalm

Don't bother your head with braggarts or wish you
could succeed like the wicked.
In no time they'll shrivel like grass clippings
and wilt like cut flowers in the sun. (vv. 1–2)

Get insurance with GOD and do a good deed,
settle down and stick to your last.
Keep company with GOD,
get in on the best. (vv. 3–4)

Open up before GOD, keep nothing back;
he'll do whatever needs to be done:
He'll validate your life in the clear light of day
and stamp you with approval at high noon. (vv. 5–6)

Quiet down before GOD,
be prayerful before him.
Don't bother with those who climb the ladder,
who elbow their way to the top. (v. 7)

Bridle your anger, trash your wrath,
cool your pipes—it only makes things worse.
Before long the crooks will be bankrupt;
GOD-investors will soon own the store. (vv. 8–9)

Before you know it, the wicked will have had it;
you'll stare at his once famous place and—nothing!
Down-to-earth people will move in and take over,
relishing a huge bonanza. (vv. 10–11)

Bad guys have it in for the good guys,
obsessed with doing them in.

But God isn't losing any sleep; to him
they're a joke with no punch line. (vv. 12–13)

Bullies brandish their swords,
pull back on their bows with a flourish.
They're out to beat up on the harmless,
or mug that nice man out walking his dog.
A banana peel lands them flat on their faces—
slapstick figures in a moral circus. (vv. 14–15)

Less is more and more is less.
One righteous will outclass fifty wicked,
For the wicked are moral weaklings
but the righteous are GOD-strong. (vv. 16–17)

GOD keeps track of the decent folk;
what they do won't soon be forgotten.
In hard times, they'll hold their heads high;
when the shelves are bare, they'll be full. (vv. 18–19)

God-despisers have had it;
GOD's enemies are finished—
Stripped bare like vineyards at harvest time,
vanished like smoke in thin air. (v. 20)

Wicked borrows and never returns;
Righteous gives and gives.
Generous gets it all in the end;
Stingy is cut off at the pass. (vv. 21–22)

Stalwart walks in step with GOD;
his path blazed by GOD, he's happy.
If he stumbles, he's not down for long;
GOD has a grip on his hand. (vv. 23–24)

I once was young, now I'm a graybeard—
not once have I seen an abandoned believer,
or his kids out roaming the streets.
Every day he's out giving and lending,
his children making him proud. (vv. 25–26)
Turn your back on evil,
work for the good and don't quit.

GOD loves this kind of thing,
never turns away from his friends. (vv. 27–28)

Live this way and you've got it made,
but bad eggs will be tossed out.
The good get planted on good land
and put down healthy roots. (vv. 28–29)

Righteous chews on wisdom like a dog on a bone,
rolls virtue around on his tongue.
His heart pumps God's Word like blood through his veins;
his feet are as sure as a cat's. (vv. 30–31)

Wicked sets a watch for Righteous,
he's out for the kill.
GOD, alert, is also on watch—
Wicked won't hurt a hair of his head. (vv. 32–33)

Wait passionately for GOD,
don't leave the path.
He'll give you your place in the sun
while you watch the wicked lose it. (v. 34)

I saw Wicked bloated like a toad,
croaking pretentious nonsense.
The next time I looked there was nothing—
a punctured bladder, vapid and limp. (vv. 35–36)

Keep your eye on the healthy soul,
scrutinize the straight life;
There's a future
in strenuous wholeness.
But the willful will soon be discarded;
insolent souls are on a dead-end street. (vv. 37–38)

The spacious, free life is from GOD,
it's also protected and safe.
GOD–strengthened, we're delivered from evil—
when we run to him, he saves us. (vv. 39–40)

Questions

1.   When did you last need God's help? Did he help you? If so, how?

2.   When did you last feel alone? Did God meet you? If so, how?

3.   Tell God what you need help with today.

4.   What circumstances do you need to commit to the Lord? Tell him you trust him.

5.   What is one special truth from Psalm 37? Share it with a friend.

Action

Write out a special thank you letter to God for being near to you, especially during difficult times.

Prayer

I thank you Lord that you are never far away.
Your ears are attuned to my cries and you love to meet my needs.

You meet them as no other because you know what my
true needs are.
Today I will seek to rest in you and wait patiently for you.
There is no need to worry or fret.
You are always with me and for me. Amen.

Chapter 20
A Mother's Prayer Journal

A mother's prayer journal is not a place to doodle. However, I have three drawings in my journal that I look at as I pray for my children. I am not an artist, but as I look at these pictures, I try to remember their significance to me on a daily basis.

At the top of one page is a crown. This is to remind me that what my children are today is not what they will be tomorrow. There are days when they act like little pagans-- bickering, moody, and obnoxious. There may even be a few days when they are more like saints—helpful, kind, and loving. Sometimes they ask deep questions and other times they think they know all of the answers. I will not give in to despair when things with the kids aren't going well. I will not be puffed up with pride when things are going better than expected. God himself is at work in my children and he will complete what he has begun.

At the bottom of this same page are four little burial mounds. All parents either consciously or subconsciously hold on to plans and desires for their kids. From the time they are born we have certain ideas of what they should be like, what they should be when they grow up, how they should act, what others should think of them, and of us as their parents. As kids grow, these plans change. Our kids are not like us when we were little. Their personalities are different. Their world is not like ours. They are not little mature adults who make wise decisions all of the time. They sometimes burp out loud or pass gas in church. What adult would pick their nose and hold up what they find on their finger in the middle of a public meeting?

Our kids may disappoint us, hurt us, amaze us and thrill us—all in one hour! Depending on how our children behave at any given moment, we may feel like the worst parents in the world or the best. However, my focus should not be on what I desire for my kids or who I desire them to be. Rather, it should be on what God is doing in their lives. I must have a funeral service for my own plans and goals for them. I must entrust them to God and let him mold them into who he wants them to be.

In the middle of this page, there is a picture of a boat on rolling waves. Being a parent is like taking a boat ride with Jesus. I thought a boat ride with Jesus would be a nice calm ride, but as the first disciples found out, boat rides with Jesus are not always calm! There are storms in which the boat is flying up and plunging down. When the boat is on top of a wave, we may be thinking, "Wow! This is great. My kids are doing so well." Then the boat dives down and we are wondering, "Oh God! How could this happen? What am I going to do to help my child?" Up and down, up and down, day after day we ride the storms of parenthood. At times, I have wanted to abandon the ship.

When I focus on the waves and the ups and downs of life circumstances and the children's choices, I feel as if it is all up to me! Fear becomes my constant companion on the ship. The secret to these boat rides is remembering who is with us and who is ultimately in charge of the waves. At no time in any storm was Jesus ever terrified. He never gave way to despair. He was always in control. When I recognize that Jesus is with me in this boat ride that is parenting, I can focus on him and not on what the boat is doing at any particular point in time.

As I look through my prayer journal, it reminds me that God is faithful. He answers prayer. He is at work in me and in my children. As I pray, I can remember a crown (what my children will be), a grave (where I need to bury my expectations for my—his—children) and a boat (reminding me that while I may be seasick, I am never alone as a parent!).

Read Mark 4:35–41

Late that day he said to them, "Let's go across to the other side." They took him in the boat as he was. Other boats came along. A huge storm came up. Waves poured into the boat, threatening to sink it. And Jesus was in the stern, head on a pillow, sleeping! They roused him, saying, "Teacher, is it nothing to you that we're going down?" (vv. 35–38)

Awake now, he told the wind to pipe down and said to the sea, "Quiet! Settle down!" The wind ran out of breath; the sea became smooth as glass. Jesus reprimanded the disciples: "Why are you such cowards? Don't you have any faith at all?" (vv. 39–40)

They were in absolute awe, staggered. "Who is this, anyway?" they asked. "Wind and sea at his beck and call!" (v. 41)

Questions

1.   What expectations of yourself or your children do you need to bury?

2.   Describe a storm of life you are in right now. Picture Jesus with you in this storm and thank him for his presence.

3.   What changes have you seen in the relationship between you and your children since you have moved overseas?

4.   How do you think the disciples felt when they
        were in the boat with Jesus during the storm?

5.   Draw a crown. Write down character weaknesses
        or difficulties that you see in your child. Make a
        list of qualities you would like to see developed in
        yourself or your children and begin praying about
        these areas.

Action

If you don't have a prayer journal, start one today.

Prayer

I exalt you today, Lord, because you are at work in us.
You never give up on us or leave us alone.
In the ups and downs of life you are with me.
I had expectations of what life would be like.
This isn't what I expected, but I know that you have a plan
and are using our experiences to make us into people who
will honor you through the process and in the end. Amen.

Chapter 21
A Godly Car?

Pastor Pyne was a godly man. He was the pastor of my home church while I was growing up. This kind man with his glorious white hair loved God and led his congregation with quiet dignity and a wonderful sense of humor. I was a bit in awe of him and could never imagine him sinning or even thinking about sinning. He was a righteous man.

One day Pastor Pyne invited my friend and me to go to a meeting with him. I was so excited. As we got into his car to wait for him to come and drive, I noticed the car was quiet, shiny, spotless and smelled clean. I said to my friend, "Isn't this a godly car?" Pastor Pyne had such influence, even his car reflected what he was like.

No one has ever said at any time that my mini-van even remotely resembles godliness. The radio usually plays country music. There are old church bulletins, directions to various places, candy wrappers, empty soda cans and hand-held games scattered throughout the interior. It doesn't look godly. It looks messy.

I want to be a godly person. I would like godliness to be so much a part of my life that without me having to say a word, people would recognize that quality in me. I would like them to look at me and say, "Now that is a godly person." At this point in my life, it just doesn't happen. Not as a result of my demeanor, nor by my speech, and definitely not by my van.
Is godliness a quality that comes only with age? Is it

something I have to wait for? Would I look godlier if I stopped coloring my hair and let it go gray? If I was neater, and my van was tidier, would people at least think my van was godly?

What made me look at Pastor Pyne as a godly man? It wasn't merely his position in the church. It wasn't just his white hair and quiet strength. I watched him, I listened to him speak, I saw how he interacted with those in pain and those in everyday, normal life, I sensed in him a great love for God and a humble dependence on the Lord. I know he prayed. I know he spent time in the Word. I know he loved others. I experienced a touch of that myself. There is no getting around it; he was godly. His life reflected Jesus every time I saw him.

I wish I could have known Pastor Pyne when he was younger. Maybe his car wasn't so tidy when his kids were younger. Maybe he wasn't always so wise. I would have loved to follow the process that made him who he was.

I have the urge to clean my van, but what I really sense is the need to clean my life. Godliness costs more than I've been willing to pay. I am challenged to love God more deeply, pray more intensely, love others more fiercely. As I daily submit my life to God's control and ask him to live his life through me, maybe I can become godly before retirement. My goal is not to impress others or try to get him to love me more. That is impossible; his love is changeless. My desire is to please him and honor his name, to reflect his character more accurately as his image bearer.

I have been in extremely neat and clean cars since that day and they just didn't have the same godly aura. So it isn't the shininess, cleanliness, or quietness of a car that makes it godly, it is the person who owns the car. By God's grace and with his mercy, I have high hopes for me and for my van.

Now where is the vacuum and turtle wax?

Read 1 Timothy 4:6-10

You've been raised on the Message of the faith and have followed sound teaching. Now pass on this counsel to the followers of Jesus there, and you'll be a good servant of Jesus. Stay clear of silly stories that get dressed up as religion. Exercise daily in God—no spiritual flabbiness, please! Workouts in the gymnasium are useful, but a disciplined life in God is far more so, making you fit both today and forever. You can count on this. Take it to heart. This is why we've thrown ourselves into this venture so totally. We're banking on the living God, Savior of all men and women, especially believers. (vv. 6–10)

Questions

1.   Define godliness.

2.   Describe the godliest person you know.

3.   Analyze your character. What are your weak points that need addressing? What are your strengths that need sharpening?

4.   According to I Timothy 4:6–10, what are the benefits of godliness?

5.   What are the challenges of growing in godliness
        in a cross-cultural setting?

Action

Choose the messiest spot in your house. It could be a junk
drawer, closet or vehicle. Clean it well. As you are
cleaning, spend some time in prayer about your desire for
Jesus to do some cleaning in your life. Be ready and open
for how he leads you.

Prayer

It is my heart's desire to live a godly life,
not so that others notice me for my glory,
 but so that you are honored in me.
Enable me to defy apathy in my spiritual development.
Empower me to chase after you and follow
wholeheartedly your purposes for me. Amen.

Chapter 22
In Appreciation of
My Thyroid

Do you remember seeing couples sharing and tasting each other's food during a romantic dinner? We don't do that anymore. Once, Don wanted to take some of my food and I tried to stab his hand with my fork. It was *my* food and I was so hungry all of the time; I didn't want any of it to go to anyone but me. One afternoon I made a 9x13 inch pan of Rice Krispies Treats for dessert, but ate them all before my husband got home. I was spending almost double what was normal for groceries, yet the items would disappear quickly. I ate and ate and ate some more, but kept getting thinner. People would tell me to go off my diet, but I wasn't on any diet.

My heart would race, even when I wasn't thinking about Don. My hands shook, I couldn't sleep and I was hot almost all of the time. I decided I was drinking too much caffeine, so I began to drink only decaffeinated drinks. It didn't seem to help. I was going to the restroom more often. I tired easily, but had a lot of nervous energy. If it wasn't caffeine, what was it?

I finally decided to go see a doctor. He looked at me, asked some questions and took some blood samples. He told me I had Grave's Disease, which is a hyperactive thyroid. I had never spent a lot of time thinking about my thyroid; in fact, I'm not sure I even knew that I had one before that day. A thyroid is a small gland that produces thyroxin. It

controls a person's metabolism. My metabolism was
extremely high and needed fixing.

It is amazing to me that something so small could affect
my entire life! It affected my heart, my hands, my weight,
my energy level, my appetite, my body temperature, my
sleep, my mood—it pretty much affected my whole being!
My body could not work well because this one little gland
was out of tune.

I spend a lot of time working on parts of my body that are
more noticeable. I brush my teeth, wash my face, fix my
hair and polish my nails. It is amazing to me that these
things on which I spend the most time, actually matter the
least! If my nail breaks or I'm having a bad hair day, it isn't
really a big deal, but if my pituitary gland breaks or my
heart valve has a bad day, it is critical and would
drastically affect my life.

Having this disease and getting it treated made me
appreciate my thyroid. It made me treasure those parts of
my body that get no respect and very little attention.
Thinking about the little valve in my heart that lets the
blood go through can make me misty-eyed. What a nice
little valve and how sad I would be if it stopped working!

My pituitary gland is another favorite. I appreciate these
little glands that work so hard to help my body function
smoothly.

Every member of the body is important. Each has a role to
fulfill and a job to do. If one of my glands, even the
smallest one, stops working, it won't be long before my
entire body begins to notice. The body of Christ is no
different. Each member needs to function—and function
well—so that the body as a whole works as it should.
Some parts get a lot of attention; other parts get little. This
attention has nothing whatsoever to do with the value of
that part to the working of the body. Some parts are
simply easier to see. It is often those parts we don't see that
work hardest and yet receive little recognition or
appreciation, like my thyroid gland.

I do thank God for my thyroid. Don thanks God that my thyroid was treated and my metabolism is back to normal. It doesn't mean that I share my dinner with him. However, it does mean that I don't usually eat his dessert before he gets home!

As you think about your body, give thanks for those parts that work so hard with so little notice. Now, thank God for each member of the body of Christ. As we work together, whether behind the scenes or before an audience, may we honor and serve him faithfully.

Read I Corinthians 12:1–11

Spiritual Gifts

What I want to talk about now is the various ways God's Spirit gets worked into our lives. This is complex and often mis-understood, but I want you to be informed and knowledgeable. Remember how you were when you didn't know God, led from one phony god to another, never knowing what you were doing, just doing it because everybody else did it? It's different in this life. God wants us to use our intelligence, to seek to understand as well as we can. For instance, by using your heads, you know perfectly well that the Spirit of God would never prompt anyone to say "Jesus be damned!" Nor would anyone be inclined to say "Jesus is Master!" without the insight of the Holy Spirit. (vv. 1–3)

God's various gifts are handed out everywhere; but they all originate in God's Spirit. God's various ministries are carried out everywhere; but they all originate in God's Spirit. God's various expressions of power are in action everywhere; but God himself is behind it all. Each person is given something to do that shows who God is: Everyone gets in on it, everyone benefits. All kinds of things are handed out by the Spirit, and to all kinds of people! The variety is wonderful:

wise counsel

clear understanding

simple trust

healing the sick

miraculous acts

proclamation

distinguishing between spirits

tongues

interpretation of tongues.

All these gifts have a common origin, but are handed out one by one by the one Spirit of God. He decides who gets what, and when. (vv. 4–11)

Questions

1.   Describe a time when a part of your body was broken or wasn't working properly.

2.   How did this affect you?

3.   How have you been fulfilling your role in the body of Christ?

4.   Thank God that Christ is the head of the body. How does a team work together as a body under his headship?

5.   Why does I Corinthians 12 stress the unity of God and the diversity of gifts?

Action

Write a short story describing what happens when in the body of Christ members aren't working properly.

Prayer

Lord, I praise you for placing me as a member in your body. You have gifted me to serve you alongside other gifted members.
May we work together under your headship.
May there be no jealously or envy.
Your love is the bond that keeps us working together in unity. I am grateful to be a part,
even a small part, of your body as you use us to work your purposes in the world. Amen.

Chapter 23
Eternity In and Out
of My Home

Years ago when my husband asked if I would be willing to go overseas to serve the Lord, I was completely willing. I began to daydream of all I was going to accomplish. I would learn the language well, meet people and tell others about the Lord. I was sure my life was going to be different, because I would be on "the field." I would be doing something really important with my life—something of eternal significance.

Well, maybe I forgot a few details—four small ones and one rather large one. My husband and children still wanted to eat. They still needed clean clothes, a tidy house, noses wiped, diapers changed, and the list goes on. Going overseas doesn't change everything.

I was studying language, trying to visit people, looking for opportunities to share the good news, wanting to do something *important*. I wanted to be involved in "ministry" and dreaded the laundry, the dishes, the diapers, and the messiness of children. I complained about the cooking and the ironing and began to look at my family as an intrusion in life. I had come overseas to do things for God, to make a difference, but it seemed I only had enough energy for the mundane and very little extra for eternity.

What did God expect of me, a mother with four small children? How could I minister for him if it seemed I was always stuck at home under a pile of laundry? I began searching through the Bible for women that God used to bring honor to him. I read of Dorcas, Mary, Lydia, Joanna, Susanna. I read of the women who "ministered to Christ" in Mark 15:40 and 41. I discovered in the inside margin of my Bible that the phrase "minister to" means "to wait on." They probably did his laundry, cooked, and cleaned!

I thought to myself and prayed, "Oh, Lord, if it were you I was serving, I would gladly wait on you. *That* would be important. It would have eternal significance. But this—all that I do in my home—is taking me away from serving you on 'the field.' Where is the ministry I want to do that really counts?"

As I thought and prayed, and studied the Word, I began to realize that what I do in the home is ministry. Ultimately, I am serving him as I serve others in my home. This service may be when no one is looking and with no fanfare and little thanks in return. It is living and serving as Christ did.

Ministry outside our home is important. We have to learn the language well. We continually seek to serve the Lord in some ways outside our home. Nevertheless, we cannot ignore, feel guilty about, or make light of our in-home ministry. It is accurate that as women missionaries, we are called "fulltime" workers! When my children were small, my ministry at home was valuable and time consuming. My ministry outside the home was also valuable, but not extensive. I now realize that I was involved in ministry fulltime all along, but in two different arenas.

Time has flown by since that fateful day I agreed to go overseas. My children are older. I no longer feel a struggle between in-home ministry and outside ministry. I have lots of time for outside ministry. Amazingly enough, it seems my in-home ministry is becoming more limited! It's possible that in only a short amount of time Don and I may be "empty nesters"! When serving the Lord in our homes and outside the home, mothers are touching lives for eternity.

"Oh Lord, give me grace to serve you faithfully inside and outside my home." Both have eternal significance.

Read Colossians 3:12–17, 22–25

So, chosen by God for this new life of love, dress in the wardrobe God picked out for you: compassion, kindness, humility, quiet strength, discipline. Be even-tempered, content with second place, quick to forgive an offense. Forgive as quickly and completely as the Master forgave you. And regardless of what else you put on, wear love. It's your basic, all-purpose garment. Never be without it. (vv. 12–14)

Let the peace of Christ keep you in tune with each other, in step with each other. None of this going off and doing your own thing. And cultivate thankfulness. Let the Word of Christ—the Message—have the run of the house. Give it plenty of room in your lives. Instruct and direct one another using good common sense. And sing, sing your hearts out to God! Let every detail in your lives—words, actions, whatever—be done in the name of the Master, Jesus, thanking God the Father every step of the way. (vv. 15–17)

Servants, do what you're told by your earthly masters. And don't just do the minimum that will get you by. Do your best. Work from the heart for your real Master, for God, confident that you'll get paid in full when you come into your inheritance. Keep in mind always that the ultimate Master you're serving is Christ. The sullen servant who does shoddy work will be held responsible. Being a follower of Jesus doesn't cover up bad work. (vv. 22–25)

Questions

1. List the things you do as a believer in Christ, a wife, a mother, and a missionary. Take a minute to let yourself feel tired.

2. Evaluate the significance of each of these activities. Whom are you serving in each of these activities? As you read Colossians 3, take a minute to recognize whom you are ultimately serving in each of these activities.

3. Begin each day this week by asking God, "What would you have me do today?"

4. Plan how to spend your week with one activity for each role that you have. For example:

    Sunday – visit neighbor
    Monday – have time with tutor
    Tuesday – go to team meeting
    Wednesday – spend extended time in prayer
    Thursday – have a date night
    Friday – play game with kids
    Saturday – take day off

5. How would planning each week help in determining priorities?

Action
Work out a way to sleep in one day this week.

Prayer
Thank you that my ministry to you takes place 24 hours a day in every area of my life. What I do for my family is ministry as I serve you faithfully in my home. My ministry outside my home is also valuable.

May I serve you diligently in each sphere of ministry and determine how to invest my time wisely according to your purposes for me. Amen.

Chapter 24
Creative Outlooks

When we lived in the Middle East, I used to take the kids to play at the park. After bringing the kids home, their shoes would be filled with sand.

Somehow, the kids always seemed to find themselves on my bed, either playing or taking a short nap. The sand would leap willingly from their shoes to slip under the comforter and onto the sheets.

Going to bed at night, my husband would complain about the sand in our sheets. Seeking to avoid having to wash even more laundry, I asked him to imagine that he was having fun sleeping on the beach.

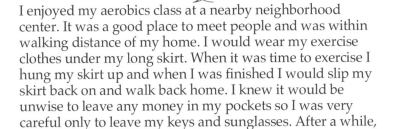

I enjoyed my aerobics class at a nearby neighborhood center. It was a good place to meet people and was within walking distance of my home. I would wear my exercise clothes under my long skirt. When it was time to exercise I hung my skirt up and when I was finished I would slip my skirt back on and walk back home. I knew it would be unwise to leave any money in my pockets so I was very careful only to leave my keys and sunglasses. After a while, I tried leaving a bit of money and that was never stolen.

One day I was going to have guests and I knew time would be short, so I decided to take more money in order to go grocery shopping on my way home. When I arrived at the center, I hung up my skirt and proceeded to do my exercises. Afterwards my skirt wasn't there. I looked everywhere: all around the floor, behind a sofa, on different hooks. My skirt was gone, along with the money, my sunglasses and my keys. I couldn't walk on the street wearing shorts! Even if I got home, I couldn't get in.

I cried and some friends offered to drive me home, suggesting I run really fast into the building and call my husband from a neighbor's phone. I went to the neighbor and couldn't find my husband's new office phone number so I called a friend. The conversation went something like this:

> Me: Someone stole my skirt.
> Friend: Were you wearing it at the time?
> Me: No.
> Friend: Well, that's good.

There is almost always more than one way to look at things that happen in our lives. Seeking to be creative in response to events that take us by surprise is an art that can be developed. I'm not simply lost, I am adventurously trying a new route and enjoying the scenery along the way. Try looking at dust on a coffee table as an opportunity for children to try some finger painting and practice writing skills. Dirty windows ensure that kids will see them and won't try to run through them, thus breaking the glass and injuring themselves.

Creative thinking can make even boring tasks more fun. It can enable us to see the brighter side of dismal events. It can help take the sting out of theft and give us a clearer perspective on life. With a little imagination, it can even make sleeping on a sandy bed an adventure at the beach!

Read Psalm 8

A David Psalm

GOD, brilliant Lord, yours is a household name. (v. 1)

Nursing infants gurgle choruses about you;
toddlers shout the songs
That drown out enemy talk,
and silence atheist babble. (v. 2)

I look up at your macro-skies, dark and enormous,
your handmade sky-jewelry,
Moon and stars mounted in their settings.
Then I look at my micro-self and wonder,
Why do you bother with us?
Why take a second look our way? (vv. 3–4)

Yet we've so narrowly missed being gods,
bright with Eden's dawn light.
You put us in charge of your handcrafted world,
repeated to us your Genesis-charge,
Made us lords of sheep and cattle,
even animals out in the wild,
Birds flying and fish swimming,
whales singing in the ocean deeps. (vv. 5–8)

GOD, brilliant Lord,
your name echoes around the world. (v. 9)

Questions

1. Choose to do one of the following to honor God today:
   Write a poem
   Sing a song
   Dance a dance

2. What sites haven't you seen yet in your host city? Choose one to go see next week.

3.   Look out your window or go for a walk. Make a list of what you see. Praise God for his creativity.

4.   Why is creativity important?

5.   Does imagination increase or decrease as a person grows older? Why is that?

Action
Tonight, look out your window up at the stars in the sky. Read Psalm 8 aloud.

Prayer
I praise your majestic name.
Your creativity amazes me: the brilliance of the stars, the small blade of grass, the wiggly worm under the rock. You have made them all.
You made each person unique and each one can praise and serve you in a different way.
You are an amazing God. Amen.

Chapter 29
I Gave God My Life, But Not My Toothbrush

One morning during my quiet time, I had such a burning desire in my heart for God to use me. My heart was reaching out to God. I poured out my soul before his throne. "Oh, God." I cried. "Use me to honor your name. Whatever the cost—prison, beatings, martyrdom—I want to serve you. Take my life today to use as you see fit. You are my King and I give myself to you."

I shared this desire with others in our team. I felt so ready to lose anything for the kingdom.

Then we had a houseguest . . . again.

Elliot used to come to our house a lot. He had no money, no job, and no place to stay. I would get so tired of serving tea, reheating dinner when he came late, washing the extra pajamas and sheets, and rearranging our kids so he could have a place to sleep. I grew to have a very poor attitude in my service toward this brother. Soon he stopped coming.

Later I heard he was sleeping at the bus station and not eating regularly. Stricken with remorse, the next time he called, I asked him where he had been and invited him to come see us again. You see I had had my quiet time and I was ready to give up my life for the kingdom.

Then he used *my* toothbrush *and* he left it bloody.

I was angry. It was my favorite toothbrush—though I hadn't realized it till then! He was my husband's friend—why didn't he choose to use my husband's toothbrush? I would have to go buy a new toothbrush. I knew I could never find another like it. The more I thought about it, the angrier I got.

"God—look what happens. I did this for you. I wanted to help this guy out and what does he do? He picks *my* toothbrush to use and get bloody. I can't believe it! I have to buy a new toothbrush. I liked my toothbrush. God, *it isn't fair!*"

Then I heard a still, small voice. "You offered me your life. You mentioned beatings, prison, and a willingness to be martyred. All I asked from you today is your toothbrush."

At times, I get so grandiose in my thinking: anything for you, Lord; anywhere for you, Lord; anytime for you, Lord. When what God is looking for is my service to him in the here and now details of my life, the small things I have to give today.

It isn't likely that I will ever be beaten, stay in prison or be a martyr. Maybe that is why I am so ready to give myself to God for these spectacular opportunities to serve (at least it sounds spectacular in a book written by someone who survives it all). What God wants from me is to be open day by day, minute by minute to serve him by giving him not only my life, but my toothbrush as well.

Read the following verses from the hymn, "Take My Life and Let it Be":

Take my life and let it be consecrated, Lord, to Thee;
Take my moments and my days—
Let them flow in ceaseless praise,
Let them flow in ceaseless praise.
Take my love—my Lord, I pour at Thy feet its treasure store;

Take myself—and I will be ever, only, all for Thee,
Ever, only, all for Thee.

Frances R. Havergal and H.A. Cesar Malan

Questions

1. Is there any area of your life that you are holding back from God or in which you angry at him for intruding?

2. What "big" things are you willing to do for God?

3. When have you been so caught up in those "big" things that you lose sight of the "little" things God might want from you today?

4. What are some little things you could do for him today?

5. Name one way, little or big, that you have served him this past week.

Action

Read through the hymn written above as a prayer.

Prayer

You know my heart and my desire to serve you.
Remind me to use every opportunity, big or small,
to honor you.
May my attitude be pleasing to you.
Please, Lord, take my life and my toothbrush,
whatever you need to bring glory to your name. Amen.

Chapter 26
Running Away from Home

We hadn't been married for more than a year or so. One day I was getting ready to go to work when Don asked me if I had any plans for the day. I couldn't think of any, and said so as I ran out the door.

During lunch at work, I read a book about keeping the romance alive in your marriage. Certain that we needed to do something drastic in case he was bored, I planned a romantic candlelight dinner for that evening. Everything was going according to plan until I walked in the front door. Don was putting on his tennis shoes. Somehow, I couldn't imagine tennis shoes and candlelight in the same scenario.

"What are you doing?" I asked nonchalantly. "I am going to play tennis with Tim," replied the traitor, I mean my husband. Silence. Uneasy glances. Tension settled over the room. Finally, a tentative question from him, "You said we didn't have plans for tonight, right?"

"Well, we didn't, but we could do something special tonight," I replied. The book had talked about the need for romance and, in my head, I had been thinking about that candlelight dinner all day. I hadn't called my husband; I had just expected him to know that we would do something together—that we *needed* to do something together, something romantic.

It was too late. Tim was already on his way over. I obviously wasn't needed so I stood up with a huff, grabbed my purse and said, "I'm leaving." I began slowly walking away, wishing he would stop me or call me back. He didn't, so I kept going. I was running away from home! (I thought only children did that.) I felt unneeded. Tim easily filled my role—he was a better tennis player than I, but *I* was the wife. Don should have wanted me and a romantic dinner; instead he was playing tennis, a game where love means nothing!

I went to a store and shopped . . . and cried . . . and shopped and cried. Tears were flowing as I walked up and down the aisles. I was angry. I was hurt. I bought some sheets. I felt betrayed. I was lonely. I bought a book on nutrition. He should have known (without me having to say anything) what I wanted and what I needed.

Then I thought about what would happen if I died in a car accident on my way home. His last memory of me would be a stiff-backed woman walking out of the house saying, "I'm leaving." I didn't want that. My anger really wasn't about my husband playing tennis with a friend. I just thought he would or should automatically know what I had been thinking about all day. I felt sorry and wanted to go home.

Taking my purchases to the car, I drove slowly and carefully home, praying that I wouldn't die in an accident before I had a chance to see my husband one more time. Tim was gone when I arrived and Don was waiting. I went into his arms and told him how sorry I was for running away. As we talked about what had happened, I told him why I had walked away so slowly—I had wanted him to call me back. I told him that *he should have known* to call me back by how slowly I was walking.

Don told me that he thought I was mature enough to come back on my own to work through our problems. I thought that if he wanted to work through our problems, he should have known to come after me. Both of us had wrong assumptions about each other. He assumed I was mature and I assumed that he could read minds!

Read Galatians 6:1–5

Live creatively, friends. If someone falls into sin,
forgivingly restore him, saving your critical comments for
yourself. You might be needing forgiveness before the
day's out. Stoop down and reach out to those who are
oppressed. Share their burdens, and so complete Christ's
law. If you think you are too good for that, you are badly
deceived. (vv. 1–3)

Make a careful exploration of who you are and the work
you have been given, and then sink yourself into that.
Don't be impressed with yourself. Don't compare yourself
with others. Each of you must take responsibility for
doing the creative best you can with your own life. (vv.
4–5)

Questions

1.   How has cultural stress affected your
relationships?

2.   When have you recently felt like running away
from a situation?

3.   Describe a time when you made a wrong
assumption about someone or something and
what the effects were.

4.   What is the difference between the *burden* in
Galatians 6:2 and the *load* in 6:5?

5.   What does Galatians 6:1–5 teach us about ourselves and others when we seek to help another person?

Action

Today, seek to communicate clearly one need that you have to a person who can help you.

Prayer

Remind me, Lord, not to make assumptions about people when I don't know all of the facts.
Help me to learn good communication skills,
 to listen well and to articulate clearly.
I know in my head that people can't read my mind,
but in my heart I want them to be able to.
Use me to build good, strong, healthy relationships. Amen.

Chapter 27
Third Culture Kids, Peanut Butter and GI Joe

Our eight-year-old son came running up the stairs, a large red handprint embedded on his cheek. "Our neighbor man hit me," he cried. "One minute he was playing with me and the next he hit me across the face."

I did what any sensible woman living in a new culture would do! I did what I always do when I face a crisis. I squared my shoulders, straightened my back with fierce determination . . . and I cried.

Should I go and confront the man? I can barely confront people in English! Should I wait for Don? Should I complain to the landlord? Does this sort of thing happen a lot here?

Before we left to go overseas, people said not to worry about the kids. If the parents adjust, the kids will adjust even more quickly. "Kids pick up the language easily," they explained. They would be okay. Because of this assurance, I had done very little to brace myself or my children for the culture shock. Nevertheless, it came.

People would pick up the baby and throw her in the air, kissing her while she screamed in terror of strangers. Women went about pinching the little one's cheeks. Adults kept teasing the older children to the point of tears. The kids were always standing out in a staring crowd. We would go sightseeing, but often our children were the ones who became the exhibits!

At school, other children laughed at their lunches. Whoever heard of peanut butter and banana sandwiches? Our kids couldn't understand the language and couldn't make themselves understood. It became easy to think of only the positive aspects of our home country and that our kids would have fit in so easily there. I can think of only one thing more painful than going through culture shock and that is watching your children go through it, knowing you are responsible for bringing them to a different country.

One morning as my son was getting ready to go to school, he was upset. He was afraid to go to school. He didn't know whether to wear his gym clothes or take them and change into them there. If he took them and changed there, the other kids would laugh at him because of his GI Joe underwear. Minutes before the bus came, I told him that God would be with him. He should wear his school uniform and when it was time to change God would take care of him. He considered this, dried his eyes and left for school.

I dropped to my knees as he left and prayed. My faith and my son's faith were out on a limb. Would God come through for us? I waited throughout the day until finally I heard my son come home. "Mom," he yelled excitedly, "I changed my clothes and not one person was around. No one teased me. God took care of me."

It doesn't always feel safe and comfortable living in a different country. We must depend on God—maybe a bit more than we would in our home country, because our other sources of stability and acceptance are gone. My children are learning that God is trustworthy. God cares and protects little boys who are afraid of being laughed at because of their underwear.

In time, my children learned some language and made friends. People came to understand that my baby was shy and stopped picking her up to throw her around. The kids learned it is okay to be different and began to find their niche.

Culture shock is hard on children and their parents. What would I do if I were getting ready to leave for the field for the first time? I would be aware that children do go through culture shock and will have some difficulties, that it will probably not be easy for anyone. However, I would also recognize that God is going before me *and* my children to that other country. I would be encouraged that each person in my family will get to know God in a deeper and more intimate way. Lastly, I would never send my children to school with peanut butter and banana sandwiches or wearing GI Joe underwear!

Read 1 Samuel 1:9–2:28

So Hannah ate. Then she pulled herself together, slipped away quietly, and entered the sanctuary. The priest Eli was on duty at the entrance to GOD's Temple in the customary seat. Crushed in soul, Hannah prayed to GOD and cried and cried—inconsolably. Then she made a vow:
Oh, GOD-of-the-Angel-Armies,
If you'll take a good, hard look at my pain,
If you'll quit neglecting me and go into action for me
By giving me a son,
I'll give him completely, unreservedly to you.
I'll set him apart for a life of holy discipline. (vv. 9–11)

It so happened that as she continued in prayer before GOD, Eli was watching her closely. Hannah was praying in her heart, silently. Her lips moved, but no sound was heard. Eli jumped to the conclusion that she was drunk. He approached her and said, "You're drunk! How long do you plan to keep this up? Sober up, woman!" (vv. 12–14)

Hannah said, "Oh no, sir—please! I'm a woman hard used. I haven't been drinking. Not a drop of wine or beer. The only thing I've been pouring out is my heart, pouring it out to GOD. Don't for a minute think I'm a bad woman. It's because I'm so desperately unhappy and in such pain that I've stayed here so long." (vv. 15–16)

Eli answered her, "Go in peace. And may the God of Israel give you what you have asked of him." (v. 17)

"Think well of me—and pray for me!" she said, and went her way. Then she ate heartily, her face radiant. (v. 18)

Up before dawn, they worshiped GOD and returned home to Ramah. Elkanah slept with Hannah his wife, and GOD began making the necessary arrangements in response to what she had asked. (v. 19)

Dedicating the Child to God

Before the year was out, Hannah had conceived and given birth to a son. She named him Samuel, explaining, "I asked GOD for him." (v. 20)

When Elkanah next took his family on their annual trip to Shiloh to worship GOD, offering sacrifices and keeping his vow, Hannah didn't go. She told her husband, "After the child is weaned, I'll bring him myself and present him before GOD—and that's where he'll stay, for good." (vv. 21–22)

Elkanah said to his wife, "Do what you think is best. Stay home until you have weaned him. Yes! Let GOD complete what he has begun!"

So she did. She stayed home and nursed her son until she had weaned him. Then she took him up to Shiloh, bringing also the makings of a generous sacrificial meal—a prize bull, flour, and wine. The child was so young to be sent off! (vv. 23–24)

They first butchered the bull, then brought the child to Eli. Hannah said, "Excuse me, sir. Would you believe that I'm the very woman who was standing before you at this very spot, praying to GOD? I prayed for this child, and GOD gave me what I asked for. And now I have dedicated him to GOD. He's dedicated to GOD for life."

Then and there, they worshiped GOD. (vv. 25–28)

Questions

1. List what you think some of Hannah's struggles might have been as she left Samuel to work at the temple with Eli and his sons.

2. What problems do you think Samuel might have had adapting to his new life away from home?

3. How have your kids had a hard time with the culture?

4. Ask them how you can help them adapt to the new culture.

5. Continue to pray diligently for your children. You may want to fast and pray for them if they are going through a particularly difficult time.

Action

Set aside some time with your children this week. Ask them how they are doing and what they are learning about the culture. Listen attentively to them as you interact with them.

Prayer

Thank you for my kids.
I hate it when they are hurting and I can't fix everything so
they won't hurt anymore.
I realize that you love my kids more than I do.
I guess when I worry or seek to overprotect them I am not
fully trusting you.
It is easier to trust you with me than my kids!
Please know my heart, Lord.
I determine to entrust them to you.
When I start to take them back through worry or despair,
remind me that they are yours.
Would you help me as I care for them to do my best while
understanding that you are the one taking care of all of us?
Amen.

Chapter 28
To Hide or to Confess, That is the Question

It was just a few days before my sister's wedding. She brought her veil to my mom's house and took it out of the box. It was quite wrinkled and she wanted to hang it up to see if the wrinkles would fall out. They didn't. She was trying to think of the best thing to do, but had to go to work. She couldn't solve the problem before she left. After she was gone, I thought to myself, "How hard can it be to steam away wrinkles? This is what professionals do—they just put the wrinkled items near steam and the wrinkles disappear, right?"

I told my mom with deep and sure confidence that I could take care of the wrinkles. I put the tea kettle on the stove and waited for the water to boil. Steam would come out and I would hold the veil over the tea kettle and watch with great satisfaction as the wrinkles disappeared. She may have questioned me a few times about the procedure, but I knew I could do it, so I dismissed her objections. The water was hot, I could see steam billowing out of the kettle so I proceeded to hold the veil up over the kettle.

It was a fairly long veil and I thought I had it held high enough over the tea kettle that only the steam would touch the veil. But in one terrible instant a piece of the veil actually touched the kettle. I watched in horror as a small portion of the veil melted away, leaving a tiny hole. I stood there in shock. What was I going to do? The wrinkles were still there and so was a new hole. My thoughts ranged from, "This didn't really happen, did it?" to "It's a small hole. Maybe if I don't say anything she won't notice."

I hadn't quite decided what to do when my mom walked into the kitchen. I think she could tell by the look on my ashen face that something wasn't quite right. I told her the veil had a hole in it. She thought that maybe it came that way. Oh how I wanted that to be the case! If I couldn't hide it like I was tempted to do, I would at least love to be able to blame someone else. But I had to confess that I had done it. How was I going to tell my sister that her new veil had a hole in it? With just a few days left until the wedding, what would we do?

I called her at work and told her, "I hope you aren't going to disown me, but not only are the wrinkles still in your veil, there is also a hole." She called the dressmaker and thankfully, they had another veil ready the next day. I wasn't allowed to touch it, go near it or even look at it until it was safely attached to my sister's head the day of the wedding.

Whenever I do something wrong or stupid, my first instinct is to hide. During my first visit at Don's house, his mother gave me a simple task. I was to fill the salt shaker. How hard is that? Thankful for a simple task I filled the salt shaker, turned it right side up and watched as the plug fell off. Some salt spilled onto the counter top, but most fell into the silverware drawer. My first instinct was to shut the drawer. I wanted to hide it and pretend I wasn't involved. Don happened to look over just as I was ready to shut the drawer and saw what had happened. "Need help?" he asked. Embarrassed, I said yes.

Hiding is a normal response for me when something goes wrong. Maybe it all goes back to Adam and Eve—they tried to hide from God when they sinned. Maybe not, it could just be me. I hate messing up and my gut reaction is to hide it from the world.

How much better it is to confess, "Yes it was me. I'm sorry I messed up."

My mom understood when I wanted to blame someone else and forgave me when I told her it was me that burned the hole in the veil. My sister forgave me and let me continue to be her sister. Don helped me clean up the salt and kept dating me. He even married me knowing my limitations in the kitchen. It is freeing to confess and not try to keep hiding the truth.

However, now that I think of it . . . Don's mom hasn't ever asked me to fill the salt shaker again. And last summer when my sister's new dress was wrinkled, I offered to take care of it for her. She politely declined. Really, how hard would it have been? I had a tea kettle and with a little bit of steam . . .

Read James 5:13-20

Are you hurting? Pray. Do you feel great? Sing. Are you sick? Call the church leaders together to pray and anoint you with oil in the name of the Master. Believing-prayer will heal you, and Jesus will put you on your feet. And if you've sinned, you'll be forgiven—healed inside and out. (vv. 13–15)

Make this your common practice: Confess your sins to each other and pray for each other so that you can live together whole and healed. The prayer of a person living right with God is something powerful to be reckoned with. Elijah, for instance, human just like us, prayed hard that it wouldn't rain, and it didn't—not a drop for three and a half years. Then he prayed that it would rain, and it did. The showers came and everything started growing again. (vv. 16–18)

My dear friends, if you know people who have wandered off from God's truth, don't write them off. Go after them. Get them back and you will have rescued precious lives from destruction and prevented an epidemic of wandering away from God. (vv. 19–20)

Read Genesis 3:6–10

When the Woman saw that the tree looked like good eating and realized what she would get out of it—she'd know everything!—she took and ate the fruit and then gave some to her husband, and he ate. (v. 6)

Immediately the two of them did "see what's really going on"—saw themselves naked! They sewed fig leaves together as makeshift clothes for themselves. (v. 7)

When they heard the sound of GOD strolling in the garden in the evening breeze, the Man and his Wife hid in the trees of the garden, hid from GOD. (v. 8)

GOD called to the Man: "Where are you?" (v. 9)

He said, "I heard you in the garden and I was afraid because I was naked. And I hid." (v. 10)

Questions

1.   How does confession help the person confessing?

2.   According to James 5:16, who are we to confess our sins to and why?

3.   When did you last feel like hiding?

4.   Why did Adam and Eve want to hide in Genesis 3:6–10? Why do we also want to hide?

5.   How would team relationships be affected by
        confessions and forgiveness? Encourage team
        members to set aside some time for reflection,
        confession and forgiveness.

Action
Spend some time reflecting about confessing. Is there
anything you need to confess? It would be helpful to confess
to God, then go to a trusted friend and confess to them. Pray
together and thank God for his forgiveness.

Prayer
You already know what I've done and what I haven't done.
You see where I've sinned and I am clueless about it.
Increase my sensitivity to you, Lord.
May I walk closely with you and not ever grow too proud to
confess to fellow believers my failures and your forgiving
grace. Amen.

Chapter 29
Eight Hours and a Camel

Eight hours! A lot can be accomplished in eight hours. Some people put in a full work day; some get a good night's sleep; others may get caught up in reading a novel and may finish the whole book in eight hours.

Eight hours took on new meaning for me as Don and I sat in a car on a mountain during a snowstorm in Spain. It was cold in Madrid and we were looking forward to going south to Grenada, thinking it would be warmer. We had a leisurely lunch with three friends and then began our trip, planning to arrive at our destination in about five hours.

Snow began to fall, lightly at first, then becoming more blizzard-like. Traffic slowed to a crawl. Darkness began to descend as the sun set. Cars everywhere on the road came to a complete halt. Stopped cars stretched for miles ahead and behind us. People carefully got out of their cars to see if they could find out what had happened. Young people got out for snowball fights and to take pictures of this abnormal weather. The five of us mostly sat in the car and waited, some occasionally got out to get some fresh air or ask questions of others who were stranded. Don took a few pictures to capture the moment.

I had to go to the bathroom. This was one time I thought how much easier it would be if I were a man. A man could just go for a short walk, turn his back, do his business and return to his car. As a woman, the process would be much more difficult.
I waited as long as I could. At last, unable to stand it any

longer, I determined to brave the snow, find a dark corner, brush aside a layer of snow, and go. I told myself that even if anybody saw anything, they would never see me again. Or if they did see something, they probably wouldn't recognize me standing up. Don went with me to stand guard as I boldly got out of the car. I tried hard to find a spot away from the public (hard to do in a crowded "parking lot" with a drop off on one side and a mountainside on the other) and in the dark (again, hard to do when car headlights are on). Finally, I returned to the car in defeat. I just couldn't do it.

Time passed. I practiced self control. I thought to myself, "You are a camel. You can hold water. You are a camel." I wasn't too convincing, so I prayed that God would make the traffic move and get me to a restroom. Nothing seemed to be happening. I munched on a few pretzels—isn't salt supposed to dehydrate a person? Too late I found out that this doesn't work if the bladder is already full.

Finally, cars began to move . . . slowly. Plow trucks were on the way and so were we. We finally made it to the apartment where we were going to stay. Instead of five hours, our trip had taken a total of twelve! I jumped out of the car, outran Don to enter the apartment first, quickly greeted our hosts and escaped into the bathroom.

I wanted to include a photograph that Don took in the blizzard with this story, but while in transit back to the Madrid airport, someone stole Don's backpack. In his backpack, along with our camera, were our airline tickets for a flight that was due to leave in four hours. We spent those next four hours rushing around from one end of the airport to another. We talked with police and filled out a report, listing all that was missing. We visited several different airline representatives who sent us from one desk to another for help, pushing our luggage cart from place to place, because we couldn't check our bags without tickets. Finally, we were able to repurchase one set of tickets and paid a fine to reissue the other ones. The only bright spot in the situation were nearby and numerous restrooms available if I needed them.

After getting a chance to sit on the flight after those hours of running around in the airport, I thought back to those eight hours with nothing to do but sit in the car. It hadn't been so bad, had it?

Then I pictured a camel . . . and looked to make sure there were restrooms on the plane!

Read Philippians 4:4–14

Celebrate God all day, every day. I mean, revel in him! Make it as clear as you can to all you meet that you're on their side, working with them and not against them. Help them see that the Master is about to arrive. He could show up any minute! (vv. 4–5)

Don't fret or worry. Instead of worrying, pray. Let petitions and praises shape your worries into prayers, letting God know your concerns. Before you know it, a sense of God's wholeness, everything coming together for

good, will come and settle you down. It's wonderful what happens when Christ displaces worry at the center of your life. (vv. 6–7)

Summing it all up, friends, I'd say you'll do best by filling your minds and meditating on things true, noble, reputable, authentic, compelling, gracious—the best, not the worst; the beautiful, not the ugly; things to praise, not things to curse. Put into practice what you learned from me, what you heard and saw and realized. Do that, and God, who makes everything work together, will work you into his most excellent harmonies. (vv. 8–9)

Content Whatever the Circumstances

I'm glad in God, far happier than you would ever guess—happy that you're again showing such strong concern for me. Not that you ever quit praying and thinking about me. You just had no chance to show it. Actually, I don't have a sense of needing anything personally. I've learned by now to be quite content whatever my circumstances. I'm just as happy with little as with much, with much as with little. I've found the recipe for being happy whether full or hungry, hands full or hands empty. Whatever I have, wherever I am, I can make it through anything in the One who makes me who I am. I don't mean that your help didn't mean a lot to me—it did. It was a beautiful thing that you came alongside me in my troubles. (vv. 10–14)

Questions

1.   What causes you to feel discontent in your new country?

2.   What does it take to learn to feel content in any and all circumstances?

3.   Describe a time this past month when you were harried.

4.   Write a short story that describes contentment.

5.   What does Philippians 4:4–14 say about anxiety and contentment?

Action

Plan a two-hour break this week away from others and enjoy some quiet time.

Prayer

Father God, Oswald Chambers wrote that you are the engineer of our circumstances.

You put me where you want me and desire for me to learn contentment.

Whether I have a lot or a little, whether I live in comfort or not, knowing you are with me is my contentment.

May I continue to learn to be content and may I be a good student! Amen.

Chapter 30
Faithfulness, Perseverance and Trusting in God

Why is it that I can always think of an appropriate response to a remark only after a two or three-hour time span? How many times have I thought, days after a conversation, "If only I had said . . . "?

Riding a bus to high school many years ago, I would sometimes sit near Rick and we would talk. One day he asked me why I was so happy. I knew I had the perfect opportunity to witness, but I was so scared. What if he rejected what I said? What if I said the wrong thing? What if . . . ? As soon I said, "I don't know," I immediately began pleading with God for another opportunity, realizing that I had blown that one. Rick asked again, "No, really, why are you so happy?" Seeking strength from God, I replied, "It's because of Jesus."

"Oh," he said, "You must be one of those religious fanatics." "Some people call it that," I said, "But he is the reason I am so happy."

I don't remember anything else about the conversation. He got off the bus and I berated myself. Why didn't I come up with a more in-depth answer? I knew I had messed up. That night I kept trying to think of what I should have said, how I should have said it, and all the things I should have done differently.

We saw each other off and on after that, but I don't remember many other conversations.

Years went by.

Don and I were working overseas. I felt guilty that we weren't seeing a greater response in the people with whom we spent time. If only I could come up with better conversation turners. If only I knew what to say to make the people realize the truth. I felt jealous of those who had the gift of sharing the good news and seeing people respond right away. I wondered if I should leave the field and let someone else come to work who was better equipped for the task at hand. I felt like I did in high school—wanting to witness but seeming to blow it time after time because of my faulty replies and weak presentations. I was not seeing any immediate, visible results. I was discouraged.

My mom called. She told me that a guy named Rick had stopped by looking for me. He told her that he was a pastor now and wanted to look up people who had influenced him for Christ and thank them.

He was looking for me? I thought I had blown it. I wasn't persuasive. I wasn't powerful. I knew I should have answered him differently. And yet God, in his grace and sovereign power, used what little I said to touch the heart of another human being! I was a link in a chain of people God put in Rick's life to draw him to himself. It didn't happen overnight and it wasn't until almost twenty years later that I discovered what God had done. God used me and I didn't even know it. I saw that, though the results may not be immediate, it doesn't mean that they won't eventually come. God uses weak people, even when they think they fail. He can take what we give, use it, and work everything together so that he is glorified by our desire to make Jesus known.

You may feel discouraged. You may not be seeing immediate results. You may not even feel wanted. Yet you serve faithfully, trusting God to work. Who will be looking for you in the next twenty years to say thanks for impacting her life for Christ?

Read 1 Corinthians 15:58

With all this going for us, my dear, dear friends, stand your ground. And don't hold back. Throw yourselves into the work of the Master, confident that nothing you do for him is a waste of time or effort. (v. 58)

Read Galatians 6:6-10

Be very sure now, you who have been trained to a self-sufficient maturity, that you enter into a generous common life with those who have trained you, sharing all the good things that you have and experience. (v. 6)

Don't be misled: No one makes a fool of God. What a person plants, he will harvest. The person who plants selfishness, ignoring the needs of others—ignoring God!—harvests a crop of weeds. All he'll have to show for his life is weeds! But the one who plants in response to God, letting God's Spirit do the growth work in him, harvests a crop of real life, eternal life. (vv. 7–8)

So let's not allow ourselves to get fatigued doing good. At the right time we will harvest a good crop if we don't give up, or quit. Right now, therefore, every time we get the chance, let us work for the benefit of all, starting with the people closest to us in the community of faith. (vv. 9–10)

Questions

1.   List the people that God used to bring you to himself.

2.   Think of the people with whom you shared the gospel. Pray for them and thank God for the opportunities as you entrust them to him.

3.   Think of ways you can continue to share the good news with others, how can you remind yourself that their responses are not dependent upon you?

4.   Why can you determine to trust God for fruit? How can you persevere?

5.   Rewrite 1 Corinthians 15:58 in your own words, addressing it to yourself.

Action
Write and send a thank you letter to some of the people that God used to bring you to Jesus.

Prayer
With your help, God, I refuse to grow weary.
With your strength, I will continue to share the good news.
By your grace, I will entrust the results to you and be faithful until you call me home.
By your grace, O Lord, Amen.

Chapter 31
Balconies, Jump Ropes and Little Girls

One Christmas many years ago, my daughters received a play kitchen. They loved making pretend coffee, washing dishes and cooking on their little stove. They enjoyed having friends over and would play happily together for hours. In time its newness wore off; it was played with less and less. We moved it onto our fifth floor balcony where they could play with it if they wanted, but where it wasn't taking up space in their bedroom.

One day months later, they invited a friend over to spend the night. Lying in bed early the next morning, I could hear their happy little voices chattering away on the balcony. I tried to go back to sleep, but for some reason I felt uncomfortable and couldn't rest. I had a nagging feeling that I should go out and see how they were doing. I tried to ignore it because I wanted to sleep in, but sleep became impossible. I got up to walk out onto the balcony to see how they were doing. My heart fell as I saw them.

One of the girls apparently had a bright idea. Tired of playing with the kitchen, they saw several plastic jump ropes lying around and decided to tie them together. They let the jump ropes out over the balcony in order to climb down to the ground below. Little did they realize that the ropes tied together didn't even reach the floor below us. Their friend was already on the other side of the railing trying to figure out how to let go and slide down the rope.

I knew that if I raised my voice or scared her in any way, my daughters' friend could fall. Slowly I walked toward the children, greeting them in a quiet voice, "Hi, what are you girls up to this morning?" They turned to look at me. As I arrived where they were, I quickly took hold of the little girl's arm and pulled her over to safety onto the solid floor of our balcony. Once I knew she was safe, my voice became less quiet. "What were you thinking? Do you realize what could have happened?" I proceeded to explain to them the dangers of such play and how they should never, never, never (I may have used this word continually for several minutes!) do this again.

My heart was pounding and, as I led them inside and locked the balcony doors, I couldn't bring myself to relax. For days, as soon as I would close my eyes, I would picture them falling to their deaths. I knew that is what actually could have happened had I not listened to that inner voice and stepped outside to check on them.

When I took this little girl back to her parents, I felt that I should tell her mom what had happened. As I explained the situation, her mother looked at me with a strange light in her eyes. She told me that a nightmare that same night had robbed her of sleep. In her dream she had seen her daughter lying dead on the ground. She had spent time in prayer during the night for her daughter and asked God to watch over her and protect her.

Praise God for one mother's prayers and God's answer to those prayers. God woke me up and wouldn't let me go back to sleep. I am so thankful that, by God's grace and mercy, I listened to that "inner voice" and checked on the children that morning.

I learned several lessons through that experience: I must pray faithfully for my children. I must listen to that inner voice that parents sometimes hear. I must clearly explain to children the proper function of a jump rope and its possible dangers, as well as teach them about distances and measurement. And most of all, I must never put a kitchen on a fifth floor balcony!

Read Psalm 59:16-17

And me? I'm singing your prowess,
shouting at cockcrow your largesse,
For you've been a safe place for me,
a good place to hide.
Strong God, I'm watching you do it,
I can always count on you—
God, my dependable love. (vv. 16–17)

Questions

1. Describe a time since you have been overseas
    when God intervened and protected you. Thank
    him for his care.

2. Remember a time when God answered your
    prayers. Thank him for answering.

3. As you live as an alien in a foreign country, what
    characteristic of God is meaningful to you from
    Psalm 59?

4. Praise God for who he is and what he has done for
    you.

5. As you look at the future and goals for cross-
    cultural ministry, what can you entrust to him?

Action

Get together with a friend. Share your answer to question number one and ask her to share one of her experiences. Together, pray together about what your response is to question five.

Prayer

Lord God Almighty, You know all things.
You know the past, present and future.
You see danger when I might think it is safe.
You know I am safely in your care even when I sense danger.
You take such good care of me.
I apologize for taking your care for granted and know that I owe you songs of thanksgiving.
Thank you for being there for me. Amen.

Chapter 32
Saying Good-Bye Twice

Grieving for the loss of my grandpa was difficult. Grieving twice was even harder as it was totally unexpected.

We were overseas when my mom called to tell me that my grandpa had gone home to be with the Lord. My kids were young and couldn't comprehend my grief. No one in our host country had ever met my grandpa. Though they knew I was sad, they couldn't talk with me about who he was, what he was like and how much he meant to me. Even Don, who knew him and loved him, didn't grieve in quite the same way.

I needed someone to share "Remember when . . ." stories with me. I wanted to talk with someone who knew him, so that we could laugh about how fun it was as children to beg him to take out his false teeth. I wanted someone who could remember simply watching him sit on his favorite chair to watch the Cleveland Indians play baseball.

Because Grandpa never learned to drive, he used to walk to and from work. He always teased the waitresses and made them laugh whenever we went to restaurants. He was always ready for smooches and hugs from his grandkids. He could sit on his porch in the summer and kill more flies with his fly swatter than anyone else I know. I couldn't find anyone with whom I could share these memories of Grandpa and ease the pain in my heart.

Returning to the states one year later, I wasn't prepared for the overwhelming sadness I felt as I visited family and saw that he really was gone. The reality of Grandpa's death hit me hard as I visited his grave and spent time with my grandma. I saw her without my grandpa for the first time in my life.

It was a comfort to be with family and to finally be able to share the "Remember when" stories, but I also felt like an outsider (a traitor?) because I wasn't there. I didn't see him suffer. I wasn't there when he died. I wasn't there for his funeral and I wasn't there to grieve with everyone else in my family.

The same month my grandpa died, I found out I was pregnant with my fourth child. I gave our daughter his name "Linzy" for her own middle name. Whenever I see my daughter and remember my grandpa, I am reminded yet again that God gives life in the midst of death and hope even in the throes of despair.

Saying good-bye is never easy. Saying good-bye twice hurts even worse. I'm so thankful that the next time I see Grandpa, I will be able to say hello, not fearing even the thought of having to say good-bye a third time . . . or ever again.

Read John 14:1-4

"Don't let this throw you. You trust God, don't you? Trust me. There is plenty of room for you in my Father's home. If that weren't so, would I have told you that I'm on my way to get a room ready for you? And if I'm on my way to get your room ready, I'll come back and get you so you can live where I live. And you already know the road I'm taking." (vv. 1–4)

Read Revelation 21:1–5

Everything New

I saw Heaven and earth new-created. Gone the first Heaven, gone the first earth, gone the sea. I saw Holy Jerusalem, new-created, descending resplendent out of Heaven, as ready for God as a bride for her husband. I heard a voice thunder from the Throne: "Look! Look! God has moved into the neighborhood, making his home with men and women! They're his people, he's their God. He'll wipe every tear from their eyes. Death is gone for good—tears gone, crying gone, pain gone—all the first order of things gone." The Enthroned continued, "Look! I'm making everything new. Write it all down—each word dependable and accurate." (vv. 1–5)

Questions

1. Whom have you said good-bye to because of death and what helped you as you grieved?

2. Describe what you know about heaven. Refer to John 14:1–3; Revelation 21:1–4.

3. What happens if people don't allow themselves time to grieve?

4. Read through Psalm 23. What is in this passage that makes it such a comfort for those who are grieving?

5. What is your favorite aspect of heaven and why?

Action

Write out a "remember when" story to send to a family member or friend who will enjoy reading about a deceased loved one you both knew. Ask them to send you one of their stories.

Prayer

I do miss my grandpa, Lord.

Thank you that he came to know you before he passed away and that now he is with you.

Thank you that I will see him again one day and for the hope that your word gives about eternal life.

I could never have eternal life without the sacrifice that Jesus made for me.

Thank you for the gift of eternal life and that one day all of your children will be with you for eternity. Amen.

Chapter 33
Thoughts About Underwear, Police and Uncertainty

The first time my husband and a co-worker were asked to go in for police questioning, they had an appointment at 9:00 p.m. As I walked him to the door, one would think that I (being a cross-cultural worker) would think of something edifying or spiritual to say. What did I say to him as he left me? "Do you think you should wear an extra pair of underwear in case you don't come back for a while?"

As the hours passed by, I waited and prayed. I watched television and prayed. I walked through our apartment and prayed, looking out the window in case I saw his car pull up on the street.

At around midnight, I thought this was it. How could I tell our children that their dad was in jail? "Kids, what do your dad, the Apostle Paul and Silas have in common?" No, that wouldn't be good. "I suppose you are wondering where your dad is . . ." What could I say? What would I do? Who would help me pack up our flat?

At 12:45 am, I heard the key turn in the lock. He was home! I ran to the door and began bombarding him with questions. "What did your interrogator ask?" "Was he nice?" "What did you say?" "How did it go?" "What do we do?" As he answered my questions wearily, he finally told me that I was asking more questions than the police did! I gave him a rest.

My self-control was admirable. I didn't cried at all until we went to bed. When my husband hugged me and told me that he was glad he was spending the night with me and not with his co-worker in a cell, I wept, soaking his tee shirt.

Don has been questioned several times since then. Each time we initially felt fear and uncertainty, yet each time our trust in God grew as we watched him provide for us and protect us.

My husband was called in again. I must have been getting more used to it, as I didn't even think to suggest an extra pair of underwear! However, this time they told him that his work permit would not be renewed. We have two months to leave our home of eight years. It is time to leave our co-workers, our national friends, our vision of serving Christ in the Middle East that had been ours for eleven years.

As we pack up, we must again sort through all that we possess to decide what to keep, sell, or give away. As we face the uncertainty of the future, we are certain in whom we trust. Psalm 27:13 and 14 are especially meaningful during this time:

> I would have despaired unless I had believed that I would
> see the goodness of the LORD
> In the land of the living.
> Wait for the LORD;
> Be strong and let your heart take courage;
> Yes, wait for the LORD. (NASB)

He is still protecting us and providing for us, and now he is pointing us in a new direction. This time I can pack the extra underwear in a suitcase!

Read Psalm 27
A David Psalm
Light, space, zest— that's GOD!
So, with him on my side I'm fearless,
afraid of no one and nothing. (v. 1)

When vandal hordes ride down
ready to eat me alive,
Those bullies and toughs
fall flat on their faces. (v. 2)

When besieged,
I'm calm as a baby.
When all hell breaks loose,
I'm collected and cool. (v. 3)

I'm asking GOD for one thing,
only one thing:
To live with him in his house
my whole life long.
I'll contemplate his beauty;
I'll study at his feet. (v. 4)

That's the only quiet, secure place
in a noisy world,
The perfect getaway,
far from the buzz of traffic. (v. 5)

God holds me head and shoulders
above all who try to pull me down.
I'm headed for his place to offer anthems
that will raise the roof!
Already I'm singing God-songs;
I'm making music to GOD. (v. 6)

Listen, GOD, I'm calling at the top of my lungs:
"Be good to me! Answer me!"
When my heart whispered, "Seek God,"
my whole being replied,
"I'm seeking him!"
Don't hide from me now! (vv. 7–8)

You've always been right there for me;
don't turn your back on me now.
Don't throw me out, don't abandon me;
you've always kept the door open.
My father and mother walked out and left me,
but God took me in. (vv. 9–10)

Point me down your highway, GOD;
direct me along a well-lighted street;
show my enemies whose side you're on.
Don't throw me to the dogs,
those liars who are out to get me,
filling the air with their threats. (vv. 11–12)

I'm sure now I'll see God's goodness
in the exuberant earth.
Stay with GOD!
Take heart. Don't quit.

I'll say it again:
Stay with GOD. (vv. 13–14)

Questions

1.   Of what are you most afraid in your new country?

2.   List the reasons you are afraid.

3.   Verbally give each reason to God and explain to
       him why you are afraid.

4.   List some characteristics of God that you know
       and describe how these qualities affect his actions.
       Meditate on who God is and what he is like.

5.   Why can you choose to trust him?

Action
Read Psalm 27 aloud. Rewrite verses 13–14 in your own
words and share them with a friend.

Prayer
You are worthy of my life and my service.
I thank you that you are with me and knowing that I really
have nothing to fear.
But sometimes I am weak.
You know my frailty.
You do not despise me for that,
but you gladly offer your help and strength to me.
With you I never need give in to despair.
You are my hope and I look to you. Amen.

Chapter 34
Jesus Is Always Undisturbed

The day before my thirty-seventh birthday, I found myself in the emergency room of a hospital. My right leg and arm felt numb. My head hurt. I couldn't eat or sleep. It was about five in the morning and, as I lay there, I wondered if I would ever see Don again. What would I wear to my funeral? Who might marry Don and how long would he wait? Who would come to my funeral? What would they say? Am I going crazy? Will I live? I found that I was wringing my hands and feeling extremely disturbed. I was scared. I was alone. I was sick and did not know with what or why.

Suddenly a thought crept into my mind—Jesus is totally undisturbed about this. He has known before the beginning of time that I would be here. He is not taken by surprise by this illness. He is here. Peace came into my heart as I remembered my quiet time from the previous morning. In *My Utmost for His Highest*, Oswald Chambers wrote, "'My peace I give unto you'—it is a peace which comes from looking into His face and realizing His undisturbedness." I knew then that God was there. He was very much in control, aware of what I was feeling and what was wrong with me. My pain didn't go away. My arm and leg still felt numb. But I knew I was not a lone victim of some awful unknown disease. God knew me and the illness. He wasn't disturbed by it at all.

As I left the hospital and underwent six more months of tests, probes, pricks, and endless speculation by doctors and friends, this thought remained with me: I knew Someone knew what my illness was! My energy failed. My appetite left. My body felt old and useless. As I prayed for healing and as others prayed as well, I had an abiding peace that God was with me and at work in me. I claimed and reviewed the promises in Scripture. God was using this for my good. God would give me all that I needed. However, I also searched for a memory verse that I could claim as my own when I became discouraged.

When I felt fearful and sicker than I had ever been before, I found Micah 7:7–8, "But as for me, I will watch expectantly for the Lord; I will wait for the God of my salvation. My God will hear me. Do not rejoice over me, O my enemy. Though I fall, I will rise; though I dwell in darkness, the Lord is a light for me." (NASB) Though circumstances seemed disturbing, I knew the One who is never disturbed. I could wait for him.

Slowly my strength returned. My appetite came back. I find that each day is brighter, each activity a blessing. Each moment of life is a gift from God. I know that whatever comes my way today, God has been there before and he is totally undisturbed.

Read Micah 7:7–8

But me, I'm not giving up.
I'm sticking around to see what God will do.
I'm waiting for God to make things right.
I'm counting on God to listen to me. (v. 7)

Spreading Your Wings

Don't, enemy, crow over me.
I'm down, but I'm not out.
I'm sitting in the dark right now,
but God is my light. (v. 8)

Questions

1.   As you live in your new country, what do you feel unsettled about today?

2.   What has surprised you recently that you know didn't surprise God?

3.   Memorize Micah 7:7–8.

4.   What does it mean to be undisturbed?

5.   Find three other verses that talk about waiting for the Lord. List them here with a summary of each verse.

Action
Remember He remains undisturbed. Pray and commit yourself to trusting the Lord, even when you are unsure what is going to happen.

Prayer
What would it be like to never be disturbed?
It is hard to imagine.
You know all things; you know the end from the beginning.
You are in control of every situation and you have no reason to fear.
Thank you for being who you are.
Thank you, too, for working out what is best for me in your perfect timing.
I do not need to give into despair.
You remain totally undisturbed. Amen.

Chapter 35
Barb's Legacy

How do you say a final good-bye to your spiritual mentor? Recently the lady who taught me in junior high vacation Bible school, church youth group, throughout young adulthood and into middle age went home to be with the Lord. After having Barb Hess as a constant in my life for almost thirty years, it was time to let her go. Yet her influence in my life, and ultimately in whomever my life touches, will continue for generations to come.

I tried to explain to my two daughters how important Barb was to me. In reality I had only spent six years in regular contact with her; her other 24 years of input were through occasional visits and letters. How could one woman have had such influence on me and on others around her? What is her legacy to me?

Barb was a woman in the Word and of the Word. She lived what she taught. She wasn't perfect, but she strived to live out what she believed. I saw her reading, teaching and living the Scriptures she loved. When I came to her as a teenager with problems, she led me to the Word. When I came to her as an adult facing difficulties, she led me yet again to the Holy Bible. Now when I encounter hardship, it is my natural reaction to turn to the Word of God for help. This is Barb's legacy to me.

Barb was a woman who loved others. She made time for me. I could call her, go out to lunch with her or just chat after church. We always seemed to be able to pick up where we left off and move quickly beyond surface issues. She was sincerely interested in me, wanting to know what I was learning, how I was doing and in what ministries I was involved. She prayed for me and let me know she was behind me, supporting me as I lived out my life before God. As I sat at her funeral, I saw other women who felt exactly the same way that I did.

Barb loved others because she knew and experienced the love of God herself. She had come to know Christ as her Savior. Her life centered on this unconditional love he had for her. When she would face difficulties, she did not doubt his love for her. She gave this love away freely to others. This is another aspect of Barb's legacy to me.

Her legacy to me will never end. The way her life touched mine is now touching others she will never have the opportunity to meet! As I come into contact with other women, this is my desire, "Lord, make me a Barb Hess to them." I want to be a woman in the Word and of the Word. When others come to me, I want to lead them to the Scriptures. I want to experience the love of God daily so that my love for others will be fresh and radiant, drawing them to a closer walk with him.

As I met with Barb's husband by her casket, he held me and called me "one of her adopted daughters." What an honor! What a calling! What a legacy!

How did I say good-bye to Barb? I didn't. It was more of a "see ya later." I know that I will see her again. I know, too, that as I put into practice all that I learned from her, her legacy lives on. I will do all I can to be a "Barb Hess" to my own daughters as well as to any adopted ones I can find along the way!

Read Titus 2:3–5

Guide older women into lives of reverence so they end up as neither gossips nor drunks, but models of goodness. By looking at them, the younger women will know how to love their husbands and children, be virtuous and pure, keep a good house, be good wives. We don't want anyone looking down on God's Message because of their behavior. (vv. 3–5)

Questions

1.   What are the challenges of cross-cultural mentoring?

2.   Look around you. Are there national women who could mentor you and whom you could mentor?

3.   What qualities are good for a mentoree?

4.   Write out how God has used the Word in your life recently.

5.   What guidelines does Titus 2:3–5 give for women mentors?

Action
Ask someone you admire to be a mentor to you in a specific area of need.

Prayer
Thank you for putting mentors into my life.
I would like to pour out my life into others and mentor them.
Please work in my life so that I would be a godly mentor,
a person who would influence others for your sake.
May I be a Titus 2 woman. Amen.

Chapter 36
An M Is Better When
Followed by "& M"!

I love to plan things—retreats, conferences, other people's lives. I like making lists and crossing things off as I accomplish them. If I do something that is not on my list, I simply add it to my list and then cross it off. I get so much more done that way. The first women's retreat I planned went really well. The speaker was good, the schedule went smoothly, women seemed to enjoy themselves; but it was a lot of work. I needed more help!

When it came time for the next retreat, I asked several ladies to help me plan. It was amazing how much they added. One lady suggested, "Let's put chocolates on everyone's pillows." I liked that idea and can't believe I hadn't thought of it before! Another lady wanted to put up some decorations so the place would look nicer and create a warmer atmosphere. This had never even occurred to me. There were much better ideas for worship time, prayer time, fellowship time, and food preparation. How much the ladies at that first retreat had missed, simply because there weren't as many people to help in the planning and to use their gifts and talents to create a more effective retreat. It was hard work to deal with more people, to work through issues and to make plans, but the end result was absolutely worth every meeting together!

I also love to teach. When teaching alone, it was easy to make up a lesson plan, think through how to present the truths I wanted to share and go for it. Students seemed to enjoy these lessons and all went smoothly. After I was married, Don and I began team teaching. We each had to give a little and take a little as we prepared to teach together. Now, after years, it still takes work to put our thoughts together into one lesson plan. It would be easier to teach alone, but much less effective. He has valuable insight, creative means and an amazing ability to put my long, wordy sentences into a few meaningful terms.

Whenever it comes to planning, teaching, or working, it would appear easier to go it alone. I have been to committee meetings where there has been conflict and agony over issues that would disappear so quickly if everyone would just see the light and agree with me! But there is something in the give and take, the sharing of ideas that spurs us on to even greater effectiveness as we work through issues together. I used to think that an absence of conflict showed unity. However, it is how we deal with conflict, how we show love and honor to one another, how we listen to the ideas presented, compromise, adjust and come together through the conflicts that not only results in a better outcome, but also deepens relationships. This process produces real, solid unity.

When Don and I are not irritated, we thoroughly enjoy how we complement each other in our marriage. Don loves to have fun, but his philosophy of life is, "Work now, play later." My philosophy tends to be the opposite, "Play now, work later (if you have to)." This has caused sparks to fly at times, and yet I know that I get more done because of him than I ever would without him. I think, too, that he has more fun because of me. We balance each other and work well together as we coordinate our differing views into our strategy for living.

When we sent our first son off to college, at almost the same time as I was saying, "Have fun," Don was saying, "Be good." We are partners and we each give our children two facets of living life. How sad it would be if they only got one viewpoint! How fun for our kids to see how we work together from two totally different outlooks and have so much joy, even through our struggles, in the process of living.

Don and I are partners in life, partners in ministry. Overseas, our team members were our partners in serving the Lord, members of the same body. Our sending center coworkers share their skills, talents and insights with us and others. Our labor together enhances our work and strengthens our relationships.

Where would the Lone Ranger be without Tonto, Lucy without Ethel, and Batman without Robin? Where would M be without the "& M"? What would a cookie be without chocolate chips? What's a bath without the bubbles? Who are the "we" without you *and* me?

We need each other. Let's have fun *and* work hard together. We are partners!

Read 1 Corinthians 12:12–26

You can easily enough see how this kind of thing works by looking no further than your own body. Your body has many parts—limbs, organs, cells—but no matter how many parts you can name, you're still one body. It's exactly the same with Christ. By means of his one Spirit, we all said good-bye to our partial and piecemeal lives. We each used to independently call our own shots, but then we entered into a large and integrated life in which he has the final say in everything. (This is what we proclaimed in word and action when we were baptized.) Each of us is now a part of his resurrection body, refreshed and sustained at one fountain—his Spirit—where we all come to drink. The old labels we once used to identify ourselves—labels like Jew or Greek, slave or free—are no longer useful. We need something larger, more comprehensive. (vv. 12–13)

I want you to think about how all this makes you more significant, not less. A body isn't just a single part blown up into something huge. It's all the different-but-similar parts arranged and functioning together. If Foot said, "I'm not elegant like Hand, embellished with rings; I guess I don't belong to this body," would that make it so? If Ear said, "I'm not beautiful like Eye, limpid and expressive; I don't deserve a place on the head," would you want to remove it from the body? If the body was all eye, how could it hear? If all ear, how could it smell? As it is, we see that God has carefully placed each part of the body right where he wanted it. (vv. 14–18)

But I also want you to think about how this keeps your significance from getting blown up into self-importance. For no matter how significant you are, it is only because of what you are a part of. An enormous eye or a gigantic hand wouldn't be a body, but a monster. What we have is one body with many parts, each its proper size and in its proper place. No part is important on its own. Can you imagine Eye telling Hand, "Get lost; I don't need you"? Or, Head telling Foot, "You're fired; your job has been phased out"? As a matter of fact, in practice it works the other way—the "lower" the part, the more basic, and therefore necessary. You can live without an eye, for instance, but not without a stomach. When it's a part of your own body you are concerned with, it makes no difference whether the part is visible or clothed, higher or lower. You give it dignity and honor just as it is, without comparisons. If anything, you have more concern for the lower parts than the higher. If you had to choose, wouldn't you prefer good digestion to full-bodied hair? (vv. 19–24)

The way God designed our bodies is a model for understanding our lives together as a church: every part dependent on every other part, the parts we mention and the parts we don't, the parts we see and the parts we don't. If one part hurts, every other part is involved in the hurt, and in the healing. If one part flourishes, every other part enters into the exuberance. (vv. 25–26)

Questions

    1.   List two of your strengths and how you have used them in your present ministry.

2.   List two of your weaknesses.

3.   Think of a teammate/friend that is strong in an area where you are weak. Describe how you have worked well together.

4.   Read I Corinthians 12:11. Who decides which spiritual gift(s) you receive?

5.   How does 1 Corinthians 12:12–27 highlight the importance of each member of the body?

Action

Write a thank you note to a team member, encouraging her to continue to use her gifts and let her know how she has helped you.

Prayer

With gratitude in my heart Lord,
I praise you for placing me in your body.
I know you have gifted me.
Forgive me when I am jealous of another person's gift or when I wish that I had a different gift and am not content with what you have given me.
May we all work together as one under your headship so that others will know our love and unity is only because of you and your work in us and through us. Amen.

Chapter 37
Of Headaches and Hospitality

Hospitality headaches can strike again . . . and again!

An hour before twenty women are coming over for tea and cookies, there is no water.

The stove runs out of gas in the middle of baking a cake for guests coming that night.

Halfway through lunch with fellow team members in my home, I realize I left the tuna out of the tuna noodle casserole.

A bachelor comes to eat dinner with us. I sample a bite and decide that it isn't too bad. I serve it along with several other dishes. After he takes his first bite, he asks for salt. I bring the salt and pepper (I wanted to be prepared) and as he salts his food, he suggests that it is often wise to taste the food before serving it to guests.

My husband laughed, and groaned at the same time, when I bought knives, forks and spoons that didn't match. I knew we needed eating utensils and I didn't have a lot of time so I bought what was available. I try to make the table look pretty, but I'm secretly satisfied just to have the food finally ready and on the table so we can eat.

What's funny to me is that according to one test, hospitality may be one of my spiritual gifts! How can this be? What is hospitality? Is it having everything perfect in our homes? Is it never burning the food or never forgetting the main ingredient in a dish? Is it the ability to set a charming table?

How could hospitality be one of my gifts if I fail at so many of these things?

Hospitality is the practice of making others feel at home. It isn't a contest to see who sets the prettiest table or who cooks the best food. You don't have to be a Martha Stewart. When you joyfully receive guests and make them feel welcome and important to you, you have practiced hospitality.

What makes you feel welcome in someone's home? It makes me feel welcome when I am in a home and the hostess's focus isn't on her performance or what she is serving, but rather on me! It's nice when things are pretty and everything is prepared when I arrive and we begin our visit. It's also fine when my friend needs help. We get to chat in the kitchen while we cut tomatoes or chop onions.

It is the visiting, the chatting that is key. Everything else simply enhances this key ingredient to hospitality.

In each of my hospitality headaches, the world didn't come to an end. I explained what happened and we laughed together. I apologized for the inconvenience, and then did my best to make my guests feel comfortable. Old friends and I still laugh about the tuna-less tuna casserole. I would laugh with our bachelor friend about the salt, but he never came back.

Read 2 Kings 4:8–10

One day Elisha passed through Shunem. A leading lady of the town talked him into stopping for a meal. And then it became his custom: Whenever he passed through, he stopped by for a meal. (v. 8)

"I'm certain," said the woman to her husband, "that this man who stops by with us all the time is a holy man of God. Why don't we add on a small room upstairs and furnish it with a bed and desk, chair and lamp, so that when he comes by he can stay with us?" (v. 9–10)

Questions

1.   What do you enjoy about being hospitable?

2.   What is the hardest thing about being hospitable in a different culture?

3.   Describe a time when someone was hospitable to you and you were blessed.

4.   Brainstorm with your family for a strategy to help make hospitality less stressful for you.

5.   How did the Shunamite woman show hospitality in 2 Kings 4:8–10? What can you learn about hospitality from her?

Action
Invite friends over for a potluck dinner. Enjoy their company. Let them help clean up afterwards. Relax. Accept help. Don't worry about being judged.

Prayer

My desire is for my home to be a haven for friends.
May it be an oasis in the desert for those needing rest.
Help me be less concerned about how it looks and how I may
be judged, and more concerned for the welfare of the souls of
those who enter. Amen.

Chapter 38

The Totaled Woman's Rest in His Everlasting Arms

When I was first married, I read a book called, *The Total Woman*. It talked about how to keep the romance alive in your marriage. After the birth of our fourth child, I was ready to write a book entitled *The Totaled Woman*. Having children made a big difference!

In motherhood, I can find moments of delight and moments of disaster. I loved hearing my children's first words, seeing their first tooth, helping them with their first steps. I also remember the awful physical tiredness. Getting enough sleep at night was almost impossible. Getting up often to feed, change or comfort babies and small children was draining. Refereeing fights during the day, keeping up with laundry, housework and meals kept me on my toes. I loved the little fistfuls of flowers and the homemade cards. I loved the hugs and kisses and the statements like, "Mommy, you have a nice nose," but other things that the kids said weren't so much fun. For example, my sister says the worst three-and-a-half words in the English language are uttered in the middle of the night, "Mom, I feel sic—." I hated it when the kids were sick and would rather have been sick myself.

Often a mother is outnumbered. She must learn to do many things at once. I remember nursing a baby, going to the bathroom and taking laundry out of the machine all at the same time! I also remember playing hide-and-seek with the kids just so I could hide behind a file cabinet for a few minutes' break!

A mom can usually spend only a little time on herself. She is constantly thinking of others. How can I meet my kids' needs? How can I meet my husband's needs? Am I doing the right thing? Am I disciplining too much or too little, expecting too much or too little? The list of all a mother must think about is endless. It is an overwhelming job filled with moments of delight and disaster. When the delight is present, we feel confident and really enjoy our roles. However, what happens during moments of disaster?

Deuteronomy 33:27 says, "The eternal God is a dwelling place and underneath are the everlasting arms." (NASB) A mother is a refuge for her children. However, a mother needs a refuge as well. She needs the support of those everlasting arms. When a child is sick, we can go to that refuge. When we are dealing with discipline problems and appear to be failing, those arms are waiting for us. When we are so tired, we don't know how we will get through the day, the everlasting arms are there to hold us up. Our Father's arms are trustworthy and sure. We can rest in his arms, knowing that he loves our children and will provide all they need. He will also provide all we need as mothers.

Mothers usually come to the place where they feel they are stretched beyond endurance. Living far away from home in a different culture magnifies it even more. Not long ago I came to a point as a mother when I honestly felt that I was the wrong person for the job. Surely, my kids would be better off without me. They needed someone who knew what she was doing! Why were there so many unknowns, so many pressures, and struggles in raising children?

God brought me through this experience, showing me that he does not make mistakes. I was the mother he wanted for my children! No one else could mother my children like me. Still, I was not able to do it on my own. I needed help. So I turned to those everlasting arms and found them—warm and snug, strong and true, ever present and everlasting—just for me. I discovered a dwelling place and a support that will see me through every moment of disaster and delight.

Read Deuteronomy 33:26–29

There is none like God, Jeshurun,
riding to your rescue through the skies,
his dignity haloed by clouds.
The ancient God is home
on a foundation of everlasting arms.
He drove out the enemy before you
and commanded, "Destroy!"
Israel lived securely,
the fountain of Jacob undisturbed
In grain and wine country
and, oh yes, his heavens drip dew. (vv. 26–28)

Lucky Israel! Who has it as good as you?
A people *saved* by GOD!
The Shield who defends you,
the Sword who brings triumph.
Your enemies will come crawling on their bellies
and you'll march on their backs. (v. 29)

Questions

1. Write a special memory from each of your children.

2. What extra stresses are you experiencing as a mother because of living overseas?

3. What does it mean to be held up by everlasting arms? to know God is with you as your parent?

4.   What has surprised you most about being a
      parent?

5.   Describe a time when you relied on those
      everlasting arms and found them ready for you.

Action
Pray quickly and silently for each child in your family. Now,
take a nap. You need a break!

Prayer
I want to be a good mother.
Please help me.
Thank you for being my refuge and dwelling place.
May my children see your faithfulness through me as I rest in
you. Amen.

Chapter 39
A Daughter's Tears

I knew something was wrong the minute my daughter got into our van. What was my first clue? She was sobbing. Soon I had tears in my eyes, also, as I held her and she told me how some girls at school had started a rumor that she was gay.

I comforted her and told her everything would be okay. As we started for home, I began thinking about how these little "twits" had hurt my daughter. How could anyone be so cruel as to start such a rumor about my daughter? It was her first year in a new school in a new city! She needed support, not discomfiture.

The more my mother's heart dwelt on her pain, the angrier I got. How dare anyone hurt her with such cruel intent. I confess to you that my response was not godly (I did mention God's name, not in a good way, but in connection with what I wanted him to do to those little girls!)

We went upstairs to her bedroom, got out her Bible, and read from Matthew 5: "But I say to you, love your enemies, and pray for those who persecute you in order that you may be sons of your Father who is in heaven; for he causes his sun to rise on the evil and the good and sends rain on the righteous and the unrighteous." (NASB)

We talked about (and felt) anger, hurt, and betrayal . . . and then went on to talk about what our response should be to these girls, because of who we are in Christ. I prayed, telling God of my anger and then asking him to bless these little girls and to help them come to know him. I asked him to give my daughter grace and strength to handle whatever would happen. I verbally thanked him for allowing this into her life and asked him to use it to make her and I more like him. We dried our tears and I left her in her room.

My heart was forgiving these girls by faith, but my feelings just weren't there. As I would drive past their house, my first reaction was tightness in my throat and a desire for revenge. I confessed this to God and reaffirmed my heartfelt desire for God to bless these girls instead of cursing them. This was what I chose to truly want because I knew it was the right response.

Forgiveness is pivotal to my own spiritual growth. If I were to harbor ungodly thoughts and desire for revenge in my heart, it would not bother my "enemies" in the least. They would probably never even know about it. However, it would bother me and cramp my spiritual life.

I can remember unkind things I did as a child. I laughed at a girl who wet her pants and ignored a young lady because of her acne. I know of unkind things I do and say as an adult. I have stuck out my tongue at my husband behind his back (how adult!). Though I pride myself on keeping secrets, I have accidentally let a confidence slip. I have been hurt and I have hurt others.

How thankful I am that God forgives me. I am deeply appreciative that my husband still loves me even when I do something childish. My heart fills with gratitude that my friends whom I have hurt pardon me. How absurd it would be for me to hold grudges when I have been forgiven so richly!

I cannot control the way people treat my family or me. I can control my response to them. May I be gracious, forgiving and compassionate like my Father. May my daughter grow up knowing her mother feels pain when hurt, and yet can forgive because of who her Father is.

The day after the rumor started, my daughter found out who had started the rumor and it didn't seem to matter to her anymore. The kids at school soon found other things to talk about. She was fine after just one day. I struggled for weeks. It almost makes me mad at her for getting over it all so quickly, but I forgive her!

Read Luke 7:36–50; Luke 23:33–34

One of the Pharisees asked him over for a meal. He went to the Pharisee's house and sat down at the dinner table. Just then a woman of the village, the town harlot, having learned that Jesus was a guest in the home of the Pharisee, came with a bottle of very expensive perfume and stood at his feet, weeping, raining tears on his feet. Letting down her hair, she dried his feet, kissed them, and anointed them with the perfume. When the Pharisee who had invited him saw this, he said to himself, "If this man was the prophet I thought he was, he would have known what kind of woman this is who is falling all over him." (vv. 36–39)

Jesus said to him, "Simon, I have something to tell you." "Oh? Tell me." (v. 40)

"Two men were in debt to a banker. One owed five hundred silver pieces, the other fifty. Neither of them could pay up, and so the banker canceled both debts. Which of the two would be more grateful?" (vv. 41–42)

Simon answered, "I suppose the one who was forgiven the most." "That's right," said Jesus. Then turning to the woman, but speaking to Simon, he said, "Do you see this woman? I came to your home; you provided no water for my feet, but she rained tears on my feet and dried them with her hair. You gave me no greeting, but from the time I arrived she hasn't quit kissing my feet. You provided nothing for freshening up, but she has soothed my feet with perfume. Impressive, isn't it? She was forgiven many, many sins, and so she is very, very grateful. If the forgiveness is minimal, the gratitude is minimal." (vv. 43–47)

Then he spoke to her: "I forgive your sins." (v. 48)

That set the dinner guests talking behind his back: "Who does he think he is, forgiving sins!" (v. 49)

He ignored them and said to the woman, "Your faith has saved you. Go in peace." (v. 50)

Luke 23:33-34

When they got to the place called Skull Hill, they crucified him, along with the criminals, one on his right, the other on his left.

Jesus prayed, "Father, forgive them; they don't know what they're doing."

Questions

1. As you examine your team and family relationships, who do you need to forgive?

2. How did Jesus teach us to forgive and why is forgiveness essential?

3. How do you see forgiveness practiced in your new culture?

4. What are the consequences to you and your ministry if you choose not to forgive?

5.   What do you learn about forgiveness from the story in Luke 7?

Action
By faith, verbally tell God who has hurt you and why you hurt. Then tell him that you forgive the person(s) who hurt you.

Prayer
Grudges feel so good some times.
They compel me to feel worthy, and that I am in the right.
I feel like I am hurting the other person, while in reality I am really hurting myself.
Thank you for forgiving me.
I remember ways I have sinned against you and hurt you.
Yet, you have forgiven me.
What would I do or where would I be without that forgiveness?
O God, make me a channel of that forgiveness.
May I not be like the man who was forgiven much yet forgave little.
Make me like you. Amen.

Chapter 40
Becoming a Mother-in-law

For over twenty years, I have been praying for my oldest son's future spouse. I prayed for her spiritual growth and development. I prayed for my son and his future spouse that, as a married couple, God would protect them from immorality and unfaithfulness. Sometimes I prayed for her parents and their role in preparing her to become a wife for my son and a mother to my grandbabies. I could not picture her. I did not know her name. For years, she has been known simply as "future spouse."

After a phone call from my son announcing his engagement, I was able to cross off "future spouse" and write in "Emily." When I prayed, I could now see her face and know her name, her character, her family, and her wedding date. My oldest son was getting married. I was going to become a mother-in-law.

This is not a role I take lightly. I have been involved in her life, albeit unknowingly, for a long time. I certainly don't want to hurt her or our relationship, now that I finally have met her! To help me prepare for my new role, I have been asking women my age and older what the secret is to being a good mother-in-law. There are different responses—pray for them, listen well to them, learn to let go, watch the comedy, "Everybody Loves Raymond," and do totally the opposite of his mother! But there is one point that almost every woman has mentioned and agreed on: "Keep your mouth shut." One woman pointed out that even if you are asked for advice, be careful what you say and how you say it.

If I had one goal, it would be that I would be like a second mom to her—a good one who listens, supports, encourages and prays; not one who interferes, takes sides or forces her husband to choose between me and her.

I want to be a good mother-in-law, but I am also beginning to recognize that my role as a mother to my son will also change as I become an in-law to his wife. My son and his wife are going to establish their own home, their own family, and their own traditions. They will take care of each other. My son is going to be a husband and his first responsibility will be to his wife, not to his dad, to his siblings or to me.

I sometimes have the hardest time remembering that he is a mature man now. He is not the same little boy who would run around in his footed pajamas with a superman cape fighting invisible enemies. Throughout his life, I have done my best to prepare him for the role of a good husband. I haven't been an ideal housekeeper, so he will be impressed if his wife makes the bed! I sometimes burn the meals, so her cooking will be superb. His job in our family has been to take out the trash—she'll love that he will do it without thinking.

What more could a woman ask for?

It was exciting to meet the woman for whom I have been praying for so long. As this young couple prepares for their marriage, I am going to put into practice what I have been learning about "mother-in-law-hood." I will seek to be their number one fan, their prayer warrior, their mother who loves them both. After they are husband and wife, I will probably breathe a huge sigh of relief as the wedding day draws to a close. I will hang my new dress in the closet and find a new candidate to take out the trash at our home. My role of mother, in some ways decreasing and in some ways expanding, is exciting. I look forward to how God will work in and through this new couple. But wait! A new role may be calling out to me in the future. I must begin preparing for this and start praying again for those whom I have not yet met—my future grandbabies. Can't you picture it? Little pajama clad feet running through the house and jumping into my arms yelling, "Granny!"

Read the following verse from the hymn, "A Christian Home":

O give us homes with godly fathers, mothers,
Who always place their hope and trust in Him;
Whose tender patience turmoil never bothers,
Whose calm and courage trouble cannot dim;
A home where each finds joy in serving others,
And love still shines tho days be dark and grim.

Barbara B. Hart and Jean Sibelius. <u>Praise! Our Songs and Hymns</u>, compiled by John W. Peterson, Norman Johnson, edited by Norman Johnson. Grand Rapids, MI Zondervan, 1979

Questions

1. What have you appreciated about your mother-in-law?

2. What has made it difficult for you to have a good relationship with your mother-in-law?

3. Have you been praying for the spouses of your children? If not, will you begin regularly remembering to bring this need to the Lord?

4. What would you do if you did not like the person your child was dating or engaged to?

5. How can you build an even stronger relationship with your in-laws while living far from them?

Action

Play a game with your children. When it is finished hug and/or kiss your children and thank them for playing.

Prayer

Lord, you know my children's future.

I ask that you would provide for each of my children a godly spouse.

Help me to be a godly mother and a loving mother-in-law who looks to you and is a support to my children and their friends. Amen.

Chapter 41

Who Will Pack My Computer?

Several workers had been asked to leave our host country or were denied entry to the country on their way back from a trip. This left their spouses to sort, pack and help the children deal with a quick, unplanned exit from their home. Now Don and a coworker had been asked to report to the police station at 9:00 in the evening. Police had been to the coworker's home. Another coworker was in jail. As I waited for Don to come home, I began thinking of all that I would have to do if he had to leave the country quickly.

I would have to pack—I could do that. I would tell the kids—I had practiced how to do that. I would have to see that all of our luggage would get to the airport and on to the plane. I could see no problem doing that. The issue for me was, who would pack the computer? I could pack clothes, toys, and house wares with no problem. But how in the world was I going to get the computer back into the box so that it would not break in transit? I had plenty of time to think about it as Don did not get home until almost 1:00 in the morning. However, the issue remained. I knew my limitations and I was convinced I couldn't get the computer back into its box.

As Don came home and two more interviews followed, by God's grace I felt positive, though uncertain, about everything. I was nervous, but I felt a peace about it all, except the computer. Why was I obsessing about the computer? I don't know. I don't remember if it was new, if we had a hard time getting it out of the box or if I had some traumatic experience involving a box when I was a child that was coming back to haunt me! But I just knew I could not handle packing the computer.

As people asked me how I was doing, I would say fine. If they pursued the subject with me, I would proceed to tell them about the computer and how impossible it would be to pack. Finally, a man (a worker from a different agency who I only saw once a week at the most) simply looked at me and said, "Sue, I will be happy to come over, if needed, and I can pack up your computer for you." I cannot tell you what a load that lifted from me. God used that one simple sentence spoken by a friend to assure me that we would be alright.

We didn't have to leave at that point in time. John didn't have to pack our computer. But I knew that God was going to take care of us and our computer, because He sent John, who offered to pack it for us.

"Tumor, suspicious mass, probably malignant, surgery, blood work, chest x-ray to see if it has spread." These were the words I heard coming from Don's mouth as he reported to me what the doctor said. I was certain that these words belonged somewhere else; this vocabulary should be foreign to our conversation, to our family; but there was no mistake. As I left that conversation, I began to wonder, what would the future hold? How would we tell our children? What would happen?

As we told friends about our situation, I heard them say: "Let me bring a meal over." "We'll be praying for you." "Let us know if there is anything you need." "I can come to the hospital and wait with you."

As I heard these words, felt their concern, and considered the future, my thoughts returned to the past. I remembered my question: who will pack the computer? The real packer was God—he simply used one of his children to be his hands. He sent John to say that he would do it. Now when I start thinking of what may happen and about things that I might not be able to handle, I know that God is the one who will take care of us. He is using his children to let me know that we are part of his body and that we aren't alone in this.

It is written, "I can do everything through him who gives me strength. Yet it was good of you to share in my troubles." (Phil 4:13–14, NIV) It is true that we can do everything with Christ's help. We don't necessarily need anybody else. It is also true that we can share in each other's troubles. We are all needed and important parts of his body. As I look at how God works and provides for us, I see these two truths. Sometimes God works alone and sometimes he uses his children to provide for us. I guess this leaves me with two questions:

Who will pack your computer?

Whose computer will you pack?

Note: After surgical removal of the tumor, it was found to be benign!

Read Philippians 4:10–20

I'm glad in God, far happier than you would ever guess—happy that you're again showing such strong concern for me. Not that you ever quit praying and thinking about me. You just had no chance to show it. Actually, I don't have a sense of needing anything personally. I've learned by now to be quite content whatever my circumstances. I'm just as happy with little as with much, with much as with little. I've found the recipe for being happy whether full or hungry, hands full or hands empty. Whatever I have, wherever I am, I can make it through anything in the One who makes me who I am. I don't mean that your help didn't mean a lot to me—it did. It was a beautiful thing that you came alongside me in my troubles. (vv. 10–14)

You Philippians well know, and you can be sure I'll never forget it, that when I first left Macedonia province, venturing out with the Message, not one church helped out in the give-and-take of this work except you. You were the only one. Even while I was in Thessalonica, you helped out—and not only once, but twice. Not that I'm looking for handouts, but I do want you to experience the blessing that issues from generosity. (vv. 15–17)

And now I have it all—and keep getting more! The gifts you sent with Epaphroditus were more than enough, like a sweet-smelling sacrifice roasting on the altar, filling the air with fragrance, pleasing God no end. You can be sure that God will take care of everything you need, his generosity exceeding even yours in the glory that pours from Jesus. Our God and Father abounds in glory that just pours out into eternity. Yes. (vv. 18–20)

Questions

1.   Describe a time in your new country when God met your need himself.

2.   Describe a time in your new country when God used people to meet a need that you had.

3.   What might be some reasons that God works in one way and not the other at different times?

4.   If there is one thing or person that intimidates you, what or who is it?

5.   Commit that thing or person to God and keep
        moving forward in ministry by faith.

Action
Choose one verse from Philippians 4:10–20 to memorize and
claim as your own.

Prayer
I can do all things through Christ.
Thank you for being sufficient for me.
Thank you, too for putting me in a body where we can share
our burdens, have our needs met and meet needs.
May I rely on you and in that reliance be available to others.
You have used others to help me. It is an amazing thing to
belong to you and each other as members of your body.
Amen.

Chapter 42
Time and a Changing Perspective

Yesterday

As I was growing up, I loved listening to a Gene Autry Christmas album during the holidays. After I was married, my cousin made a cassette tape of that album for me. It has been one of my treasured possessions. Just listening to Gene croon those songs brings back so many cherished family memories. When our children were little, I wanted them to have the pleasure of Gene's music as well, so I would play it for them during Christmas on my tape player. One day my small son, fascinated by all of the buttons on the tape player, pushed the record button. He interrupted Gene's singing of the reindeer song with a few mumbled words, then clearly "go" and "daddy." I was angry that he had ruined my tape.

During my children's early years, I gave up having a quiet time. If it was quiet, I would fall asleep. So I had a "loud time" when I would read my Bible and pray as the kids played or watched television. I remember having one of the kids in my lap as I read. She grabbed an ink pen and, after scribbling in Hebrews, she tore the top right hand corners off of the book of James.

I wanted to be a good mother to our children so I read books and listened to tapes on parenting. One afternoon I was preparing dinner in the kitchen and listening to a tape about motherhood. My children came into the kitchen clamoring for a snack. I couldn't hear the tape. I bellowed, "Would you be quiet? I am listening to a tape so I can be a good mother!"

Today

My favorite part of Gene's Christmas tape is listening to our son's voice. When it gets to the reindeer song, the whole family groans as I always turn up the volume so that I can hear my son's young voice say "Go! Daddy!" As I read through my Bible and come to the book of Hebrews and James, it is with special fondness that I recall those precious moments with my small daughter on my lap. I love it when my grown children come into the kitchen to chat with me. Their voices, not heard so often in the house anymore, sound better to me than any music or tape in the world.

With the passing of time, perspectives change! I watch tired mothers at the grocery store, yelling at their kids and wishing their kids were more mature. I listen as mothers talk about the busyness of diapers, dishes and parent-teacher conferences. They can't seem to wait for their kids to grow up and become more independent. It is regrettably common for worker moms to be anxious for their kids to grow up so they can be more involved in "real" service, as if serving in their home isn't real!

I want to say to young mothers what others tried to tell me in the past. Enjoy this time of your life and the lives of your children! You will look back with fondness on these days. Lay a foundation of joy. Take the time to build into your children as a primary ministry. Listen to them; have fun with them. It's fine if they mess up a tape and in the future you have the sound of their voice instead. It's okay if they doodle a bit in one of your books. Let them interrupt you in the kitchen. In time, they will be grown and you will miss their sticky kisses, pounding footsteps and marker drawings on the walls. Time will fly. All too soon, they will grow up. They will leave to make their own homes.

Hold them in your lap a little longer today—if they let you! Color in a coloring book or read a book with them. Build a Lego tower. Watch the clouds. Play hide and seek. Give kisses and hugs.

I still have opportunities to serve in my home with laundry to do, meals to serve and a house to clean. I still have opportunities to serve others outside of my home. However, I have no small children to hold in my lap, hug or play hide and seek with me.

Tomorrow

Tomorrow will take care of itself. I will not rush into it. I plan to enjoy interacting with my teenage girls and try to sneak a few minutes with my grown sons. I cannot change the past, giving more or less time to my children. I cannot know the future or what it holds for them or for me. Nevertheless, I can relish today and live it in light of what I've learned from the past, with a view to the eternal.

Read Matthew 6:25–34

"If you decide for God, living a life of God-worship, it follows that you don't fuss about what's on the table at mealtimes or whether the clothes in your closet are in fashion. There is far more to your life than the food you put in your stomach, more to your outer appearance than the clothes you hang on your body. Look at the birds, free and unfettered, not tied down to a job description, careless in the care of God. And you count far more to him than birds. (vv. 25–26)

"Has anyone by fussing in front of the mirror ever gotten taller by so much as an inch? All this time and money wasted on fashion—do you think it makes that much difference? Instead of looking at the fashions, walk out into the fields and look at the wildflowers. They never primp or shop, but have you ever seen color and design quite like it? The ten best-dressed men and women in the country look shabby alongside them. (vv. 27–29)

"If God gives such attention to the appearance of wildflowers—most of which are never even seen—don't you think he'll attend to you, take pride in you, do his best for you? What I'm trying to do here is to get you to relax, to not be so preoccupied with *getting,* so you can respond to God's *giving.* People who don't know God and the way he works fuss over these things, but you know both God and how he works. Steep your life in God-reality, God-initiative, God-provisions. Don't worry about missing out.

You'll find all your everyday human concerns will be met. (vv. 30–33)

"Give your entire attention to what God is doing right now, and don't get worked up about what may or may not happen tomorrow. God will help you deal with whatever hard things come up when the time comes. (v. 34)

Questions

1.   What worries you about tomorrow?

2.   What does Matthew 6:25–34 say about worrying?

3.   What are you or should you be enjoying today?

4.   How do you think your perspective may change five years from now?

5.   Think of a treasured memory. Write it down. Did you realize it would be treasured at the time it happened?

Action
Write down a recent event that may one day become a treasured memory.

Prayer
Today is what I have.
I cannot alter the past and I do not know what lies ahead.
I can guess. I can plan.
But today is what I know I have, this moment in time.
I choose to spend this moment loving you,
loving those around me and being content with where I am.
I leave the past where it is buried.
I entrust the future to your care.
You've given today to me.
May I choose wisely. Amen.

Chapter 43
Loneliness and a
Swiss Mountain Man

Don and I had been married for two months and we were going to our first married couples' party. It was a costume party.

As we brainstormed together about what to do, we thought of going as salt and pepper shakers, but couldn't figure out how to do that. Because we couldn't afford to buy anything, we looked at our closet and tried to be creative Then, Don had a brilliant idea. We would go as a swing set. We would wear matching shirts and jeans, take a broomstick (minus the broom) and attach it to paper bags covering our heads. We would cut out swings and a teeter-totter from brown paper bags to hang from the pole! How clever we were.

We didn't really stop to consider how we would walk. Would we really be able to meet or talk with anyone with paper bags covering our faces?

The answer was no. It was terribly difficult to walk—we couldn't even hold hands because we were separated by that stupid pole between our heads. I could not see well through the cut out holes in the bag and I can't remember if we even had holes cut out for our mouths. However, we did win the prize for having the most original costume.

As the party went on, we were able to take off our masks and the restrictive pole. We ate and mingled with the other guests. Don was off talking with some guys he had met. I tried to join one of the other groups, but for some reason I ended up in the middle of the room, alone. There I was, standing in a room full of people, and I felt lonelier than I had ever felt in my entire life. Maybe I should have left the bag on my head!

I didn't know where to go. Everyone seemed so engrossed in their own conversations that there wasn't a place for me. I remember looking at the door feeling very close to tears. I started walking towards the door thinking that I would escape and wait for Don in the car. Somehow feeling lonely when I am alone is so much more comfortable than feeling lonely in a crowded room.

Just seconds before running to the car, a "Swiss mountain man" approached me. "Hi!" he said. He had on a feathered cap, bib shorts and knee socks—I almost expected him to yodel! I began talking with him. Soon he drew me into a group and I felt like I belonged somewhere once again. My feelings of loneliness diminished.

That wasn't the first time, or the last time, that I have felt so out of place. During those early days of our marriage, we were new to the city; I kept waiting for someone to invite us, the newcomers, over for dinner or out to see a movie, anything! Nothing happened. Loneliness seemed to be the only visitor I had.

It was some time after the party that we decided to take the initiative. We invited Jeff, the Swiss guy, and his wife Dorian over to watch a movie and eat dessert. We had a little one-bedroom apartment on the second story of a house. Our big, old black-and-white television set would only fit in our bedroom, so there we sat. Two of us were on the bed and two of us were on chairs beside the bed watching *The Sound of Music* and eating chocolate cake!

Our hospitality was nothing fancy. It was, however, the beginning of a wonderful friendship. It seemed appropriate to watch the *Sound of Music* with them. I think I saw the same feathered hat and shorts in the movie that Jeff wore the night he stepped in and rescued me from loneliness!

Read Psalm 25:16–22

Look at me and help me!
I'm all alone and in big trouble. (v. 16)

My heart and kidneys are fighting each other;
Call a truce to this civil war. (v. 17)

Take a hard look at my life of hard labor,
Then lift this ton of sin. (v. 18)

Do you see how many people
Have it in for me?
How viciously they hate me? (v. 19)

Keep watch over me and keep me out of trouble;
Don't let me down when I run to you. (v. 20)

Use all your skill to put me together;
I wait to see your finished product. (v. 21)

GOD, give your people a break
From this run of bad luck. (v. 22)

Questions

1.   Describe a time you have felt lonely.

2.   How has living overseas intensified or decreased feelings of loneliness?

3.   Why is it sometimes a tendency to sit back and wait for others to meet our needs?

4.   After reading Psalm 25:16–22, how do you think God can help us when we feel lonely?

5.   What adjectives would you use to describe the feeling of loneliness?

Action

At the next social gathering, intentionally look for someone who appears lonely. Reach out and initiate a friendship with her.

Prayer

I know I have you, Lord.
You never leave me, yet at times I feel lonely.
I stand in a crowded room and it looks like everyone has found their niche except me.
There is laughter, talking, and even some hugs and pats on the back.
Please send me a good friend.
 I want to develop my friendship with you, but I also want a flesh-and-blood buddy with whom I can share my heart.
I will wait, trusting in you for what is best for me. Amen.

Chapter 44
The Power of Words

When my kids were younger, they enjoyed playing with PlayStations and Game Boys and thought it would be fun to have either of those. One year for Christmas my parents gave them each a Game Boy as a present. I wasn't up on all of the terminology and I often got those two names confused. So I would mistakenly tell people that my parents gave my children Playboys. They would just stare at me looking somewhat taken aback. My kids were quick to correct me, "Mom! It's Game Boys! You can say either PlayStation or Game Boy. Don't mix the two names. Remember—they gave us *Game Boys*!"

It is amazing how messing up words can cause so much consternation and confusion. I mixed up two little words, yet the mixing of those two simple words created a huge difference in what I communicated.

The older I get, the more I realize how powerful words are. One hot and sticky night when Don and I were in the Middle East, I reached over to give him a hug. He felt cool to my touch, so I told him he was cool. As he hugged me back, he told me I wasn't too hot.

Now, those two words are approximate in their meanings, right? Being cool and being not too hot are similar temperature-wise. However, in colloquial terms they have quite opposite meanings!

Words are powerful. They can elate, sadden, anger, disappoint, encourage, discourage, destroy or build up. James

3 talks a lot about the power of the tongue. The tongue is small, but can cause huge problems or bring great encouragement.

I want to be careful in my use of words. What I say can have far-reaching effects. Just as a rock thrown in a pond causes ripples, so can the words that come out of my mouth.

Before speaking, we should ask ourselves some questions like: What kinds of words are we using? What effect are my words having on people? What words can I use to build up and encourage those around me? What words do I use that bring discouragement and heartache? What words would I love to hear?

As I ponder the power of words, I remember their impact once when I was struggling as a mother of a teenager, wanting to trust God, but worrying at the same time. *What if I am doing something really wrong? What if circumstances continue to worsen?* As I was standing in the back of church, an acquaintance who could tell I was troubled asked me, "Are you fighting the good fight?"

That question took my eyes off my situation and myself, my worries and concerns, and refocused them on my purpose for living. My friend reminded me that I was indeed in a battle and that I needed to continue to fight on in prayer and faith. My heart had to be centered on the Lord, not my situation.

Six little words. She didn't give a sermon or reach out and give me a hug. She used words to lighten my load and uplift my thoughts.

Think about the last six words that you spoke when talking with someone. Will someone remember them years later as a turning point in his or her life? I was able to thank this person eight years after her encouraging words. She was delighted that God had used her to encourage my soul in the midst of a difficult time.

Words! They can make a world of difference, especially if they are the right ones!

Read Ephesians 4:29

Watch the way you talk. Let nothing foul or dirty come out of your mouth. Say only what helps, each word a gift. (v. 29)

Read Ephesians 5:4

Though some tongues just love the taste of gossip, those who follow Jesus have better uses for language than that. Don't talk dirty or silly. That kind of talk doesn't fit our style. Thanksgiving is our dialect. (v. 4)

Read Proverbs 15:1-4

God Doesn't Miss a Thing

A gentle response defuses anger, but a sharp tongue kindles a temper-fire. (v. 1)

Knowledge flows like spring water from the wise; fools are leaky faucets, dripping nonsense. (v. 2)

God doesn't miss a thing—
he's alert to good and evil alike. (v. 3)

Kind words heal and help;
cutting words wound and maim. (v. 4)

Questions

1.   Describe an experience with your team that showed you the power of words.

2.   To which do people pay the most attention: the words people speak or how they are spoken. Describe the difference.

3.   What do Ephesians 4:29 and 5:4 warn us against
        and encourage us to do?

4.   Rephrase Proverbs 15:1–4 in your own words.

5.   How have words helped or hurt your team
        relationships? Set aside some time to talk about
        this as a team.

Action

Make a list of positive adjectives and encouraging phrases.
Keep it on hand and use it with those around you. Good job!
That was wonderful! How delightful! Keen insight!

Prayer

Help me to guard my mouth, Lord.
 May my words edify and encourage those around me.
Empower me to speak truth gently and to refrain from
harshness, even when I am angry.
May it be evident to those around me how much I love you
by the words I choose to speak and the manner in which I
speak them. Amen.

Chapter 49
Unexpected Opportunities Meet Faith

I was nervous when my husband asked me if I would go with him to Northern Iraq. Just thinking about going to Iraq made me somewhat squeamish. I had never been there before. I didn't know what to expect. What would I wear? How would I be received? What would be my role? How could I best prepare for the trip? Because he had already traveled there once, he told me about that trip and answered some of my questions so that it didn't seem as scary. As the Director of Women's Ministry, it would be good for me to interact with Christar women serving there. I also reasoned, what kind of leader would I be if I didn't at least visit where others choose to live for the purpose of sharing the Gospel with people who haven't heard it? Trusting God and his plan for me, I agreed to go. As our plane neared the airport where we were going to land, it began to descend in circles. I was alarmed. I asked Don, "Why are we going around and around as we go down?" He calmly replied, "Oh, I heard they land this way in Baghdad. I didn't know they did spiral landings here! It is a security precaution so that if anyone wants to take potshots at us, the plane will be harder to hit."

Potshots? No one mentioned potshots to me before the trip!

After landing safely (with no potshots taken), another traveling companion, Nan, and I discussed spiral landings and decided to give them a new name. We dubbed them "air swirlies."

As we began to visit with missionaries and interact with national believers, we found our common language to be Arabic. Don and I had lived in the Middle East for twelve years. I used to do quite well in Arabic, but we had lived in the States for eight years and my Arabic language skills were rusty. Don would ask questions and as I listened to the Arabic responses, I would translate them into English for Nan. There were times I couldn't keep up, especially after several hours of interacting! At one point I remember listening and trying to put into words what I had heard. I looked at Nan and said, "This woman says she has gone through some terrible experiences. It was difficult for her, but she got through them. I don't know what they were and I'm not sure exactly what happened. However, I clearly understood what she said at the end. She left in peace." I don't think this was helpful to Nan!

> *Translating?* No one mentioned this to me before the trip! However, I got so used to doing it that several times I even translated what I heard in English into English for Nan!

As we traveled from one city to another, we would go through countless checkpoints. I heard bits and pieces of conversation. "Hmmm, we are closer to Mosul than I thought we would be." "We left the Kurdish area and are now in the Iraqi controlled areas." "Where does this road go? The sign says Mosul." *Mosul—weren't there bombings there not too long ago? How close are we? How far down the road are we going? What does it mean exactly to leave the Kurdish area?*

> *Mosul?* No one mentioned Mosul before the trip, except to say that we shouldn't go near there!

One missionary wanted us not only to get a picturesque view of his host city, but also to have the opportunity to see ancient Phoenician carvings near some caves. He took us to the top of a mountain where we could see the city. We were going to hike down the mountain to see the caves. Our friend didn't realize that Nan and I had only brought long skirts (imagine "Little House on the Prairie" styles) and sandals. We couldn't really hike so we decided to wait on the side of the mountain for the guys to return. We walked around a little bit. Nan took pictures from different vantage points. Then we sat on a rock and chatted. Time passed. We received a cell phone call from them telling us that they came up a different way and were waiting for us at the van. "By the way," the missionary warned us, "Be careful to not step on any round, shiny disks. We think they removed them all, but we aren't sure. So watch your step."

> *Round, shiny disks?* He meant land mines! No one mentioned landmines to me before the trip!

We were able to meet with two of Don's former seminary students. One couple had just moved to this city in Northern Iraq from Baghdad and shared some of their struggles there. As we were visiting with them and their two young children, the children had to ask their parents a few questions about us. "Are they Americans?" When they heard that we were, their very next question was, "Do they carry guns?" Once they determined that we were Americans and that we had no guns, their next question was, "Do they believe in Jesus like we do?"

> *Children afraid of me because I am an American?* No one mentioned this to me before the trip!

You know, it's probably good that I didn't know then what I know now. What good would it have done to know? I guess I could have been too afraid to go. But think of all that I would have missed! The missionaries I met who work so faithfully inspired me. The believers I met who persevere in their faith and share the gospel despite opposition and persecution encouraged me. I saw with my own eyes the open doors and the opportunities for church planting and can now share that with others. I was challenged to grow spiritually, to walk more boldly by faith and keep on praying! I would be much poorer in spirit had I missed any of these faith-building opportunities.

I guess if I had known what was ahead, I could have better prepared myself. I could have sped in my van down a steep, circular hill to prepare for "air swirlies." I could have studied up on what landmines looked like, or brushed up on my Arabic. Still, there would be other unexpected encounters and challenges. We can never know everything. That's why we walk by faith in the One who does!

It is all too easy to wait to do something until we have at least most of the answers to all of our questions. Fear often dissuades us from living more courageously, forcing faith to take a back seat to fear.

Only in this life on earth can we can walk by faith. One day when we see Jesus, we will no longer need faith; we will walk by sight. So for now I must determine daily to let faith be the driving force of my life. Fear should never govern my actions as a believer. Whether I am prepared or caught by surprise, my response should be the same. I will walk by faith in Jesus Christ.

Read Habakkuk 2:4

"Look at that man, bloated by self-importance—
full of himself but soul-empty.
But the person in right standing before God
through loyal and steady believing
is fully alive, really alive. (v. 4)

Read Habakkuk 3:17-19

Though the cherry trees don't blossom
and the strawberries don't ripen,
Though the apples are worm-eaten
and the wheat fields stunted,
Though the sheep pens are sheepless
and the cattle barns empty,
I'm singing joyful praise to God.
I'm turning cartwheels of joy to my Savior God.
Counting on God's Rule to prevail,
I take heart and gain strength.
I run like a deer.
I feel like I'm king of the mountain! (vv. 17–19)

Questions

1. List the main differences between living/walking by faith and living/walking by sight.

2. What adjectives would you use to describe a life ruled by fear?

3. Why was Habakkuk able to exult in the Lord even when everything seemed to be going wrong?

4. Now that you are living in a new country, what unexpected challenges have you encountered?

5. How does faith grow?

Action

Write out some ways that your faith has grown since leaving your home and arriving in your new country.

Prayer

I realize that you are trustworthy.
Sometimes I am afraid; I don't know what is going to happen and the situation looks bad.
You are either who you say you are or you are not.
I choose to live by faith and trust that you are the one true God.
I will keep pressing on by faith until I see your face. Amen.

Chapter 46
Welcoming a New Neighbor . . .
or Not

The house across the street had seemed barren for some time. I had not seen anyone go or come from it for months after the "For Sale" sign was posted. One day, the sign gave notice that the house was sold. I watched each day to see if someone was moving in to be our new neighbor so that I could greet them.

Finally, I saw a moving truck pull in their driveway. I thought it was perfect timing as I had just finished baking some cookies. I filled a cute basket with cookies and prepared my welcome speech. "Hi, my name is Sue. I live across the street and wanted to come over and welcome you to the neighborhood." I thought this would be a great way to make new friends and possibly have more opportunities to witness.

I crossed the street and knocked on the door. Greeting the woman who opened the door, I gave her my spiel to welcome her to the neighborhood. The woman looked a bit confused as she said, "I'm sorry, but we are the ones moving out."

I hadn't even known anyone was living there! I came up with a quick response, "Well, I'm sorry I didn't get to know you. Here, have some moving out cookies and I hope your move goes smoothly." She seemed to appreciate them.

I returned home feeling a bit dejected. I had such high hopes of making a new friend. How could I not have seen there were people living there? Who takes cookies over to people moving out of a house?

Though I thought I would be too afraid to go back over, I watched and waited to see a moving truck. I never saw it arrive. I never saw it leave. Did they move in under the cover of darkness? I don't know. However, I do know that there are people living there now. I have seen them and their dog. I have not taken over any cookies to welcome them into our neighborhood. With the way things go, I would probably have met their movers at the door instead of the neighbors!

I come up with great plans for meeting people with the goal of sharing Christ. When I was pregnant with my youngest and ready to deliver at a Middle Eastern hospital, I intentionally requested a semi-private room. I would be in a room with a woman from a different religious background. She would have had a baby and family members would visit. I would have a new baby and Don would visit. We would chat and get to know each other. Our families would become friends. We would share the gospel with them. It was a great plan.

I didn't know they didn't always place people according to their reason for being in the hospital. My hospital mate had gall bladder surgery. She didn't want to talk with anyone. She was in pain. Her family came to console her. The curtain that separated our beds remained shut. I don't think I ever saw her face.

More often than not, my plans don't always come together the way I had hoped they would. I don't know why. I do know, however, that God's plans always succeed. His purposes are never thwarted; his ways are always best.

My plans may seldom work out as I envision them. I don't know all of the details, the future or people involved. God does. I know I can trust God to always work out his plans in his will. His strategies and timing are better than I could ever imagine.

Read Proverbs 3:5–6

Trust God from the bottom of your heart;
don't try to figure out everything on your own.
Listen for God's voice in everything you do, everywhere

you go;
he's the one who will keep you on track. (vv. 5–6)

Read Proverbs 16:1–3

Mortals make elaborate plans, but GOD has the last word.
(v. 1)

Humans are satisfied with whatever looks good;
GOD probes for what is good. (v. 2)

Put GOD in charge of your work,
then what you've planned will take place. (v. 3)

Questions

1. What has not gone according to plan in your move overseas?

2. How does God guide us in our planning and how can we determine his will?

3. How can a person tell if their plans start taking precedence over God's plans?

4. What are some different ways that God guides or directs our paths?

5. How does living in a different culture exacerbate making plans?

Action

Grab a calendar for the coming year. Spend some time in prayer before planning what you would like to see happen. What are some goals you have for yourself? Your family? Your team?

Prayer

My plans don't mean much if you are not leading me.
Help me to consider you before I make plans.
I submit my planning process to your will and ask you to intervene where necessary.
I want my walk with you to be vibrant and growing.
As I get to know you better and seek to know you more, it could be that more and more plans will fall into place.
Lead on, Lord. Amen.

Chapter 47
God's Will Is Better Than Life

I felt awful. I hurt all over and had felt sick for months, but the doctors were confused. Although test results were normal, something was wrong with me. I became convinced that I was going to die. I didn't want to die! I wanted to see my children grow up. I wanted to meet my grandchildren. I didn't want Don to marry anyone else—what if he ended up liking her more than me?

I had been praying for a husband for my single friend. Now I was afraid that the answer to my prayer would precipitate my own death. I would die and the husband that I was asking for her would turn out to be mine! I stopped praying for a husband for her, since it seemed to coincide with my imminent departure from this world. Whenever I would lie down at night and think about God's will for me being death, I would fight him, explaining to him why I shouldn't die. I was so afraid he wouldn't listen to me.

At my lowest point, we were visiting family and I had to stay home from church. I was in bed once again wrestling with God about his will for my life. I did not want his will, if it included my death. I was feeling so sick and so tired, not only of the illness, but of fighting with God. I came to the point that I knew that my struggling was useless. More than that, I knew in my soul that his will would be better than my will. After deciding to trust him for what is best, I surrendered to him my soul and my body. I waited impatiently for his will to be done and for my death to come.

I thought I should let God know I was sincere so as I lay on the bed, I crossed my arms over my chest, striking a burial pose, and closed my eyes. I told the Lord I was ready to go home. I didn't want to fight him anymore. I loved him and wanted his will for my life . . . and death. His will was far more crucial to me than my life. I waited.

Some time passed. Nothing happened. I peeked. I was still in the same room and I was alive. Maybe it wasn't God's will for me to die that day. It occurred to me that in the midst of my difficulty, I didn't have to assume that the will of God would be bad. It might feel bad, look bad and seem bad, but he promises me that his will for me is perfect and good.

That day was a turning point for me both spiritually and physically. My soul rejoiced that I did not have to be afraid of God's will. My body became less of a focal point than seeking God. Though I was willing to stay sick or die if it was God's will for me, in time I eventually felt better. I continue to learn not to dread God's will, but to trust him—even when life is difficult. I know his will is far superior to my own plans and my own attempts to control life. God's will is always best.

Even though I had stopped praying for my friend to find a husband, she did, and I didn't have to die in the process. God led her to a husband and I was able to live and keep mine.

Read Ephesians 5:11–20

Don't waste your time on useless work, mere busywork, the barren pursuits of darkness. Expose these things for the sham they are. It's a scandal when people waste their lives on things they must do in the darkness where no one will see. Rip the cover off those frauds and see how attractive they look in the light of Christ.
   Wake up from your sleep,
   Climb out of your coffins;
   Christ will show you the light!
So watch your step. Use your head. Make the most of every chance you get. These are desperate times! (vv. 11–16)

Don't live carelessly, unthinkingly. Make sure you
understand what the Master wants. (v. 17)

Don't drink too much wine. That cheapens your life.
Drink the Spirit of God, huge draughts of him. Sing
hymns instead of drinking songs! Sing songs from your
heart to Christ. Sing praises over everything, any excuse
for a song to God the Father in the name of our Master,
Jesus Christ. (vv. 18–20)

Questions

1.   How does a person understand what the will
of the Lord is? (Eph. 5:17)

2.   Describe a time recently when you were afraid
of God's will.

3.   Why is it fairly common to expect God's will to
be bad?

4.   How does being filled with the Spirit change a
person's life?

5.   In reality, is it possible to always give thanks
for all things? How does one put this into
practice?

Action

Think through what your biggest fear is about the will of God for your life. Spend some time in prayer giving that fear to him, intentionally submitting it to his authority.

Prayer

When things are going well, I feel good about you, Lord.
When things are not going my way, you are so easy to blame.
I know what I deserve and apart from your grace, I would be destitute.
Your plans are good for me.
Enable me not to fear, but to know you and entrust even my greatest fear of your will to your wisdom and power.
I respectfully submit to you, Amen.

Chapter 48
Praying for Safety

Because I had never traveled to the Central Asian country we were planning to visit, I was a bit nervous. I had heard stories about the airline that would take us there. There were tales of delays, cancellations, and crashes. I decided that if we were going to go, we would need to make sure people were praying for flight safety. Not only did I make it a matter of prayer, but when others would ask how they could pray, I would mention the name of the airline and ask them to pray that our flight would go smoothly.

When the day for travel came, everything went smoothly on the way to our destination. There were no delays; nothing was cancelled; we didn't crash. I was thrilled. The only blight to the whole trip was being sprayed by some kind of insecticide while on the plane. A man sprayed the aisles and in the air as he walked down the aisle with his canister. I did not know what it was, nor did I hear any explanation. I held my breath as much as I could. But as we disembarked, hopefully bug free or germ free—whatever he sprayed for—we felt fine and chalked it up to a new experience. I thanked God for answering prayer and getting us to our destination safely.

After gathering out luggage, we headed out with our host. He picked us up in his big white car and off we went. As we headed out of the city and towards the town where he lived, I noticed that there was only one lane of the highway for both traffic directions. As we were heading straight toward another vehicle, it finally pulled off in the sand beside the road until we passed through; then it got back on the road to continue the trip. Our host proceeded to explain that since there was just one lane, the bigger vehicle claimed the right of way. Everyone else in smaller cars had to get off the road until the bigger car passed. I was thankful that our host's car was bigger than most. No sooner had that thought crossed my mind that I noticed a big, colorful truck heading towards us. Closer and closer we came until we simply swerved off the road until the truck passed before we continued on our way.

"Lord," I said silently, "I wasted too much time praying about the flight. That was much less scary than the drive on these roads. Please take care of us." I watched more and more vehicles either get off the road or make us get off the road, and grew apprehensive. What if the cars were about the same size?

I decided the best thing to do was to sit back and close my eyes. Ignorance was bliss—well almost. I couldn't see cars coming. I didn't have to worry if they were bigger or smaller than ours. I intentionally sat back, tried to relax and let God know that I was trusting in him for every aspect of the journey, not just the flight!

This trip reminded me of what life can be like. It sometimes resembles a roller coaster ride—up and down, all around, thrills and chills! Our end destination is fixed. We are secure. It's just a bit of a ride from where we are to where we're going. Sometimes we need to keep our eyes open, enjoy the view and plan for what's ahead. Other times we may feel the need to close our eyes and pray, "Lord you know what's ahead. Help me trust you to see me through."

And he does.

Read Acts 12:1–17

Peter Under Heavy Guard

That's when King Herod got it into his head to go after some of the church members. He murdered James, John's brother. When he saw how much it raised his popularity ratings with the Jews, he arrested Peter—all this during Passover Week, mind you—and had him thrown in jail,

putting four squads of four soldiers each to guard him. He
was planning a public lynching after Passover. (vv. 1–4)

All the time that Peter was under heavy guard in the
jailhouse, the church prayed for him most strenuously. (v.
5)

Then the time came for Herod to bring him out for the kill.
That night, even though shackled to two soldiers, one on
either side, Peter slept like a baby. And there were guards
at the door keeping their eyes on the place. Herod was
taking no chances! (v. 6)

Suddenly there was an angel at his side and light flooding
the room. The angel shook Peter and got him up: "Hurry!"
The handcuffs fell off his wrists. The angel said, "Get
dressed. Put on your shoes." Peter did it. Then, "Grab
your coat and let's get out of here." Peter followed him,
but didn't believe it was really an angel—he thought he
was dreaming. (vv. 7–9)

 Past the first guard and then the second, they came to the
iron gate that led into the city. It swung open before them
on its own, and they were out on the street, free as the
breeze. At the first intersection the angel left him, going
his own way. That's when Peter realized it was no dream.
"I can't believe it—this really happened! The Master sent
his angel and rescued me from Herod's vicious little
production and the spectacle the Jewish mob was looking
forward to." (vv. 10–11)

Still shaking his head, amazed, he went to Mary's house,
the Mary who was John Mark's mother. The house was
packed with praying friends. When he knocked on the
door to the courtyard, a young woman named Rhoda
came to see who it was. But when she recognized his
voice—Peter's voice!—she was so excited and eager to tell
everyone Peter was there that she forgot to open the door
and left him standing in the street. (vv. 12–14)

But they wouldn't believe her, dismissing her, dismissing
her report. "You're crazy," they said. She stuck by her

story, insisting. They still wouldn't believe her and said, "It must be his angel." All this time poor Peter was standing out in the street, knocking away. (vv. 15–16)

Finally they opened up and saw him—and went wild! Peter put his hands up and calmed them down. He described how the Master had gotten him out of jail, then said, "Tell James and the brothers what's happened." He left them and went off to another place. (vv. 16–17)

Questions

1.   As you moved overseas, what new challenges were you prepared for and what has taken you by surprise?

2.   After reading Acts 12, what might Peter have been thinking about as he was in prison?

3.   How did the church respond to Peter's situation? What result did it have?

4.   How has fear been a problem for you in your host culture?

5.   Describe a time when you were amazed when God answered your prayer.

Action

Write out a time line of your life showing the ups and downs of your roller coaster ride. Remember how God met you at each of those times and spend time praising him. Share with a friend the "ride" of your life and how God has been present with you through the highs and the lows.

Prayer

Thank you, Lord that you know all about tomorrow.
I can prepare for what I think might happen today and only guess at what tomorrow holds.
I am grateful that you answer prayer.
Help me not to be amazed when you do answer, but instead to have confidence that you will respond to my prayers.
Amen.

Chapter 49
Why Am I Still in Culture Shock?

We were on our way home! After being in our host country far away from family and all that was familiar to us, we headed back. On the plane, we tasted root beer and grape soda—things we had not tasted in several years. Anxious to see family, friends, and McDonald's, excitement gripped my heart.

As we went through US customs, the unsmiling officer grilled us, "How will you support yourselves in the States, if you live overseas? Where have you been? Why were you there? What will you be doing?" It wasn't exactly the welcome I was looking for. He looked at my young daughter and asked her where she was from. She looked at him, paused, and replied, "Now, that is a good question." He soon waved us through and family awaited us with open arms.

As we visited with friends and shared our work and experiences with churches, they responded with interest and affirmation, although in one church, someone did ask, "Hey, we haven't seen you in awhile—where have you been?" We loved getting caught up on our friends' news and experiences.

We wanted to see more friends and asked how we could get in touch with them. It broke our hearts to hear stories of divorce, separation, and infidelity. These, too, were our church friends and their lives had changed drastically. It seemed whenever I asked about someone there was a sad story. I grew fearful to ask and soon stopped inquiring if I didn't see someone at church. It hurt too much to hear so much sad news all at once.

Going to the grocery store for just one simple item, a bag of regular chips was overwhelming. I grew frustrated with so many options: low salt, barbecue, sour cream and onion, cheese, ranch. . . . On another occasion, I thought I would try the Hyper Mart just to see what it was like. I needed some dish detergent, but just seeing the 99 checkout lines sent me into a tailspin. I got out of there as quickly as possible . . . in one of the many lines! How do I use the credit card? There are so many different machines with different ways to swipe the cards!

People had changed. We had changed. Our culture had changed. Overseas I had learned not to look men in the eyes or talk freely with them. What was I supposed to do when a man in the grocery store commented to me about the weather? Should I respond? What was his purpose?

Who had I become? I didn't really fit in overseas, though I was learning more about life there. I didn't really fit in back into my home country, though I was learning to readapt. I didn't feel like I fit in either place. I was a foreigner overseas and a foreigner in my home country. Where did I belong?

"For our citizenship is in heaven, from which also we eagerly wait for a Savior, the Lord Jesus Christ" (Phil 3:20, NASB).

Read 1 Peter 2:9–12

But you are the ones chosen by God, chosen for the high calling of priestly work, chosen to be a holy people, God's instruments to do his work and speak out for him, to tell others of the night-and-day difference he made for you—from nothing to something, from rejected to accepted. (vv. 9–10)

Friends, this world is not your home, so don't make yourselves cozy in it. Don't indulge your ego at the expense of your soul. Live an exemplary life among the natives so that your actions will refute their prejudices.

Then they'll be won over to God's side and be there to join
in the celebration when he arrives. (vv. 11–12)

Questions

1.   How have you experienced reverse culture shock?

2.   If a coworker was returning to the states for a time,
what advice would you give them about how to
prepare for reverse culture shock?

3.   What are some of the benefits and challenges of
feeling like a foreigner?

4.   Reread I Peter 2:9–10. What does it mean to be a
people for God's own possession? What sense of
purpose do these verses give you?

5.   Why does Peter move from who we are to address
our behavior in I Peter 2:11–12?

Action

Gather a list of the most common ways people experience
reverse culture shock. Keep it on hand to review before you
travel and share it with someone who is getting ready to go
back to their home country.

Prayer

When I don't feel like I belong, help me to remember,
Lord God, that I belong to you.
I am a citizen of heaven.
I am a member of a *chosen race,* a *royal priesthood* and a *holy nation.*
You chose me out of darkness into your light, so that I might proclaim your excellences.
It doesn't matter where I live or how I feel, I am in your family.
Thank you that I belong to you. Amen.

Chapter 30
Forgiving Dirty Old (and Young) Men

I hailed a taxi. I don't remember why I didn't get in the back seat as I normally did. Maybe the driver had opened the front door for me. We weren't going far so I climbed in and told him where I needed to go. I was looking out the window. I had been in the country long enough to know not to converse with him beyond what was culturally appropriate. We arrived at our destination and as he reached over to open the door for me, he intentionally brushed his arm repeatedly against my breasts. I leaned back as far as I could to avoid him and left the car as fast as humanly possible. I felt angry, dirty, used, and guilty. Why did I sit in the front seat? Did I do or say anything to elicit this type of action?

When I told someone about what happened, this person did not empathize with me or appear to be as concerned with my well-being as with lecturing me about what to do to make sure it did not happen again. This response reinforced my guilt and made me angry with myself. It took all of the blame away from the person who had inappropriately fondled me and placed it on me. Yes, I should have been in the back seat. No, I didn't invite his attention in any way. Nevertheless, he was in the wrong!

Another day I was walking down the street. I was modestly dressed and minding my own business. A man was walking toward me. Keeping my eyes downcast, I kept walking on the opposite side of the walkway only to have him walk toward me and make inappropriate gestures with his body. I sped up to get as far from him as possible. *What a jerk!* I thought. I had not one ounce of compassion in me, only indignation. Unaccustomed thoughts crossed my mind such as, *God, damn him to hell! How dare he treat me like that and show such disrespect.* Filled with anger, I kept walking and asked God to punish this loathsome creature. Immediately his Holy Spirit convicted me of my lack of forgiveness and spiteful attitude. "How much have you been forgiven, Sue? That man is lost. Unless he turns to me, he will be damned. He will be separated from my presence. Is that what you really want for him?"

Tears came to my eyes. "But God, he is a jerk." His response, "Yes, child, but he is a lost jerk." I asked that God would have mercy on his soul. I prayed for this man's salvation and for God's blessing on his life. I spent time thanking God for forgiving me and saving me by his grace. I was God's enemy, as lost as the man who insulted me, yet God forgave me. In my heart, I really did not want this man to go into a Christless eternity.

As women facing unwanted advances from lost men, we must always remember their eternal fate and what ours would have been apart from God's mercy. When men make rude remarks and touch us inappropriately, yes, we need to defend ourselves and uphold our honor in these cultures. It is imperative to find culturally suitable ways to deal with harassment. "Don't you have a mother?" is something that can be yelled in certain cultures. Asking for help from bystanders is another.

Whether we address the harassment through confrontation, help from others, or physical action, it is imperative to the well being of our souls that we also aggressively forgive those who harm us. We must bless, pray for, and love even our enemies. We must beware of bitterness, anger, and bias. By God's grace, he commands us to forgive.

How thankful I am that though God had every right to condemn me to an eternity outcast from his kingdom of light, he reached into my dark world to forgive me. He saved me from what I deserved in order to give me more than I could ever have imagined. May these lost men also experience

God's grace as we return their curses on us with a prayer for God's blessing on them.

Read I Samuel 1:1–17

There once was a man who lived in Ramathaim. He was descended from the old Zuph family in the Ephraim hills. His name was Elkanah. (He was connected with the Zuphs from Ephraim through his father Jeroham, his grandfather Elihu, and his great-grandfather Tohu.) He had two wives. The first was Hannah; the second was Peninnah. Peninnah had children; Hannah did not. (vv. 1–2)

Every year this man went from his hometown up to Shiloh to worship and offer a sacrifice to GOD-of-the-Angel-Armies. Eli and his two sons, Hophni and Phinehas, served as the priests of GOD there. When Elkanah sacrificed, he passed helpings from the sacrificial meal around to his wife Peninnah and all her children, but he always gave an especially generous helping to Hannah because he loved her so much, and because GOD had not given her children. But her rival wife taunted her cruelly, rubbing it in and never letting her forget that GOD had not given her children. This went on year after year. Every time she went to the sanctuary of GOD she could expect to be taunted. Hannah was reduced to tears and had no appetite. (vv. 3–7)

Her husband Elkanah said, "Oh, Hannah, why are you crying? Why aren't you eating? And why are you so upset? Am I not of more worth to you than ten sons?" (v. 8)

So Hannah ate. Then she pulled herself together, slipped away quietly, and entered the sanctuary. The priest Eli was on duty at the entrance to GOD's Temple in the customary seat. Crushed in soul, Hannah prayed to GOD and cried and cried—inconsolably. Then she made a vow:
Oh, GOD-of-the-Angel-Armies,
If you'll take a good, hard look at my pain,
If you'll quit neglecting me and go into action for me
By giving me a son,

I'll give him completely, unreservedly to you.
I'll set him apart for a life of holy discipline. (vv. 9–11)

It so happened that as she continued in prayer before
GOD, Eli was watching her closely. Hannah was praying
in her heart, silently. Her lips moved, but no sound was
heard. Eli jumped to the conclusion that she was drunk.
He approached her and said, "You're drunk! How long do
you plan to keep this up? Sober up, woman!" (vv. 12–14)

Hannah said, "Oh no, sir—please! I'm a woman hard
used. I haven't been drinking. Not a drop of wine or beer.
The only thing I've been pouring out is my heart, pouring
it out to GOD. Don't for a minute think I'm a bad woman.
It's because I'm so desperately unhappy and in such pain
that I've stayed here so long." (vv. 15–16)

Eli answered her, "Go in peace. And may the God of
Israel give you what you have asked of him." (v. 17)

Matthew 5:43–48

"You're familiar with the old written law, 'Love your friend,'
and its unwritten companion, 'Hate your enemy.' I'm
challenging that. I'm telling you to love your enemies. Let them
bring out the best in you, not the worst. When someone gives
you a hard time, respond with the energies of prayer, for then
you are working out of your true selves, your God-created
selves. This is what God does. He gives his best—the sun to
warm and the rain to nourish—to everyone, regardless: the
good and bad, the nice and nasty. If all you do is love the
lovable, do you expect a bonus? Anybody can do that. If you
simply say hello to those who greet you, do you expect a
medal? Any run-of-the-mill sinner does that. (vv. 43–47)

"In a word, what I'm saying is, Grow up. You're kingdom
subjects. Now live like it. Live out your God-created
identity. Live generously and graciously toward others,
the way God lives toward you." (v. 48)

Questions

1.   How was Hannah harassed by Peninnah and misunderstood by Eli?

2.   What was Hannah's response in these two situations?

3.   In what ways have you been harassed in your new culture?

4.   How does Jesus say to respond to your enemies? (Matthew 5:44)

5.   What are some culturally appropriate ways to respond to sexual harassment in your host culture?

Action

Interview several national friends and ask them about how to respond to harassment in their culture. Ask them to help you know how to avoid it and how to deal with it when it happens.

Prayer

Thank you for saving me from the darkness of my world and
bringing me into the light of your presence.
 I am not always treated the way I would like to be treated;
I can get really angry about that.
I am sometimes disrespected; my rights are trampled upon;
my personhood is humiliated.
No woman should be mistreated by another human being.

When it happens to me, Lord,
may I be aware of your love and forgiveness for me.
May love and forgiveness flow through me to such an extent
that your light, grace and mercy are evident in me. Amen.

Chapter 31
To Adapt or Not to Adapt:
That Is the Question

My neighbor stopped by my home. She and I were developing a growing friendship and I was enjoying opportunities to share my faith with her. When she came in, she noticed that the caretaker's son was playing with our children. She seemed a bit confused and asked why we allowed the caretaker's son to play with our children. I shared with her God's love for all and that we tried to show his love to everyone. After we chatted for a while, she left and I wondered what would happen to our friendship. Maybe I should adapt culturally and keep my children separate from the poorer children in my neighborhood. Then I remembered the Scripture: James 2:5 is about God choosing the poor of this world to be rich in faith and heirs of his kingdom; in Proverbs 31:20, the virtuous woman extended her hands to the poor and needy; "He who is gracious to a poor man lends to the Lord" is found in Proverbs 19:17. Because I knew that God shows no favoritism, it would be sin for me to differentiate between poor and wealthier children. I decided to obey God and continued to allow our children to play with the caretaker's son.

Several weeks later, my friend stopped by again. She said, "You know, one of the things I admire about you is your love for everyone." I was then able to share with her again about the depth of God's love for all people and how I experienced this love personally. For me not to share that with all others would be heartless. She was touched by my life when I refused to adapt culturally as a matter of principle. However, a co-worker and I were at a religious meeting in another friend's house. One of the women asked how people like us could believe in three gods. My co-worker stood and said loudly, "God forbid that we would ever believe such a thing!" She went on to explain more about our faith. I sat and prayed silently for her. The next day my friend commented on that event. She said, "Your friend has a stronger faith than you do, doesn't she?" Unsure how to answer, I asked her why she thought so. She replied, "She really stands up for what she believes."

I didn't know that in that culture, if a person really believes something, she is very vocal about it. Because I did not change my behavior to fit the culture, I actually appeared less certain and less supportive of my faith. I was not a good testimony because I didn't understand the cultural implications of staying quiet and not speaking forcefully about my faith.

How do we know when we should adapt and when we shouldn't? We let Scripture be our guide. No matter where we live, our home countries or different ones, we always need to determine our course of action based on the Word of God. By comparing a practice with Scripture, there is more clarity regarding whether something is right or wrong.

How should I dress? What time do I need to be in at night? When is it appropriate to interact socially with men? What places are off limits for me as a woman in this new culture? What if all my friends are having their future told by someone reading coffee grounds in their cups? Do I follow the culture on these points or not?

Many times the issues aren't about whether something is right or wrong, but rather what is culturally appropriate. Sometimes, what is culturally appropriate is fine and when we adapt the result is that our message is more easily heard. However, sometimes what is culturally appropriate may be wrong. In that case, we need to act counter-culturally and let Scripture be our guide. As we live for God, our light will shine before the people so that the Lord is glorified by our obedience to him above all else.

There are times to adapt and times to act outside cultural norms, even in our home cultures. May God give us wisdom and a comprehensive knowledge of his Word and our cultures so that we are able to choose wisely.

Read Acts 10:9–33

The next day as the three travelers were approaching the town, Peter went out on the balcony to pray. It was about noon. Peter got hungry and started thinking about lunch. While lunch was being prepared, he fell into a trance. He saw the skies open up. Something that looked like a huge blanket lowered by ropes at its four corners settled on the ground. Every kind of animal and reptile and bird you could think of was on it. Then a voice came: "Go to it, Peter—kill and eat." (vv. 9–13)

Peter said, "Oh, no, Lord. I've never so much as tasted food that was not kosher." (v. 14)

The voice came a second time: "If God says it's okay, it's okay." (v. 15)

This happened three times, and then the blanket was pulled back up into the skies. (v. 16)

As Peter, puzzled, sat there trying to figure out what it all meant, the men sent by Cornelius showed up at Simon's front door. They called in, asking if there was a Simon, also called Peter, staying there. Peter, lost in thought, didn't hear them, so the Spirit whispered to him, "Three men are knocking at the door looking for you. Get down there and go with them. Don't ask any questions. I sent them to get you." (vv. 17–20)

Peter went down and said to the men, "I think I'm the man you're looking for. What's up?" (v. 21)

They said, "Captain Cornelius, a God-fearing man well-known for his fair play—ask any Jew in this part of the country—was commanded by a holy angel to get you and bring you to his house so he could hear what you had to say." Peter invited them in and made them feel at home. (vv. 22–23)

God Plays No Favorites

The next morning he got up and went with them. Some of his friends from Joppa went along. A day later they entered Caesarea. Cornelius was expecting them and had his relatives and close friends waiting with him. The minute Peter came through the door, Cornelius was up on his feet greeting him—and then down on his face worshiping him! Peter pulled him up and said, "None of that—I'm a man and only a man, no different from you." (vv. 23–26)

Talking things over, they went on into the house, where Cornelius introduced Peter to everyone who had come. Peter addressed them, "You know, I'm sure that this is highly irregular. Jews just don't do this—visit and relax with people of another race. But God has just shown me that no race is better than any other. So the minute I was sent for, I came, no questions asked. But now I'd like to know why you sent for me." (vv. 27–29)

Cornelius said, "Four days ago at about this time, midafternoon, I was home praying. Suddenly there was a man right in front of me, flooding the room with light. He said, 'Cornelius, your daily prayers and neighborly acts have brought you to God's attention. I want you to send to Joppa to get Simon, the one they call Peter. He's staying with Simon the Tanner down by the sea.' (vv. 30–32)

"So I did it—I sent for you. And you've been good enough to come. And now we're all here in God's presence, ready to listen to whatever the Master put in your heart to tell us." (v. 33)

Questions

1. In what ways have you adapted to your host culture? Why?

2. In what areas have you decided not to culturally adapt? Why?

3. How did God prepare Peter to adapt in Acts 10?

4. Why were the Jews who were with Peter amazed that the Holy Spirit came? (Acts 10:45)

5. How did Peter respond to those who criticized him for adapting in Acts 11:1–18?

Action

Determine if there are any areas where you are not sure whether or not to adapt. Discuss these areas with teammates and together look to Scripture for guidance.

Prayer

I will look to your Word, O Lord, to determine my actions. May I be effective in proclaiming your word, and please, God, don't let any of my actions detract from the integrity of your Word.

Help me be sensitive to the culture and my new friends.
Open doors for your message and may my speech and actions
only enhance it. Amen.

Chapter 52
Do the Possible,
Trust God for the Impossible . . .
Don't Confuse the Two

One day when I was on the staircase with my neighbor, we stopped to chat. We were discussing the different aspects of our two religions. As I shared the gospel with this very religious woman, she looked at me and said, "I have never heard that before."

What an amazing moment in history! Imagine being the first person to explain the good news to another who has never heard it. I was ecstatic, thankful, humbled, and eager to see her response. She went on to share other things with me. Throughout our time as neighbors, we continued to chat. She would try to convince me of truth and I would try to convince her of truth. Neither of us changed, and despite my prayers for her, as far as I know she hasn't come to know Christ.

Another friend finally understood the gospel as I shared with her. She was not an overly religious person; she seemed more interested in material things and getting ahead in the world. Her response to me was, "Do you know what would happen to me if I believed?" She seemed to be seriously considering Christ's claims. The next time I saw her she was more entrenched in her own religion and not eager to talk with me anymore about spiritual things.

At a neighborhood gathering, though frightened, I shared about the importance of Jesus Christ in my life. My friends said, "It is only right that you feel this way about your prophet."

Time after time, year after year, sharing the gospel, seeking open doors, turning conversations towards spiritual issues . . . I saw no visible results. I grew discouraged. Was there something wrong with me? How effective was I? Or was the area in which we were working so difficult that it would just take more time and prayer?

Whenever I feel that I should quit, give up, surrender, admit defeat, or go home, I have usually taken over God's role rather than keeping mine. My job is to do the possible—to share my faith as effectively as possible, pray, give, love, obey, live wholeheartedly for the Lord, walk by faith, trust God, persevere, lean on him, and keep loving. I must do my part, but I feel defeated when I take on God's job as well.

Only God can change hearts, reveal light, save souls, open the eyes of the blind and the ears of the deaf, heal bodies and souls of people, and adopt his enemies as his children. He can work the impossible. If I confuse God's role with my own, I grow discouraged because I am not God and cannot fulfill his role.

Remember . . . do the possible, trust God for the impossible and don't confuse the two!

Read Nehemiah 2:11–20

And so I arrived in Jerusalem. After I had been there three days, I got up in the middle of the night, I and a few men who were with me. I hadn't told anyone what my God had put in my heart to do for Jerusalem. The only animal with us was the one I was riding. (vv. 11–12)

Under cover of night I went past the Valley Gate toward the Dragon's Fountain to the Dung Gate looking over the walls of Jerusalem, which had been broken through and whose gates had been burned up. I then crossed to the Fountain Gate and headed for the King's Pool but there

wasn't enough room for the donkey I was riding to get
through. So I went up the valley in the dark continuing
my inspection of the wall. I came back in through the
Valley Gate. The local officials had no idea where I'd gone
or what I was doing—I hadn't breathed a word to the
Jews, priests, nobles, local officials, or anyone else who
Then I gave them my report: "Face it: we're in a bad way
here. Jerusalem is a wreck; its gates are burned up.
Come—let's build the wall of Jerusalem and not live with
this disgrace any longer." I told them how God was
supporting me and how the king was backing me up.

They said, "We're with you. Let's get started." They rolled
up their sleeves, ready for the good work. (vv. 17–18)

When Sanballat the Horonite, Tobiah the Ammonite
official, and Geshem the Arab heard about it, they
laughed at us, mocking, "Ha! What do you think you're
doing? Do you think you can cross the king?" (v. 19)

I shot back, "The God-of-Heaven will make sure we
succeed. We're his servants and we're going to work,
rebuilding. You can keep your nose out of it. You get no
say in this—Jerusalem's none of your business!" (v. 20)

Read Nehemiah 4:4–9, 13–20

Nehemiah prayed, "Oh listen to us, dear God. We're so
despised: Boomerang their ridicule on their heads; have their
enemies cart them off as war trophies to a land of no return;
don't forgive their iniquity, don't wipe away their sin—they've
insulted the builders!" (vv. 4–5)

We kept at it, repairing and rebuilding the wall. The
whole wall was soon joined together and halfway to its
intended height because the people had a heart for the
work. (v. 6)

When Sanballat, Tobiah, the Arabs, the Ammonites, and
the Ashdodites heard that the repairs of the walls of
Jerusalem were going so well—that the breaks in the wall
were being fixed—they were absolutely furious. They put

their heads together and decided to fight against
Jerusalem and create as much trouble as they could. We
countered with prayer to our God and set a round-the-
clock guard against them. (vv. 7–9)

So I stationed armed guards at the most vulnerable places
of the wall and assigned people by families with their
swords, lances, and bows. After looking things over I
stood up and spoke to the nobles, officials, and everyone
else: "Don't be afraid of them. Put your minds on the
Master, great and awesome, and then fight for your
brothers, your sons, your daughters, your wives, and your
homes." (vv. 13–14)

Our enemies learned that we knew all about their plan
and that God had frustrated it. And we went back to the
wall and went to work. From then on half of my young
men worked while the other half stood guard with lances,
shields, bows, and mail armor. Military officers served as
backup for everyone in Judah who was at work rebuilding
the wall. The common laborers held a tool in one hand
and a spear in the other. Each of the builders had a sword
strapped to his side as he worked. I kept the trumpeter at
my side to sound the alert. (vv. 15–18)

Then I spoke to the nobles and officials and everyone else:
"There's a lot of work going on and we are spread out all
along the wall, separated from each other. When you hear
the trumpet call, join us there; our God will fight for us."
(vv. 19–20)

Read Nehemiah 6:15-16

The wall was finished on the twenty-fifth day of Elul. It had
taken fifty-two days. When all our enemies heard the news and
all the surrounding nations saw it, our enemies totally lost
their nerve. They knew that God was behind this work. (vv.
15–16)

Questions

1.   How do you see a balance of God working and people working in these passages from Nehemiah?

2.   When do you find it difficult to separate your role from God's?

3.   What happens when you try to take over God's job or you leave your job to him?

4.   What role does prayer play in this struggle to do the possible and trust God for the impossible?

5.   Why do people sometimes tend to confuse these two roles—doing the possible and trusting God for the impossible?

Action

Read through the book of Nehemiah and note his prayers and how he responds to obstacles confronting his goals.

Prayer

I am incapable of doing the impossible.
Only you can do that.
By your grace, I am capable of doing the possible.

I confess to you my frustration when I try to do your job.
Your timing is different from mine and your goals may differ
from mine.
Enable me to grow in my faith and to trust you for the
impossible.
You are able. Amen.